Silent Voices Speak

The Wadsworth Modern Anthropology Library

Richard de Mille: The Don Juan Papers: Further Castaneda Controversies

Philip R. DeVita: The Humbled Anthropologist: Tales from the Pacific

Conrad Phillip Kottak: Prime-Time Society: An Anthropological Analysis of Television and Culture

Mac Marshall and Leslie B. Marshall: Silent Voices Speak: Women and Prohibition in Truk

R. Jon McGee: Life, Ritual, and Religion Among the Lacandon Maya

Serena Nanda: Neither Man nor Woman: The Hijras of India

Silent Voices Speak

Women and Prohibition in Truk

Mac Marshall *and*
Leslie B. Marshall
University of Iowa

Wadsworth Publishing Company
Belmont, California
A Division of Wadsworth, Inc.

Anthropology Editor: *Peggy Adams*
Editorial Assistant: *Karen Moore*
Production Editor: *Angela Mann*
Designer: *Donna Davis*
Print Buyer: *Barbara Britton*
Copy Editor: *Stephen McElroy*
Compositor: *Kachina Typesetting*
Cover: *Donna Davis*
Cover Illustration: *Adriann Dinihanian*

Printed in the United States of America 49

1 2 3 4 5 6 7 8 9 10—94 93 92 91 90

Library of Congress Cataloging in Publication Data
Marshall, Mac.
Silent voices speak : women and prohibition in Truk / Mac Marshall and Leslie B. Marshall.
p. cm.—(The Wadsworth modern anthropology library)
Includes bibliographical references.
ISBN 0-534-12384-8
1. Trukese (Micronesian people)—Alcohol use. 2. Women, Trukese (Micronesian people)—Social conditions. 3. Prohibition—Micronesia (Federated States)—Moen Island. 4. Alcoholism—Micronesia (Federated States)—Moen Island. 5. Moen Island (Micronesia)—Social conditions. I. Marshall, Leslie B. II. Title. III. Series.
DU568.T7M37 1990
362.29'2'089995—dc20 89-35287
CIP

ISBN 0-534-12384-8

Acknowledgments

Blocker, Jack S., Jr. 1985. *"Give to the Winds Thy Fears:" The Women's Temperance Crusade, 1873–1874.* Contributions in Women's Studies, No. 55. Westport, CT: Greenwood Press. Copyright © 1985 by Jack S. Blocker, Jr. Quotations in chapters 1, 5, 6, 7, 9 are reprinted with permission of the author and publisher.

Forman, Charles W. 1982. *The Island Churches of the South Pacific: Emergence in the Twentieth Century.* American Society of Missiology Series, No. 5. Maryknoll, NY: Orbis Books. Quotations in chapter 8 are reprinted with permission of the publisher.

Hezel, Francis X. Personal correspondence. Quotation in chapter 5 is printed with permission of the author.

Lemert, Edwin M. 1967. Alcohol, values and social control. In *Human Deviance, Social Problems, and Social Control,* by E. M. Lemert. Englewood Cliffs, NJ: Prentice-Hall. Quotations in chapter 1 are reprinted with permission of the author.

Millay, John R. 1987. Prohibition Pacific style: The impact of a law banning alcohol in a Micronesian society. In *Contemporary Issues in Mental Health in the Pacific Islands,* eds. Albert B. Robillard and Anthony Marsella. Social Science Research Institute Monograph Series. Honolulu: SSRI, University of Hawaii Press. Quotations in chapter 6 are reprinted with permission of the author.

Áán fiin Chuuk meyinisin.
To all Trukese women.

Contents

Foreword to the Series

Modern cultural anthropology encompasses the full diversity of all humankind with a mix of methods, styles, ideas, and approaches. No longer is the subject matter of this field confined to exotic cultures, the "primitive," or small rural folk communities. Today, students are as likely to find an anthropologist at work in an urban school setting or a corporate boardroom as among a band of African hunters and gatherers. To a large degree, the currents in modern anthropology reflect changes in the world over the past century. Today there are no isolated archaic societies available for study. All the world's peoples have become enveloped in widespread regional, social, political, and economic systems. The daughters and sons of yesterday's yam gardeners and reindeer hunters are operating computers, organizing marketing cooperatives, serving as delegates to parliaments, and watching television news. The lesson of cultural anthropology, and this series, is that such peoples, when transformed, are no less interesting and no less culturally different because of such dramatic changes.

Cultural anthropology's scope has grown to encompass more than simply the changes in the primitive or peasant world, its original subject matter. The methods and ideas developed for the study of small-scale societies are now creatively applied to the most complex of social and cultural systems, giving us a new and stronger understanding of the full diversity of human living. Increasingly, cultural anthropologists also work toward solving practical problems of the cultures they study, in addition to pursuing more traditional basic research endeavors.

Yet cultural anthropology's enlarged agenda has not meant abandonment of its own heritage. The ethnographic case study remains the bedrock of the cultural anthropologist's methods for gathering knowledge of the peoples of the world, although today's case study may focus on a British urban neighborhood or a new American cult as often as on efforts of a formerly isolated Pacific island people to cope with bureaucracy. Similarly, systematic comparison of the experiences and adaptations of different societies is an old approach that is increasingly applied to new issues.

The books in the Wadsworth Modern Anthropology Library reflect cultural anthropology's greater breadth of interests. They include introductory texts and supporting anthologies of readings, as well as advanced texts dealing with more specialized fields and methods of cultural anthropology.

However, the hub of the series consists of topical studies that concentrate on either a single community or a number of communities. Each of these topical studies is strongly issue-focused. As anthropology has always done, these topical studies raise far-reaching questions about the problems people confront and the variety of human experience. They do so through close face-to-face study of people in many places and settings. In these studies, the core idiom of cultural anthropology lies exposed. Cultural anthropologists still, as always, go forth among the cultures of the world and return to inform. Only where they go and what they report have changed.

James A. Clifton
Series Editor

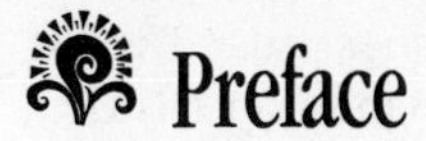

Preface

Legal prohibition of alcoholic beverages is a controversial subject. It is also an emotional topic that frequently elicits an irrational reaction when raised. Many people find controversial, emotional topics like prohibition, abortion, gun control, and nuclear disarmament difficult to discuss in a calm, reasoned way, particularly as these subjects bear on individual rights or personal control. With regard to prohibition, many Americans say, "It's crazy! We tried it in the United States and it failed miserably. It just goes to show that you can't legislate morality. You can't force people to give up something if they want it badly enough."

Given the strong feelings surrounding the subject of alcohol prohibition we wish to make clear that we are not necessarily advocates of this particular means of alcohol control. We are neither teetotallers nor strong proponents of the idea of legal controls over other people's morality, *but* we do not simply reject the idea of prohibition without consideration and discussion. Draconian as it may appear to many Americans, prohibition is among a range of alcohol control measures that policymakers might decide to try in certain sets of circumstances, such as happened in Truk. Defining those sets of circumstances and assessing the actual impact of prohibition are legitimate and important questions for social science inquiry.

In this book we offer a detailed account of prohibition and its aftermath in a relatively small, somewhat isolated community in the western Pacific. When we examine the impact of prohibition in this particular case, a number of issues of more general import for alcohol control policies emerge. These issues make the book of more than passing interest for those concerned with larger questions of public control of alcohol and drug abuse in many different human communities.

We must also comment on our use of geographical names. Recent political changes in the Pacific have led to new names for many islands, which is sometimes confusing to those unfamiliar with the area. Geographically, Micronesia refers to the small island groups of the west-central Pacific, on a par with Polynesia to the east and Melanesia to the south. However, after World War II, Micronesia came to be used as a synonym for those islands under U.S. Trust Territory administration (specifically, the Caroline, Marianas, and Marshall Islands). The Trust Territory consisted of six districts (Marianas, Marshalls, Palau, Ponape, Truk, and Yap) that have since developed into new political entities. The former Marianas District is now the Commonwealth of the Northern Marianas Islands (CNMI). The Marshalls District is now the Republic of the Marshall Islands. Palau District has become the Republic of Belau, and Ponape, Truk, and Yap Districts have joined together with Kosrae (which earlier split off from Ponape District) to form the Federated States of Micronesia (FSM). Two major islands in FSM have changed the spelling of their names: Kusaie to Kosrae, and Ponape to Pohnpei. In the following pages, where we refer to historical events that occurred in the old Trust Territory districts we retain the older spellings (Kusaie, Palau, Ponape); otherwise, we use the new ones. We follow the same rule in regard to other Pacific Island locations where name changes have occurred (Gilbert Islands to Kiribati and New Hebrides to Vanuatu).

The field research on which this book is based was underwritten by a grant to the senior author from the National Science Foundation (BNS-8418908) and was carried out on Moen Island by both authors during summer 1985. During the following summer with the support we received from an Interdisciplinary Research Grant awarded through University House at the University of Iowa, we analyzed our data and began writing. The book also draws on our earlier field research experiences in Truk State for 18 months in 1969–1971 on Namoluk Atoll, under auspices of the National Institute of Mental Health, and for 8 months in 1976 in Peniyesene village, Moen Island, with a University of Iowa Faculty Developmental Assignment and a grant from the American Philosophical Society, Johnson Fund. We have relied also on archival research we conducted in Honolulu in summer 1974 on the history of beverage alcohol in Micronesia. The 1974 research was made possible by a National Institutes of Health Biomedical Sciences Support Grant awarded through the University of Iowa. We are most grateful for these various sources of research support over the years.

Many different individuals aided our work in significant ways. In Truk, Koschy Reuney and Antero Rawit served as paid research assistants during the data-gathering phase of the project. Their perseverance made it possible to gather detailed, high-quality, general population survey data for a sample of 1,000 respondents during the summer of 1985. Many other people in Truk, too numerous to name, willingly shared documents, observations, and recollections with us. We are indebted especially to our Trukese friends—men and women, drinkers and abstainers—who offered insights into their culture and on the events in their society and lives discussed in this book. They know who they are and we hope they know the extent of our *kinissow.* Without their contributions we could not have written this book.

Fran Hezel, S.J., shared his usual keen observations, good humor, and friendship, as well as providing ready access to the Micronesian Seminar Library. John Millay, who also has investigated certain aspects of the liquor ban in Truk, was generous with data, ideas, and helpful suggestions. Robin Room made the rich library resources of the Alcohol Research Group in Berkeley available, and he and Margery Wolf commented usefully on the entire manuscript. Linda Kerber provided an incisive criticism of Chapter 7. Renée Heyum and Karen Peacock warmly opened the Pacific Collection in the Hamilton Library, University of Hawaii to us during January 1986, and the Reverend Edith Wolfe shared some particularly valuable information with us on the Woman's Board of Missions for the Pacific Islands. Captain Boisse Correa of the Honolulu Police Department patiently answered questions and helped confirm specific events that occurred during the early days of prohibition in Truk in 1978–1979. Kelsey Marshall actively assisted us with data collection on Moen. While living with us in Iowa City during 1986, Larry Gabriel assisted with the translation and transcription of taped interviews. Our research assistants at the University of Iowa, Julie Duncan, Kathy Jackson, Blane Nansel, and Chris Reichl have helped with interview transcription, bibliographic searches, data entry, and analysis. Jay Cook, Program Analyst in Iowa's Computer Resources Laboratory, cheerfully and efficiently helped us juggle apples and turn them into stars. The Graduate College of the University of Iowa provided funds to prepare the photographs for publication. Peggy Adams, Jim Clifton, Sheryl Fullerton, Angela Mann, and Stephen McElroy all provided excellent editorial assistance and support. Reviewers Ward Goodenough, University of Pennsylvania; Dr. Robin Room, Alcohol Research Group, Medical Research Institute of San Francisco; and Craig Severance, University of Hawaii, Hilo all provided helpful comments.

Our warm thanks to everyone who has contributed to this work.

List of Illustrations

List of Tables

List of Abbreviations

AA	Alcoholics Anonymous.
ABCFM	American Board of Commissioners for Foreign Missions.
ACAP	American Council on Alcohol Problems.
ADAB	Alcohol and Drug Abuse Branch [State of Hawaii].
AMA	American Medical Association.
CCM	Community College of Micronesia.
CNMI	Commonwealth of the Northern Marianas Islands.
DISCUS	Distilled Spirits Council of the United States.
EOSC	Eastern Oregon State College.
ERA	Equal Rights Amendment [to the U.S. Constitution].
ESCAP	Economic and Social Commission for Asia and the Pacific.
FSM	Federated States of Micronesia.
LMS	London Missionary Society.
MH	*Missionary Herald.*
NIAAA	National Institute of Alcohol Abuse and Alcoholism.
PCV	Peace Corps Volunteer.
PICS	Pacific Islands Central School.
PITTS	Pacific Islands Teacher Training School.
SDA	Seventh Day Adventist.
THC	Tetrahydrocannabinol.
TTC	Truk Trading Company.
TTPI	See USTTPI.
UCC	United Church of Christ.
USTTPI	United States Trust Territory of the Pacific Islands.
VCR	Videocassette recorder.
WBMPI	Woman's Board of Missions for the Pacific Islands.
WCTU	Woman's Christian Temperance Union.

In Truk, there'll be no Schlitz
So we'll have to use our wits
We'll sail to Palau
Or Kolonia for Sakau
For having no beer is the schitz!

(*Marianas Variety News & Views,*
August 18, 1977, p. 6)

CHAPTER ONE

The Social Control of Alcohol

> Neither drinking nor drunken behavior is a historical absolute, and a multitude of possible links may be traced between them and those major historical phenomena which too often have been the first resort of temperance historians. Changing class structures, work experiences, and family relationships can all affect attitudes toward drinking and drinking behavior itself. Public policy toward liquor control helps create the context in which drinking takes place, and itself derives from a changing political situation (Blocker 1985b:145).

On January 15, 1978, following nearly 20 years of legal drinking, citizens of the Pacific island of Moen in Truk, Federated States of Micronesia, inaugurated a self-imposed prohibition against the sale and consumption of alcoholic beverages. This book tells the story of the events that led to this political action and of its consequences for Trukese life.

Anthropology's most enduring contribution to the interdisciplinary arena of alcohol studies has been to record the social and cultural variation that attends the human encounter with alcoholic beverages. This cross-cultural record, as it is widely known, reminds us that the attitudes toward alcohol and the times, ways, and places in which it is consumed are much more varied than those represented by European and Euro-American societies. We present this book as an addition to the anthropological record of the myriad ways members of human communities have sought to deal with the behavioral changes usually associated with drinking. Although it is, first and foremost, an ethnography of prohibition in a Pacific island society, we think the book also reflects important changes that have occurred within the field of cultural anthropology.

One such change is that history and cultural anthropology have grown closer together, cultivating common topics, sharing some methods, and mutually enriching one another through the borrowing of data and ideas. A substantial portion of our account is a social history of alcohol use and abuse in Truk. This work relies on primary documentary sources, together with oral histories of events that took place between 1976 and 1985 obtained from persons who lived through and participated in them. At times we have supplemented these information sources with secondary sources addressed to prohibition itself or to related issues.

A second change having profound effects within cultural anthropology is the impact of feminist scholarship and a focus on gender as a subject requiring greater research attention. As feminist scholars have often remarked, "When women become a focus in a detailed study of a specific locality they emerge from their relegation to the 'fuzzy, shadowy, background' to become conscious, active, human beings sharing an important part of the action, although constrained by the male dominated structures of society" (Bryson and Wearing 1985:359). The feminist literature has influenced our account, which pivots on fundamental differences between Trukese women and men over beverage alcohol. As such, we hope it makes a modest contribution to the links between cultural anthropology and women's studies.

A third important change transpiring in anthropology in recent years is a shift toward applied research—toward practical affairs rather than purely academic discourse. Questions of alcohol control policies—informal and implicit or formal and explicit—confront all human communities in which alcoholic beverages are consumed. Although this book is not a policy-oriented study with specific recommendations for action, we do address and assess the consequences of an effort at total prohibition in a relatively small, homogeneous, island society. Our findings concerning the effects of prohibition in Truk are situated within a broader comparative framework including examples from elsewhere in Oceania and from other parts of the world. Although we do not attempt an exhaustive survey of every known instance of legal prohibition, we feel we do present enough evidence of its use to allow a dispassionate evaluation. In the end, we draw some general conclusions about the pros and cons of prohibition in different kinds of human societies, along with some specific conclusions about the net effect of prohibition in Truk.

Trukese women played an active political role as agents of change in instituting and maintaining prohibition from 1978 to the present (January 1989). In addition to chronicling women's involvement in these events, we evaluate the impact of the temperance movement on women's continued involvement in public policy issues and community political life in Truk. Finally, we assess the overall social, economic, and political effects of prohibition on Trukese society and culture by taking advantage of a before-and-after "natural experiment" (a set of events that could not be designed in advance). Because we had carried out an extensive investigation of alcohol use and drunkenness on Moen two years before the liquor ban was established, we were able to compare data gathered for the present study, conducted seven and one-half years after prohibition began, with information obtained in 1976. This material provided a baseline for discussing changes in attitudes and actions surrounding alcohol use that occurred over this period.

The consumption of alcoholic beverages is subject to some kind of social control in all known human societies. In small-scale, face-to-face tribal societies such controls may consist merely of social pressures on drinkers to conform to culturally appropriate patterns of drunken behavior. Such societies usually also restrict who may drink, what and how much they may consume, when they may partake of such beverages, and when alcoholic beverages may be manufactured. Among the more widespread bases for social controls on alcohol use are age and gender. Children frequently are not allowed to drink until they reach a state of maturity based either on external physical signs or on age. In some human societies women are not supposed to drink at all, and even in most of those where women may drink they are enjoined to consume smaller amounts and to drink less often than men. Larger, more complex societies typically have written laws regulating alcohol use, along with legal penalties imposed on those who break the rules.

Recently, a committee of the Institute of Medicine observed that much additional study is needed on outlining how and when formal community responses to alcohol problems are initiated. The committee noted the particular importance of studying "natural experiments," that is, opportunities to investigate the effects of changes in law, policy, or circumstances surrounding drinking, and lamented the limited progress made in this direction. Advocating comparative studies and studies of change, the committee targeted a number of research areas for greater development. Prominent among these were "historical studies that chart patterns of change," qualitative studies that permit the examination of "processes of change as people experience them," and "studies of natural experiments . . . that chart the effects on drinking practices and problems of policy interventions and other social changes" (Institute of Medicine 1987). Our research directly addresses all of these concerns.

SYSTEMS OF CONTROL

When dealing with modern societies, as opposed to traditional tribes and chiefdoms, we may define alcohol control as the state's intervention in the production, trade, or purchase of alcoholic drinks. Such a definition allows for examination of all control systems and actions related to alcohol, "not only those with the explicit aim of preventing alcohol-related problems" (Mäkelä 1985:15). This definition of alcohol control excludes those policies concerned with direct management of alcohol-related problems that do not intervene in the market for alcoholic beverages (Ibid.). Among the several major formal community responses to alcohol control governments employ (almost always in some combination) are substitution, regulation, education, and prohibition.

In his discussion of such community responses, Lemert assumes the goal of social control over alcohol use is to reduce or minimize the costs of drunken behavior. Drawing on the experiences of whole societies, and the beliefs and efforts of power elites who have sought to control alcohol use, he derives four hypothetical models of social control. The first of these is the substitution model in which "the costs of intoxication and drunkenness can be reduced by substitution of functional equivalents of drinking" (Lemert 1967:83). This model rests on "the assumption that values satisfied through drinking or drunkenness can be fulfilled through other activities" (Ibid.:84). Its advocates seek to reorganize community life so that athletics, games, recreation, and other diversions will replace the time and effort previously devoted to drinking.

Lemert's second model of social control is the regulatory approach. Its supporters believe they can diminish the social costs of intoxication by manipulating such things as the kinds of alcohol available, the price of alcohol, how the beverages are distributed, the hours and locations in which drinking takes place, and the availability of drink according to the consumer's age, sex, and other characteristics (for example, ethnicity). Public support and the cooperation of law enforcement officials are required for the regulatory model to work effectively.

In the third, or educational, model the ". . . costs of intoxication and drunkenness can be reduced by a system of indoctrination or information about the consequences of using alcohol—thus leading to moderate drinking or abstinence" (Ibid.:80). This model is problematic. We have no conclusive evidence that exposing people to information leads them to change either their actions or their values.

Lemert's final model for the social control of alcohol is the most drastic one from the point of view of social engineering. Proponents of this model—the prohibition approach—argue that we can limit or eliminate the social costs of drunkenness "by a system of laws and coercive controls making it illegal to manufacture, distribute, or consume alcoholic beverages" (Ibid.:78). Lemert comments that the prohibition model has been tried in a number of different societies and that it has failed consistently to prevent people who want to drink from doing so. He attributes "the well-documented failures of the model" to "its high costs, the instability of power elites favorable to prohibition, the limitations of power and available means of control, and the growth of resistance unresponsive to coercion" (Ibid.). Lemert also notes serious problems inherent in the prohibition model: It sacrifices the positive values derived from moderate drinking and the economic vested interests of those who earn a living from the production and distribution of alcohol; its supporters face great difficulty in enforcing laws that attempt to regulate the more personal aspects of human behavior; and it increases the scarcity value of alcoholic drink, encouraging bootlegging and smuggling that in turn undermine respect for the law. He argues that for this model to succeed:

> Probably it would require conspicuously high costs of drunkenness on one hand and on the other a positive replacement of the drinking values or substitution of new means for achieving the old values. A precondition of this would be relatively complete geographic isolation,

> similar to that found on islands, where behavior deviations have a high visibility. A social structure in which power is concentrated and little affected by public opinion or is upheld by supernatural sanctions perhaps would make for successful prohibition (Ibid.:79–80).

As an alcohol control strategy, prohibition has acquired a bad reputation in the United States and other Western countries since the 1930s. The very word is anathema to many; it smacks of moralistic judgment, prudery, and infringement of individual rights. The very idea of prohibition is rejected out of hand as old-fashioned and unworkable, a viewpoint that may represent one more example of the blinders members of the "wet generations" have worn (Room 1984) over the past half century. Such closed-mindedness may well have prevented recognition of the positive side of prohibition as a prevention strategy *for certain kinds of societies and in certain sets of circumstances.* Specifically, in those communities that rely mainly on external, social rather than internal, personal systems of control (Howard 1979), prohibition—whatever its faults—may prove acceptable to a majority of the general population and provide a helpful preventive measure against alcohol-related problems. In such cases, a prohibition movement may produce an overall social benefit.

A SHIFT IN FOCUS

Over the past 15 years there has been a marked shift in alcohol studies away from an emphasis on treatment of alcoholism as a disease of special populations to a concern with the prevention and control of alcohol-related problems in general populations (e.g., Gusfield 1976, 1982; Mäkelä et al. 1981; Popham, Schmidt, and de Lint 1975, 1976; Room 1978, 1982; Single, Morgan, and de Lint 1981). Although Fager (1984) has labeled this return to prevention "the New Temperance movement," it is more generally known as the "public health model" (Bruun et al. 1975; Holder and Stoil 1988). Its proponents seek nonmoralistic ways to reduce alcohol consumption in a population as a means of lessening the personal and social costs of alcohol abuse. This approach predicates that lower levels of consumption will result in fewer alcohol-related problems.

One source of support for this premise comes from the experience of national Prohibition in the United States from 1920 to 1933, during which total alcohol consumption decreased and rates of liver cirrhosis declined. It is thought these reductions occurred because a restricted supply greatly increased the effective price of alcoholic beverages (Gusfield 1976; Room 1978). Thus, whereas in some respects Prohibition failed as a social experiment in America, it *did* produce certain desirable public health results. Given the well-known problems that accompany prohibition (e.g., enforcement, resistance, the development of black markets, etc.), the challenge to advocates of the public health model is to devise a system of prevention that achieves the laudable public health consequences of prohibition without producing all of the negative effects historically associated with it.

In pursuing such a goal a better understanding of prohibition is required. Detailed, specific policy alternatives concerning the control of alcohol-related problems in human communities should be based on studies of the benefits and drawbacks of *all* the various control options, including prohibition (May and Smith 1988). Yet aside from a few well-documented instances of prohibition in complex, Western industrialized societies (e.g., Finland, Norway, and the United States), we know only that prohibition has been tried in many times and places and that it always has failed to prevent some people from drinking. At present we have no detailed case studies of the development, imposition, and impact of prohibition on nonwestern, nonindustrialized societies. The few sketchy reports that exist (e.g., Marshall 1975a; Millay 1987a, 1987b; Piau-Lynch 1982; Talyaga 1982; Thakur, Sharma, and Akhtar 1982) tell us very little about the actual workings of prohibition in Third World countries and next to nothing about how a variety of persons in those societies—nondrinkers as well as tipplers—view prohibition. Edwards (1979) claims that drinking problems are "putting the Third World on the map"; yet data about alcohol-related problems and prevention strategies in developing countries remain extremely limited (see, e.g., Edwards 1978; Marshall 1982b, 1984; Moser 1979). Our primary aim in this book is to help remedy this deficiency.

THE CASE AT HAND

From the introduction of alcohol to Truk in the late nineteenth century, its use has been restricted almost exclusively to males (Marshall 1979a:82–97). This marked gender difference in access to alcohol is quite unusual cross-culturally although it appears to form part of a general pan-Pacific pattern (Marshall 1982b:4–5, 1987b). In a major comparative study of gender differences in alcohol use, Child, Barry, and Bacon (1965) found that drinking was limited to members of one sex (always males) in only 4 out of 113 societies for which they had adequate information.[1] Far more typical than societies in which only men drink are those in which both males and females are allowed to consume alcohol, but where males—especially young men—drink in greater quantities and more frequently than females (Ibid.; Marshall 1979b:454–455). We corroborated the observational and interview data documenting the existence of a gender gap in Trukese drinking in 1976 (Marshall 1979a) by a general population survey of a sample of 1,000 adults on Moen Island aged 15 years or older in 1985. Our sample was stratified for age, gender, and residential location on Moen based upon the most recent census data then available for Truk (U.S.

Department of Commerce 1983; see Table 2.1). The completed sample consisted of 516 males and 484 females.

Only 11 women in the sample (2.3 percent) reported themselves ever to have consumed alcohol.[2] Three women claimed to be current drinkers (0.6 percent), and the other eight listed themselves as former drinkers. Thus, at the time of our survey, more than 99 percent of the women sampled were abstainers. By contrast, 85.5 percent of the male respondents were current or former drinkers. Furthermore, the preponderance of the male abstainers were in the 15–19 age cohort, and it seemed likely that the majority of them would become drinkers eventually since 83 percent of male current drinkers had begun to drink by age 19, and 96.5 percent had done so by age 24. Clearly, then, Truk was a dramatic example of a society in which most men consumed alcoholic beverages and most women did not. We might anticipate then that these men and women would have quite different attitudes toward and feelings about alcohol. And we might also expect that when members of only one sex indulge heavily in a substance that may lead to family problems and community disruption, the stage is set for disagreement and confrontation along gender lines.

In most tribal and peasant societies, women do not participate actively in public political life. Men denigrate women in many such societies as at best flightly and at worst stupid, and in either case as certainly not fit for weighty deliberations over public policy. Today we recognize that women encounter similar attitudes and impediments in complex, industrialized Western societies as they seek to engage more fully in the political process. Except under unusual circumstances, the tribal societies of Micronesia did not grant women an active, public political role, although women, acting as a group, could influence the decisions of their district chief on matters such as men's drinking habits (Figirliyong 1976:17). Even as many Micronesian women have obtained higher education in recent years (e.g., Marshall and Marshall 1982), sex role stereotypes regarding "women's place" and the overt opposition of many men have effectively prevented them from direct involvement in political activities.

Throughout Oceania, prohibition was one of the first laws colonial governments enacted (Marshall 1980). With independence movements leading to self-government following World War II, deprohibition—ushering in "the right to drink"—was a common change, often made even before the end of colonial rule. Given this background and the symbolic value of drinking as a sign of equality, it is surprising and somewhat ironic to discover recent instances where islanders themselves have reimposed prohibition. For example, there was a three-month ban on liquor sales in Simbu Province, Papua New Guinea, from November 1980 to January 1981, and a continuing ban began in nearby Enga Province in January 1981. Longer and more dramatic than either of these cases, however, has been the prohibition law on Moen Island, Truk, in effect since January 1978.

This law was in response to a social situation that most Trukese perceived as escalating rapidly beyond control. Many Trukese drinkers exhibited a hostile, disruptive, public style of drunkenness associated with verbal aggression and physical violence that often led to serious injury and not infrequently to homicide or suicide (Hezel 1981, 1984; Mahoney 1974; Marshall 1979a; Rubinstein 1983, 1987). Socially disruptive drinkers in Truk came overwhelmingly from the ranks of young men between the ages of 15 and 35, and in Truk as in the United States in the previous century, ". . . no family, no matter what its background or standing, could justifiably feel secure from the threat of young men's drinking and potential alcoholism" (Blocker 1985b:114). We designed our study to examine Truk's recent prohibition experience to see if and how it changed young men's alcohol use, and simultaneously, to explore several related questions. For example, did prohibition effectively reduce alcohol-related violence in Truk? Why did Trukese women finally publicly mobilize to oppose alcohol abuse in 1976–1977 after enduring many years of problematic drunkenness without public protest? Did their successful political action alter the balance of power between men and women in the political arena? What are the long-term implications of this change?

Blocker has observed that "the study of alcohol control policies and their effects upon the number of outlets, consumption levels, and alcoholic damage is still in its infancy" (1985b:123). Most such studies have been done in large, heterogeneous political units (usually nation states), and few of them have examined change over time. We give special attention to the changes in attitudes and policies toward drinking in Truk, especially over the period from 1976–1985.[3] The social and political unit we examine is small by world standards—approximately 47,000 people—and homogeneous in langauge and culture. The Truk case conforms quite well to the set of conditions Lemert prescribed for success of the prohibition model (see above). Prohibition has not eliminated alcohol use in Truk, nor has it stopped all alcohol-related problems. However, it *has* reduced what had become intolerable costs of intoxication and drunkenness, and it *has* worked reasonably well as a means of social control over drinking. Given the many "well-documented failures" of prohibition Lemert mentioned (1967), discovery of a case in which prohibition has succeeded, at least partially, is significant for our understanding of systems of prevention and control. However, changes in alcohol control policies in Truk must be understood in terms of changing gender relations there.

During the late nineteenth century in the United States, the nascent women's rights movement joined forces with the temperance movement as activists "attempted to carve out a distinctly women's position on the liquor problem" (Levine 1980:44). For those like Elizabeth Cady Stanton, president of The Woman's New York State Temperance Society, "a distinctly woman's perspective on the liquor question necessarily raised the question of women's oppression" (Ibid.:50), and women's suffrage and the antiliquor cause remained wed throughout the rest of the century. Particularly prominent in this regard was the Woman's Christian Temperance Union (WCTU) that Levine (Ibid.:53) has called "the most important and influential women's organization in 19th-century America." The WCTU gave previously nonactivist women a cause and an opportunity to participate in a broad range of public and political activities. Frances Willard's WCTU and Carry Nation's saloon smashings placed women in the forefront of efforts to eliminate alcohol use or to control alcohol-related problems. Such organizations and events helped pave the way toward women's fuller participation in the American political process. The history of American women's involvement in temperance activities was bound up in traditional notions of women as the mainstays of home and family, as the watchdogs of public morality, and as pillars of the church (Levine 1980).

Comparable ideas about women, combined with the influence of American missionaries, stimulated some Trukese women to play similar roles vis-à-vis alcohol in their own society. As in nineteenth-century America, alcohol-related problems galvanized the previously uninvolved Trukese women to joint political action. Approximately 100 years after women gained control of the American temperance movement, Trukese women repeated much of their historical experience. What is not clear is whether Trukese women's organized political opposition to problems linked to alcohol abuse in their communities presages the development of a full-scale women's rights movement there, as occurred in the United States.

In this book we will first concentrate on the circumstances that led to women's mobilization against alcohol, building on our 1976 community study of alcohol use and drunken behavior. We give particular attention to the political role of women's groups and to gender relations in seeking to understand how prohibition works as an alcohol control policy in a small Pacific island setting. We include a discussion of recent sociopolitical changes on Truk, a historical chronicle of alcoholic beverages in the islands, an examination of alterations in gender roles—particularly women's roles—and an assessment of the impact of prohibition on Trukese society and drinking behavior. Following this, we compare the Truk case with women's involvement in temperance and prohibition activities in the nineteenth-century United States, after which Truk's experience with alcohol control is discussed in relation to other alcohol policies in Oceania. Finally, using the cross-national literature, we assess prohibition as a control strategy and reach some conclusions for the case at hand.

CHAPTER TWO

Moen, Truk, 1985

> It is impossible to say a thing exactly the way it was, because what you say can never be exact, you always have to leave something out, there are too many parts, sides, crosscurrents, nuances; too many gestures, which could mean this or that, too many shapes which can never be fully described, too many flavors, in the air or on the tongue, half-colors, too many (Atwood 1986:134).

Moen is among a dozen major islands and a multitude of smaller ones scattered about the relatively sheltered waters of Truk Lagoon (see Figure 2.1). This huge geological formation, known technically as a complex atoll, has a surrounding reef about 40 miles across enclosing over 820 square miles, although the total land mass of all the islands combined is only 32.7 square miles (Manchester 1951). As with all but one of the inhabited islands of Truk Lagoon, Moen is an intensely green, mountainous volcanic island thrusting out of an azure sea. Stunning in their physical beauty, these islands stand in close proximity to one another and are home to a people who speak mutually intelligible dialects of a single language (Goodenough and Sugita 1980) and who share a common historical and cultural tradition. Individual village, district, and island origin remain important social markers, but the political consolidation of the islands during the colonial experience of the past century has led today to a meaningful ethnic identity as "Trukese," an identity shared vis-à-vis foreigners with the inhabitants of the atolls in the Hall, Mortlock, Namonuito, and Western Islands (see Figure 2.2).

Like other Pacific island port towns, Moen has grown rapidly in the years since the end of World War II. Prior to the war Moen's population did not exceed 2,300 persons (Japan 1931, 1937), but by 1967 it had risen to 5,687 and stood at 9,562 in 1973 (Kay 1974). The official census carried out on September 15, 1980, recorded a de facto population of 10,351 for Moen Island (U.S. Department of Commerce 1983; see Table 2.1). Their median age was 17.7 years and 46 percent were under age 16. Moen's population in 1985 was approximately 12,000 persons, who constituted about one-quarter of the total population of Truk State, in turn the most populous of the four political entities forming the Federated States of Micronesia (FSM; see Figure 2.3).[1]

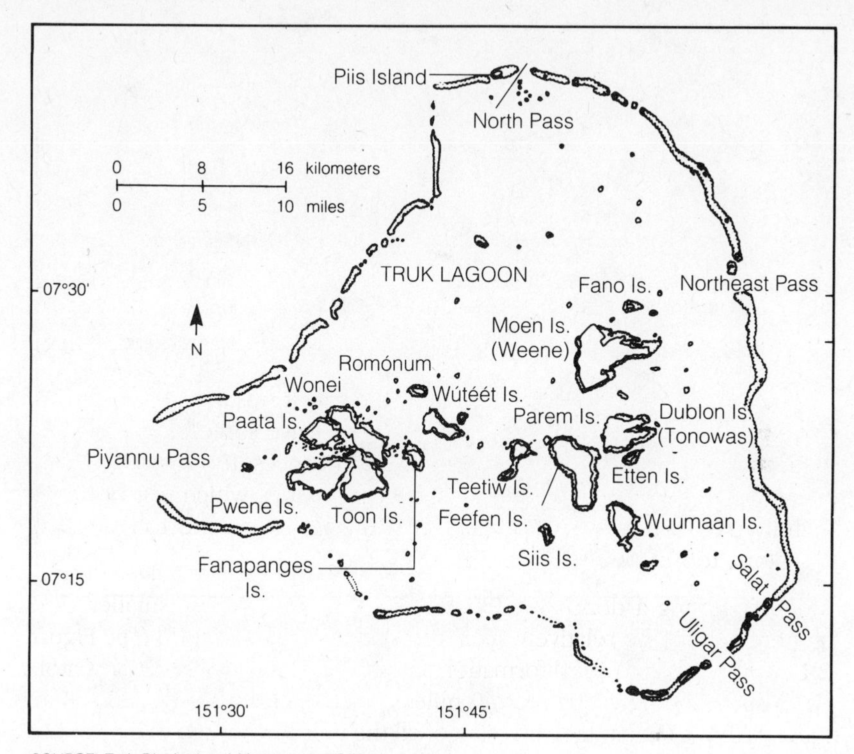

SOURCE: Truk District Land Management Office.

FIGURE 2.1 *Truk Lagoon.*

Although Truk's population has a very high rate of natural increase by contemporary world standards (over 3.5 percent per annum), most of Moen's growth in the postwar period is a result of urban migration. This migration occasionally has led to tensions among people from different islands, and especially to resentments on the part of Moen citizens to the "invasion" of their island by "outsiders." As early as 1971, an article appeared in a local newspaper entitled, "Whose island is Moen?" One of the author's major complaints was that migrants to Moen did not abide by its municipal laws, and that they frequently caused trouble or got into fights, behavior that presumably would not have occurred back home (*Micronitor,* December 4, 1971, p. 1; see also Rubinstein 1980:16). These sentiments on the part of at least some citizens of Moen Municipality contributed, a few years later, to the passage of a local prohibition law.

Second in size only to the Toon complex among the islands of Truk Lagoon, Moen consists of 7.3 square miles of land, rugged and forested in the interior, with a narrow coastal littoral where most of the people reside. Moen's highest peak looms 1,200 feet above the surrounding waters. A

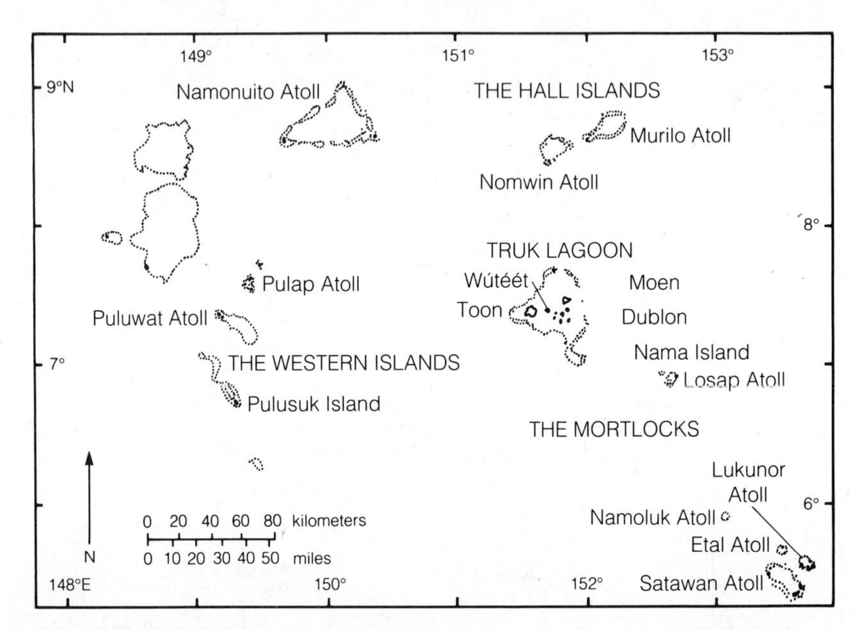

SOURCES: Association for Social Anthropology in Oceania after Trust Territory of the Pacific Islands and Truk District Land Management Office (1969).

FIGURE 2.2 *Truk State, Federated States of Micronesia.*

TABLE 2.1 *De facto population, Moen Island, Truk, September 15, 1980.*

AGE COHORT	NO. MALES	NO. FEMALES	TOTAL PERSONS
0–4	944	847	1,791
5–9	807	686	1,493
10–14	689	607	1,296
15–19	550	545	1,095
20–24	461	483	944
25–29	484	447	931
30–34	397	342	739
35–39	203	190	393
40–44	190	179	369
45–49	202	150	352
50–54	132	122	254
55–59	126	117	243
60–64	101	95	196
65–69	68	63	131
70–74	41	35	76
75+	21	27	48
TOTAL	5,416	4,935	10,351

SOURCE: U.S. Department of Commerce (1983).

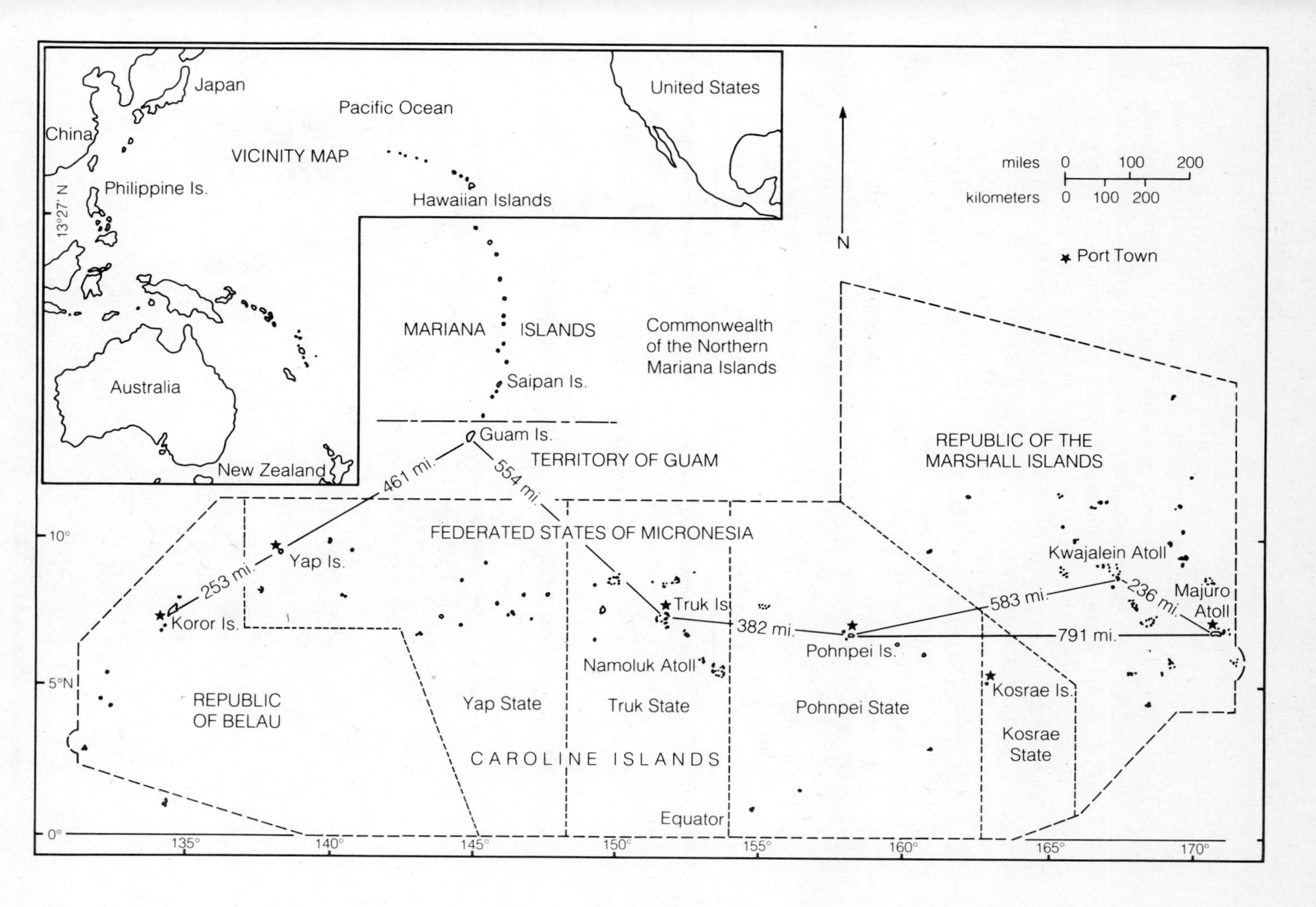

FIGURE 2.3 *Micronesia.*

SOURCE: Office of the High Commissioner.

fringing reef, interspersed with mangrove swamps, provides rich marine habitat, varied resources, and a palette of colors from aqua to dark turquoise that mediates between the greens of the island and the deep blue of the lagoon (see Figure 2.4). Unfortunately, this natural beauty is often marred by the detritus of human activity: rusting hulks that once were instruments of war; broken-down automobiles now covered with weeds; and—seemingly everywhere—aluminum cans emblazoned with names like Schlitz, Fanta, Meister Brau, Coca-Cola, Strohs, and the ubiquitous Budweiser. Socially, Moen is divided into 10 separately named districts that continue to play an important role in the kinship and political organization of the community (Figure 2.5). Under American protectorate since the end of World War II, these 10 districts have been amalgamated into a single Moen Municipal Government with a mayor, elected council, and other administrative offices such as a secretary and a municipal police force.

Before the Second World War, Spanish, German, and Japanese colonial administrations were headquartered on the adjacent island of Dublon. Dublon is less than half the size of Moen, but it was selected as the first seat of government because of its superior ship anchorage, particularly for sailing vessels. The American military government relocated the administrative headquarters from Dublon to Moen soon after the formal Japanese surrender in 1945 because of the large amount of unexploded ordnance

FIGURE 2.4 *Island scene, looking from Moen toward Feefen Island.*

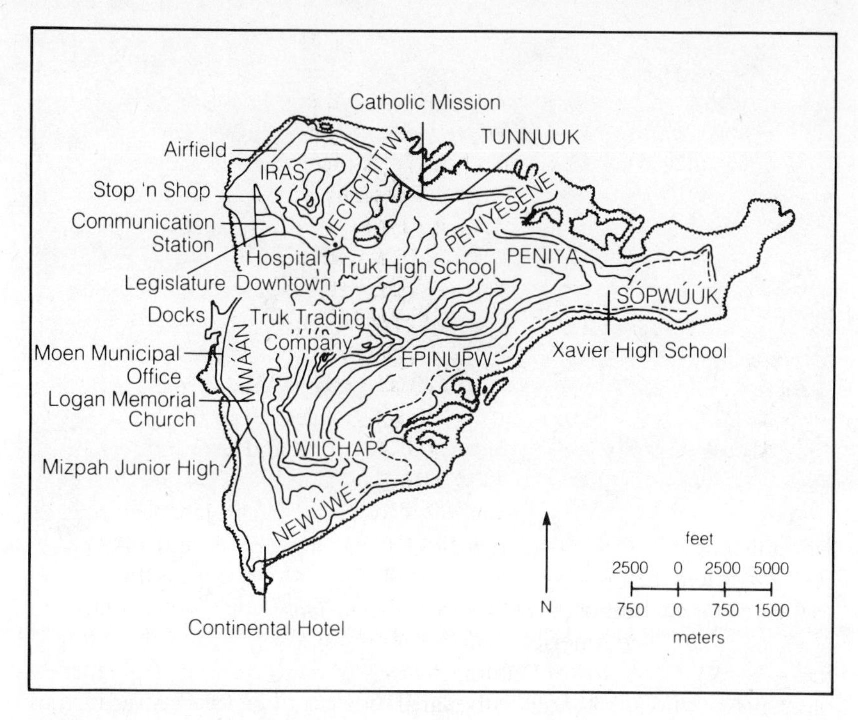

SOURCE: Hawaii Architects and Engineers (1968) Moen Island, Truk District. Final Report, Trust Territory Physical Planning Program.

FIGURE 2.5 *Moen Island, Truk.*

that remained on Dublon. Hence, Moen's history as a port town island dates back only a little over 40 years.

Moen typifies the port towns that dot the Pacific region in the late twentieth century. Moen links the people of Truk State to the rest of the world—it is the node in the international network of transportation and communication that binds us all together. As with other port towns, Moen has dock and warehouse facilities to handle imports—processed food, clothing, machinery, and a remarkable diversity of manufactured goods for Truk's consumer economy—and to take on copra, Truk's only significant export (See Figure 2.6). Near the dock area are petroleum storage tanks that fuel the diesel generators that provide the island's electricity and run the growing crowd of sedans and pickup trucks imported from Japan. Moen's port facility also serves as the transshipment and debarkation point for a fleet of small interisland government freighters making regular voyages to the outer island atolls comprising the remainder of Truk State (see Figure 2.2). A number of privately owned, converted Japanese fishing boats and other vessels of great diversity also ply between Moen and the outer islands, and a few locally based fishing boats are home ported on

FIGURE 2.6 *Dock and warehouse area, Moen, Truk, July 1985.*

Moen. Near the dock area is a small boat pool always aswarm with outboard motorboats laden to the gunwales with passengers, produce, and store-bought items as they zip back and forth between Moen and the other islands in the Lagoon.[2] Quite a few paid Moen workers commute daily by boat to their jobs in town from neighboring islands such as Dublon or Feefen. This necessity has led one enterprising businessman to purchase an elegant Chris Craft motorized yacht, replete with snack bar, VCR, and other amenities, that he uses as a water taxi to ferry commuters to and from their jobs. The fee is $1 per person each way from Dublon, Feefen, and Wuumaan to Moen.

At least as important for any modern Pacific port town as wharves and warehouses is a good airport offering access to commercial jet travel. Prior to 1982, Moen's airport consisted of a marginally adequate terminal facility and a rather short, crushed coral runway that could not accommodate landings after dark. Today, Moen boasts an excellent paved runway, lighted for night landings, and a small but adequate terminal complex for handling passengers, baggage, and air freight. All these improvements have been completed within the past decade. By summer 1985, flights on Air Micronesia's Boeing-727s passed through Moen's airport at least daily, either heading east to Pohnpei, the Marshall Islands, and Hawaii or northwest to Guam.[3] At that time the airport also handled military cargo planes supplying the U.S. Air Force Civic Action Team engaged in public works projects on Moen and elsewhere in the Lagoon, and even now small private planes, usually from Guam, land at Moen.

LIFE IN THE FAST LANE

Truk has become increasingly modernized during the last century, beginning with the Japanese period from 1914–1945 and accelerating over the past 25 years, particularly with the Kennedy administration's decision to vastly increase the annual budget of the Trust Territory, which brought notable changes in the social landscape. Much of the old life has vanished, been destroyed, or altered almost beyond recognition. Customs have been eroded. Modern substitutes have supplanted traditional material culture. The survivors of these changes have hammered out different ways of interacting from the remnants of the old life and the bits and pieces of the new. Contemporary Truk is significantly different from what existed 30 years ago.

The Trukese are keenly aware of these changes, but like humans everywhere have found it difficult to direct or control the force of the storm that has swept over them. As early as 1970, an editorial in a local newspaper drew attention to the rise of social classes based on wealth, and to the modern buildings, new machines, and seemingly endless variety of material goods arriving in the stores (*Met Poraus,* October 2, 1970, p. 5). This same editorial also drew readers' attention to population growth, an increase in crime, and to widespread drunkenness. Alcohol use and abuse have long been an element in the rhetoric of change in Truk linked to such negative aspects of modern life as crime and confusion. Youngsters and young adults argue that Truk today is electricity, jet airplanes, and frozen chickens, not the wood fires, paddling canoes, and fresh fish of their parents' and grandparents' childhoods. In this context, alcohol—and marijuana—is looked upon as a new thing to be mastered, just like computers, flush toilets, break dancing, and algebra.

By comparison with the inhabitants of other islands in Truk State, persons on Moen live in the fast lane. They have regular access to many of the technological devices of the modern world that are represented elsewhere in Truk only minimally, if at all. For example, with the steady increase in the urban population, with the availability of money via a government salary scale the envy of other Pacific island countries,[4] and with the paved roads that have increased the lifespan of most vehicles, the number of registered motor vehicles on the island has climbed from 6 in 1955 to 710 in 1985.[5] These vehicles represent a considerable cash investment. For example, in the summer of 1985 a new Suzuki jeep cost $6,000 on Moen, a Toyota pickup sold for approximately $7,500, and fancier cars such as the Toyota Cressida cost considerably more. Moen now has a morning rush hour. Between 8:00 and 8:30 on several different weekdays vehicles pass the Post Office at a rate of more than 12 per minute, or one vehicle approximately every 5 seconds.

All villages on Moen now have access to electricity from the central power plant, although not all private homes are wired to receive it.

Electricity, even if often intermittent, has allowed wealthier citizens to purchase refrigerators, freezers, VCRs, electric fans, and other home appliances unknown in Trukese villages until quite recently.[6] Most major businesses and government offices have photocopiers, and there are several computers on the island, with the prospect of many more to come in the next few years. Air conditioning is de rigueur in the newer stores and mandatory in many government offices to maintain computers and similar sensitive machinery in Truk's humid tropical climate.

In the late 1970s a piped water system with storage tanks located in different parts of the island was constructed that tapped artesian wells under Moen's mountains. As a conservation measure, the water is usually on for only a few hours per day, but its very availability has reduced reliance on wells and streams that, given Moen's population growth, were often contaminated. In addition to the piped water supply, most of Moen's people also use rain catchment systems employing corrugated metal roofs, gutters, and cisterns or 55-gallon drums for storage. In 1982–1983, a cholera epidemic in Truk spurred development of an islandwide sanitary sewer system, and elimination of the overwater toilets the Japanese had introduced years before. Although the new sewer system is not without its flaws and problems, it represents a step toward modernization not yet taken elsewhere in Truk State.

And with the obvious material changes—motor vehicles, home and office appliances, and a public works infrastructure—when people walk the streets of Moen there is an excitement in the air that they do not experience in the rural island communities away from the center. They encounter strangers; they see foreigners; they hear other languages. There are video games to be played, laundromats to be tried, restaurants to be sampled, and numerous stores to be visited, filled with an astonishing variety of consumer goods from North America, Asia, and Australia. Daily commercial jet flights carry friends and relatives off to far places, and bring others back, sometimes transformed by their experiences abroad. Huge ocean-going freighters tie up regularly at the wharf downtown while tankers anchor at an offshore buoy to deliver their cargo via an underwater pipeline. Motorboats buzz almost continuously about the waterfront area, with first one and then another darting off across the lagoon, inscribing long white arcs on the clear blue water. Radios blare from storefronts. Young men wearing T-shirts proclaiming "Budweiser" or "Marlboro" saunter along, the latest rock tunes blasting from their portable tape decks. Young women stroll in pairs or groups, alternately flirting with the young men and appearing totally disinterested in their surroundings. Children giggle in the shade, sipping cans of cold Coke or Fanta. Compared to the sleepy outer islands with their highly predictable daily round, broken only by an occasional "ship day" or natural disaster, Moen is an exciting place to be.

Tourism in Truk has developed only since the late 1960s with the advent of commercial jet service from Guam and Honolulu on Air Micronesia. Once regular air travel was established, hotel development began as well. In late October 1968, the U.S. Navy released 14 acres of military retention land it controlled at South Field (Newúwé), the site of a former Japanese seaplane base, for development into a first class resort hotel (*Met Poraus,* November 7, 1968, p. 3). The Continental Travelodge Hotel opened in 1970, but was preceded by the now defunct Hotel Maramar and by Christopher's Inn, both of which opened in 1969 (*Met Poraus,* June 19, 1969, p. 17). Today, a small but steady stream of tourists visit Truk, primarily scuba enthusiasts who come to dive on the sunken wrecks of the World War II Japanese fleet off Dublon. Two different dive shops cater to their needs, and plans are afoot for other small-scale tourist-oriented developments.

Moen is where the jobs are in Truk, and most jobs are in state government.[7] Moen is where the accoutrements of the outside world offer the promise, or the illusion, that one has left the village behind and is participant in a new, exciting, consumer-oriented lifestyle. Moen is where Truk's young people must venture to complete high school, once they finish the regional junior highs that educate them through tenth grade. Moen is the place from which Trukese people depart to pursue higher education abroad, whether on Pohnpei, Guam, in the United States, the Philippines, Papua New Guinea, or elsewhere, and Moen is the place to which most graduates return with their newfound skills, hoping to find a job in the government sector. Increasingly, in recent years, with seniority of government workers who entered the workforce 20 or more years ago, with the sharp growth in the number of young adults who have obtained postsecondary education, and with the reduction in U.S. aid with termination of the Trust Territory, many college-educated young persons find themselves either unemployed or underemployed and form part of a rather resentful urban outgroup. Now that the Compact of Free Association with the United States has been implemented it seems likely that some—perhaps many—of these young adults will migrate permanently to Hawaii and the west coast of the U.S. mainland in search of employment, much like Samoans have done over the last three decades (Lewthwaite, Mainzer, and Holland 1973).

The governmental and commercial center of Truk State is concentrated in an area of the island bracketed by Iras on one side and Mwáán on the other (see Figure 2.5). Nestled in a natural saddle between two of the island's larger peaks is the heart of Truk's governmental complex, known by its Japanese name of Nantaku. In this complex are the hospital, courthouse, Truk High School, and the offices of most state government departments. Here, too, are found the fancy houses once reserved for American contract employees of the Trust Territory administration and now occupied by senior public servants. Nantaku provides an excellent focal point from which to locate and identify the town's other major buildings, facilities, and areas (see Figure 2.7).

The power plant, the Police Station and Fire Department, the Truk

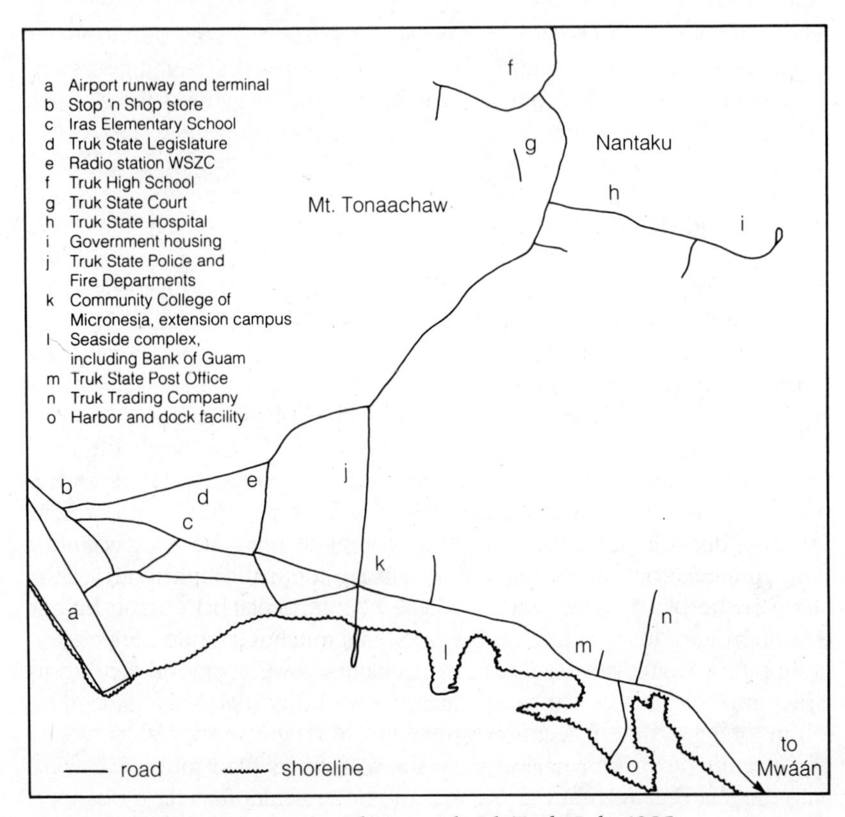

FIGURE 2.7 *Port town area of Moen Island, Truk, July 1985.*

branch of the Community College of Micronesia (CCM), and several modern stores line the winding, paved road down the hill from Nantaku toward the lagoon. This road ends in a T-intersection with the main coastal road that runs most of the way around the island. A right-hand turn leads past more stores and a restaurant to the huge satellite dish of the Communications Station where it is now possible to talk with persons almost anywhere in the world via long distance telephone. Opposite the communications facility is the large grassy playfield and the campus of Iras Elementary School, adjacent to which are the government radio station (WSZC),[8] and the state legislature building. Not far past the communications complex are more stores and a few houses on the right, and the airport terminal and runway on the left. Turning around 180 degrees and backtracking to the T-intersection leads directly into Moen's commercial center—the mercantile mile—wherein are located many modern stores, restaurants, the Bank of Guam, the Post Office, other government offices (e.g., Public Works), and the boat pool and dock facilities (see Figure 2.8). Here, too, is a cluster of small vans (serving as mobile stores catering to commuters who do not wish to carry their purchases from the regular stores to their boats), the farmer's market, a fishing cooperative, a couple of movie theaters, Slick Mick's Video Arcade,[9] the Truk Travel Company, one or two prominent churches, and some extremely well-appointed new apartment buildings. Anchoring this commercial area at the far end, and separating it from Mwáán village and the Moen Municipal Government offices, is the Mobil Oil dump, whose large white tanks loom like giant sea slugs at the water's edge.

Modern Moen is a study in contrasts. Paved roads extend from the town area to the villages of Iras, Mechchitiw, and Tunnuuk in one direction and to Mwáán and Newúwé in the other.[10] These roads give way to rough, rock-strewn, and pothole-laden dirt feeder and linking roads that produce heavy wear and tear on vehicles. Attractive cement block homes with glass louvered windows, fancy wooden doors, and bright paint stand side by side with squatter settlements of crowded, unpainted wooden boxes, raised on posts and crowned with rusted tin roofs. Upper-level politicians and public servants in their shiny, air-conditioned Japanese cars, replete with tape decks and tinted windows, glide past their unemployed country-men trudging along the hot streets under the relentless tropical sun. Fancy new stores selling frozen beef and chicken, commercial baby food, dispos-able diapers, brightly colored clothing, digital watches, and portable radio/ tape decks compete with small, ramshackle, family-run operations selling little else but canned mackerel, cigarettes, and flashlight batteries.

A significant development on Moen in the last two decades is the rise of a monied elite in a formerly egalitarian society with no traditional class differences. Social class has now become a significant feature of contem-porary Trukese life, although it is not formally labeled in the Trukese language. Other than a few extremely wealthy upper-class families, town dwellers sort into middle class and lower class on the bases of education, wage employment, and traditional kinship affiliation. Thus, we refer to upper-class and middle-class persons collectively as the elite. By rough approximation about 500 adults on Moen in 1985 made up the elite. Typically, citizens in this category had at least a high-school education (and usually more); a household income of at least $10,000; ties by kinship, marriage, or adoption to a traditional chiefly lineage (or similar ties to senior public servants or high-ranking politicians in the new political system); an important church position (e.g., lay minister, Fin Anisi leader); and significant material assets on Moen in land and personal property (businesses, vehicles, homes, etc.). In most cases, both spouses in elite married couples were employed for wages in government or private enterprise.

We have some misgivings about using class labels derived from the American system to describe Trukese society, and we are convinced that a class analysis by itself cannot explain the reality of modern Trukese social organization. For Truk remains a society organized primarily and fun-damentally along kinship lines, and the lineages and clans still serve as the

FIGURE 2.8 *Part of the Seaside complex and Bank of Guam, Moen, Truk, June 1985.*

basis for the social structure, whether in the realm of politics or of economics. What we label "incipient social classes" overlay and crosscut the undergirding kinship structure in significant ways, and failing to discuss these emergent differences would produce an inaccurate picture of life in the islands today. A recognition of nascent social classes in Truk is also essential to an understanding of women's involvement in the prohibition movement over the past decade. In Truk, as in the United States a century ago, middle-class women provided the leadership and the energy to launch and sustain prohibition (see Chapter Seven).

Some of today's elite are part Japanese, the progeny and descendants of unions between Trukese women and Japanese men in an era when few Japanese women lived in the islands. Truk's elite, as with elites in developing countries elsewhere in the world, have more money, material possessions, and sophistication than their compatriots, largely because they have had greater access to education—particularly higher education—and wage employment, opportunities that have been passed along to their children in most cases. A considerable number of elite families on Moen own two cars, one of which they operate as a taxi to generate extra family income. On a good day a taxi driver can earn $75–$100 on Moen at a set fare of 25 cents/ride (50 cents to the outermost villages).

Many elite couples on Moen in 1985 enrolled their children in one of the church-run private schools because they could afford the tuition[11] and because the students were believed to get a better education there, particularly in mastery of the English language. Education, employment, financial capital, and travel experiences all have equipped elites for leadership positions in the modern political system, bringing their power and prestige full circle. Those Trukese aspiring to elite status harbor dreams and ambitions not unlike those of upwardly mobile young Americans. They want a piece of land on Moen on which to build a nice house and enough money to afford a car. The port town's rapid growth from immigration has fueled land speculation, and today a small plot on which to build a home may sell for several thousand dollars.

Moen's urban and urbane elite often have useful and important connections outside of Truk, either elsewhere in the FSM or on Guam, in Hawaii, or on the U.S. mainland. Many such connections result from interethnic marriages that occur at an accelerating rate on Moen. Not only do outer islanders marry persons from Truk Lagoon in greater numbers than before (see, e.g., Marshall 1975b), but those who leave Truk for education or employment abroad also find non-Trukese spouses with greater frequency. Such spouses include Americans, Chamorros, Tongans, Papua New Guineans, Marshallese, Filipinos, and persons from other parts of the FSM (e.g., Kosraens, Pohnpeians, and Yapese). These interethnic marriages offer potential access to places and resources outside of Truk and may enhance elite status if manipulated wisely. Some elites on Truk, for instance, send one or more children to Guam or Hawaii to live with relatives and to be educated there.

Truk's elite travel more widely and more frequently than most islanders. Many think little of taking a shopping trip to Guam's modern, air-conditioned, duty-free malls—especially before Christmastime—or to combining business with pleasure in Honolulu. Truk's wealthiest citizens now have investments abroad, either in land, homes, apartment buildings, or businesses. Presently, most such investments are on Guam, but the number of Trukese with such connections to Hawaii or the U.S. mainland is increasing and may be expected to grow further in the post-Compact of Free Association era.

EDUCATION IN THE TOWN CENTER

American Board (ABCFM) missionaries first brought Western-style education to Truk in the 1880s, and formal education remained exclusively in missionary hands (both Protestant and Catholic) during the Spanish and German colonial periods. During World War I and following the establishment of the League of Nations Mandate, the Japanese set up elementary schools primarily to instruct Trukese in the rudiments of Japanese language and culture (Fischer 1963; Ramarui 1976; Singleton 1959). Even the most promising student was limited to about five years of formal instruction, and no Trukese student was sent out of Micronesia to continue formal education abroad (Singleton 1959). "The system was geared . . . to produce a supply of general laborers and domestic servants who understood the Japanese language, plus a small elite of skilled laborers and petty officials" (Fischer 1963:516). Although the Japanese did not appear to have a specific policy favoring males over females, fewer young women than young men in Truk obtained even the basic three years of schooling then available.[12]

The Japanese schools ceased to function during World War II. Postwar (1948–1951), the U.S. Navy set up a school on Truk to teach English to promising young Micronesians to prepare them as elementary teachers and for jobs in the civil administration. This Pacific Islands Teacher Training School (PITTS) first had a two-year and then a three-year course of studies (Hezel 1979). From 1945–1965, when high-school training was still at a premium in the islands (cf. figures in Hezel 1979:172), Micronesian gender-role notions clearly influenced parents' decisions to support education for their sons rather than their daughters.[13] Only 22 Trukese women completed high school between 1948 and 1964; since 1967, however, they have entered high school in greater numbers. In 1975, more than 100 Trukese women graduated from high school, and three years later the number of female graduates exceeded the number of males for the first time (Hezel n.d.a). Between 1978 and 1983, females comprised 47 percent of all high-school graduates in Truk (Ibid.; see Table 2.2).

With the advent of civilian administration in 1951, PITTS changed into PICS (Pacific Islands Central School). PICS functioned as the only public high school in the Trust Territory until the early 1960s when public high schools were established in the six district centers and elementary schools were given the responsibility for educating pupils through eighth grade. Truk High School began at this time on Moen as an amalgamation of the Intermediate School and PICS. Due both to limited facilities (including dormitory space for students from other parts of the district) and budgetary constraints, Truk High School has never been able to accommodate more than a small percentage of the district's elementary school graduates. Hence, from the beginning, admission to Truk High was based on a competitive examination administered to eighth graders throughout the state. Starting in 1970, the Peace Corps helped establish public junior highs on Satawan, Ulul, Toon, and Moen. These four schools educate students through tenth grade and serve as "feeders" for Truk High. Today Moen has three high schools: Berea Christian School (run by the Liebenzell Mission), Truk High School (operated by the state government), and Xavier High School (sponsored by the Catholic Mission).

Beginning in 1966, U.S. Peace Corps volunteers (PCVs) were sent to the Trust Territory in large numbers as part of the Kennedy administration's plan to bind the Micronesian people more closely to the United States in preparation for the end of the U.N. trusteeship. By December 1968, Truk District hosted 110 PCVs (*Met Poraus,* December 13, 1968, pp. 2, 8, 10),

TABLE 2.2 *Secondary school enrollment figures for Truk District/Truk State by year and gender.*

YEAR	NO. MALES	NO. FEMALES	% FEMALE	TOTAL
1950[a]	227	11	5	238
1977	1,056	780	42	1,836
1981	1,034	850	45	1,884
1985	1,225	948	44	2,173

[a]*For this year only the figures reported combine Intermediate School enrollment with enrollment of Trukese in PITTS because regular high-school education was not yet available on Truk in 1950.*

SOURCES: Truk State Office of Planning and Statistics (1981); U.S. Department of the Navy (1951); U.S. Department of State (1985); U.S. Trust Territory of the Pacific Islands (1977b:119).

although plans were under way to reduce their number to between 70 and 80 over the next nine months (in 1985 there were only 12 volunteers in all of Truk State). During the late 1960s in Micronesia it seemed that PCVs were everywhere; in fact, the ratio of one volunteer for every 240 Micronesians was the highest in the world. Every municipality in Truk District had at least one volunteer, and some had several at the same time or in succession. Most volunteers taught, especially English as a second language. Generally, these educational efforts were successful, and they provided some of the groundwork necessary to enable numerous Trukese young people to enroll in American colleges and junior colleges during the 1970s and 1980s. Energetic PCV women also provided significant new role models for young Micronesian women.

The main campus of the Community College of Micronesia (CCM), an accredited two-year institution that awards Associate of Arts degrees, is on Pohnpei. CCM began an extension program in Truk in 1973 that by 1978 was locally administered. Quite a few Trukese high-school graduates attend CCM on Pohnpei, but a sizable number also enroll in extension courses at the branch campus on Moen.[14] A great many of these students are young women working in the wage economy or seeking job skills that will permit them to obtain such employment.

In 1980 Eastern Oregon State College (EOSC) began to offer summer school extension classes on Moen with visiting faculty on assignment from the main campus, and in 1984–1985 a year-round program for as many as 70 students was started. These classes made it possible for some Trukese who had begun college in the United States, but who had returned home before completing their studies, to obtain their baccalaureate degrees. Fifty students graduated from this program on July 16, 1985, eight of whom were women. By the end of summer 1985 EOSC had awarded close to half of all bachelor's degrees held by Trukese, and the college also had a sizable Micronesian enrollment at its home campus in La Grande, Oregon. In 1986, EOSC held a second graduation ceremony at the Logan Memorial

Church on Moen for another 37 Trukese students who earned B.S. degrees in General Studies (Martin 1986c).

Higher education for more than a tiny handful of Trukese is something very recent. In the early 1950s, a few men were sent to intensive programs on Guam and Fiji for careers as medical practitioners, and at approximately the same time some Trukese women obtained nurse's training on Guam (Singleton 1970). The first Trukese college graduate did not return to the islands until 1967, although a handful of students had attended two-year programs, had entered college but not graduated, or had acquired specialized postsecondary vocational training at such institutions as the East-West Center in Honolulu (Ibid.). In 1972, the U.S. government extended programs for low-income and minority students to attend college to the Trust Territory. Nearly every Micronesian student qualified for these programs on both income and minority status grounds, and large numbers of them left for junior colleges and colleges in the United States (Hezel 1979).

RELIGION ON MOEN

Churches and church-related activities are the single most important social institutions in Truk today, with the possible exception of local and state government. Certainly, churches are the center of village life on a day-to-day basis. As elsewhere in the Pacific (see, e.g., Forman 1982), Christianity filled the social vacuum created by the onslaught of rapid political and economic change (under four different colonial regimes in Truk).

Nearly all Trukese are nominally Christian, although many retain strong syncretistic beliefs in elements of traditional religion (e.g., a fervent belief in "ghosts," a reverence for ancestral spirits, etc.). Well over 90 percent of Trukese identify themselves either as Protestant or Catholic. In this context *Protestant* refers to the Congregationalism the American Board of Commissioners for Foreign Missions (ABCFM or American Board) from Hawaii introduced via Pohnpei beginning in the 1870s. Beginning in 1907 the German colonial government forced the ABCFM missionaries in Truk and Pohnpei to relinquish their stations to an evangelical German Lutheran group known as the Liebenzell Mission (Forman 1982:63; Kohl 1971). Today both American Board and Liebenzell churches exist in Truk and their adherents all refer to themselves simply as Protestants. Presently, the Protestant category is divided three ways. The Liebenzell Mission supervises the churches of Namoluk and the Lower Mortlocks, together with those in Fááyichuk. The American Board churches split in 1980, following factional competition and infighting that had gone on for several years. The two groups resulting from the division are known as Nómwoneyas and UCC (United Chuch of Christ). Catholicism was introduced to the Mortlock Islands in 1911, and the first Catholic Church in Truk Lagoon was founded on Dublon a year later (Hezel 1970:223, n.d.b). Catholicism did not gain a permanent foothold on Moen until a church was constructed in Tunnuuk in 1922. The complex has served as headquarters for the Diocese of the Caroline and Marshall Islands during most of the post–World War II period (Hezel n.d.b). Particularly on the outer islands, almost everyone in a community is either Catholic or Protestant.

Catholics and Protestants each sponsor women's organizations, a focus for most women's activities outside of the kin group. The Catholic women's groups are known as Mwichen Maria; those of the Protestants are called Fin Anisi, "Helping Women." The Protestant women's groups, in particular, have a long history in Truk, dating to the early Christian missioners a century ago. Women play important roles within local church congregations and women's groups are involved in a host of community activities. Over the years, and until quite recently, church women's organizations have been the *only* forum where women could meet and organize activities independent of men. Even today, church women's groups are central to women's lives and remain the sole setting within which all women can come together to discuss, plan, and implement activities.

However, the Fin Anisi women's groups have been undermined by the 1980 split within the American Board Churches. Initially, the two American Board church factions (Nómwoneyas and UCC) broke over economic issues. Before 1980–1981 a few large, wealthy, and active congregations on Moen raised most money available to the church as a whole; however, the majority of the American Board clergy who represented poorer congregations located elsewhere than on Moen controlled these funds. Although this appeared to be a simple port town–rural division, in fact the situation was more complex. In the nineteenth century the ABCFM first established itself in the Mortlocks and from there undertook the evangelization of Truk Lagoon. From the 1880s onward, a disproportionate number of Trukese American Board ministers has been from the Mortlocks or from Mortlockese migrants to Truk proper. Before the Nómwoneyas–UCC split, Mortlockese ministers allied with ministers from Dublon controlled the American Board church leadership. Clergy with strong kin ties to Moen who led congregations on that island comprised the other faction. Eventually, five Moen churches split off as the UCC faction; the remaining eight Moen churches stayed with the rural Nómwoneyas faction, which included churches on Dublon, Feefen, Fano, and Piis (see Figure 2.1).[15]

The UCC–Nómwoneyas division involved the Fin Anisi groups almost from the beginning and has weakened women's attempts to maintain themselves as a powerful political pressure group. In the mid-1970s, the non-Moen ministerial leadership of the American Board denied funds to a group of Fin Anisi from Moen wishing to attend a church conference in Hawaii. The Moen women resented this decision since at other times *men* had been given financial support to attend conferences abroad. In 1976, relations between the Fin Anisi and the ministers' group deteriorated further after a misunderstanding over the expenditure of money sent by the Woman's Board of Missions for the Pacific Islands (WBMPI) in Honolulu for relief efforts following devastation wrought by Typhoon Pamela.

After this argument, the atmosphere between the members of certain Moen churches and the remainder of the American Board churches in Nómwoneyas slowly worsened. Finally, in 1981, the group of Moen churches requested a charter from the Trust Territory government and, upon receiving it, formally separated. Only the UCC faction retained the tie to the Hawaii Conference of the United Church of Christ (the descendant of Congregationalist missionaries' efforts in Hawaii beginning in 1820). In the years since, a united front between these two church groups has been difficult to achieve, and the consequent division of the Fin Anisi has weakened Protestant women's political influence on Moen. The disagreements between the two groups of ministers have prevented women in one faction from participating in meetings or workshops the other sponsors. Protestant women no longer act and speak as one body.

In recent years, a few minority religions have become established in the port town or on nearby islands in Truk Lagoon. The oldest of these, Jehovah's Witnesses, first came to Moen in the mid-1960s and had 43 converts as of spring 1984 (Buthing et al. 1984; Kohl 1971). Other groups represented are the Bahais (who have a very small following), the Seventh-Day Adventists (with 40 members in 1984 after eight years of preaching the faith in Truk), the Mormons (who first came in 1977), Assembly of God, Baptists, and the Apostolic Pentecostal Church (brought to Truk in 1983) (Buthing et al. 1984). Of these groups, the Mormons have been far and away the most successful. They counted 300 adherents in 1984, had built an attractive church in Mwáán, and had plans to erect a building on Wuumaan Island starting in late 1985.

With the exceptions of Jehovah's Witnesses and the Catholic Church (which preaches moderation), Christian religious organizations in Truk strongly oppose their members' use of alcoholic beverages (DuPertuis 1988). To be a true Christian from these points of view is to eschew alcohol; indeed, some men give up drinking when they reach their 30s in order to enter the competition to become a church deacon or other important religious official. Despite this general opposition to alcohol use, most religious organizations in Truk have not mounted serious education, prevention, or treatment programs. The sole exception is the *mwiichen asór,* a program the Catholic Mission introduced in 1968 to reduce abusive drinking (see Marshall 1979a:142–143; Chapter Three).

SUMMARY

General social changes over the past 30 years have profoundly altered life on Moen. The population has doubled, largely as a consequence of immigration to the town by people seeking education, employment, and the excitement of a new lifestyle. The cash economy has grown dramatically over this period, primarily through U.S. foreign aid to the government. Increased political autonomy has been undertaken with the establishment of the Truk State government within the FSM. Secondary schooling has become concentrated on Moen and opportunities for a high-school diploma—particularly for women—have expanded markedly. Religious alternatives to Congregationalism and Catholicism have grown apace, and some new religious organizations have supported schools as part of their mission activities. Jet air service linking Moen to the rest of the world has become a daily occurrence; ship traffic inside and beyond Truk State has increased. The patina of a modern consumer society has formed unevenly on the surface of Moen's now class-stratified communities. In the midst of these changes, public attitudes toward and laws governing alcoholic beverages have shifted. We now turn to a discussion of the Trukese experiences with alcohol and the laws surrounding it.

CHAPTER THREE

Dry Dreams

> Michael handed me a flask of brandy: "Enjoy this because there's no booze here. The Moen men were the most violent drunks in the Pacific. Their women decided to bring prohibition to the tropics. They went to the polls one Sunday morning while their men were too hung over to vote. Democracy in action—the women won 100 percent. Booze is banned on Moen, so let's drink this precious liquid" (Barbach 1984:196).

THE INTRODUCTION OF ALCOHOL INTO TRUK

No traditional alcoholic beverages were produced in Polynesia, Melanesia, and Micronesia prior to outside contact (Loeb 1943; Marshall 1976). Although Pacific peoples lacked alcohol, most used indigenous drug substances such as kava and betel nut. Kava is a beverage made from the chewed or pounded root of a shrub in the pepper family, *Piper methysticum,* and before European contact was not found outside Oceania. The kava ceremony was most elaborated in Fiji, Samoa, and Tonga, although kava was known and used over most of Polynesia and in various Melanesian societies—especially in Vanuatu, Papua New Guinea, and Irian Jaya (Brunton 1988; Lindstrom 1987). In Micronesia, kava consumption was limited to Pohnpei and Kosrae. Betel nut is a misnomer for a pharmacologically active mixture of the *Areca* palm nut *(Areca catechu),* the leaves, stems, or catkins of a plant related to kava *(Piper betle),* and slaked lime made from crushed seashells or coral. This combination usually is chewed as a quid to which other substances (e.g., tobacco) sometimes are added. In Oceania, betel chewing is found in much of Melanesia and in westernmost Micronesia (Belau, Yap, and the Marianas), but is absent from the Polynesian Triangle.[1] Much less common than kava or betel were various plant-derived hallucinogens the inhabitants of parts of Melanesia took (see Marshall 1987a for details).

Tobacco, imported from the New World by European voyagers via Island Southeast Asia, was introduced between the late 1600s and the 1800s, depending on the island group in question (Ibid.). Tobacco has a long history on the island of New Guinea (Haddon 1947), but did not reach most of Island Oceania until well into the nineteenth century.

Trukese were rare in that they made no use whatsoever of any traditional mind-altering substances. Other Micronesians chewed betel nut or drank kava, but not the Trukese. Once introduced to tobacco and liquor in the nineteenth century, however, Trukese avidly adopted these substances (Marshall 1979a:35–41; Marshall and Marshall 1975:450–453). For most Pacific islanders, trade alcohol or the knowledge of how to produce fermented or distilled beverages for themselves came in the early-to-mid nineteenth century, accompanying beachcombers and whalers who roamed the Pacific during those years. By comparison, Truk's encounter with alcohol was quite late, due largely to the islanders' reputation for ferocity toward outsiders (Hezel 1973).[2] Trukese were not introduced to drinking by European and Japanese traders until the early 1890s. By this time Protestant missionaries had been at work in Truk Lagoon for a decade, resident traders had been around a bit longer, and German colonial control was imminent.

That Trukese did not have any traditional alcoholic beverages is reflected in their vocabulary for these substances. Generically, beverage alcohol is called *sakaw,* a loan word from Pohnpei where it means kava. In Trukese, *sakaw* can refer both to alcohol and to the state of inebriation. All but two of the words for beverage alcohol the Trukese recognize are English-sounding cognates. Thus *piyé* is beer, *wayin* is wine, *yiis* is yeast, and *wiisiki* is whiskey or any other distilled alcoholic beverage (also referred to as *meyi pwich,* hot stuff, because it burns the throat as it is swallowed). Yeast is a home brew made by mixing baker's yeast with sugar and water in a large covered container and allowing the liquid to ferment for a day or two. Sometimes yeast is flavored with instant coffee or canned fruit syrup to mask its normal soapy-water taste. Trukese specify two other kinds of beverage alcohol: *chooriyú* and *áchi. Chooriyú* is Trukese moonshine made from distilled yeast.[3] *Áchi* is fermented coconut toddy.

The Trukese encounter with alcoholic beverages seems to have been violent from the start. Having no tradition of alcohol use, Trukese, like others in Oceania and Native North America who were without indigenous alcoholic beverages, were strongly influenced by those who introduced them to drinking (MacAndrew and Edgerton 1969). Those people who drank in Truk in the 1890s—primarily resident traders—often behaved in a rowdy, belligerent manner, and Trukese could not help but notice this. In 1904 the German colonial regime began to suppress the traditional interisland or interdistrict warfare in Truk, and drunken brawling provided an alternative (Marshall 1979a). The earliest written accounts of Trukese drinking all emphasize heavy intoxication, fighting, and general disruption as its accompaniment.

Bracketing the turn of the century was a period of 20 to 25 years during which Trukese men became thoroughly familiar with alcohol and its effects. Then, soon after the outbreak of World War I, Japan moved into the political vacuum left by the withdrawal of German military personnel from Micronesia to the European theater. It is not clear whether the Japanese governors forbade the Trukese to use alcohol immediately, but with the war's end and the granting of Japanese control over Truk under a League of Nations Mandate in 1921, legal prohibition became the law of the land. Although prohibition did not entirely dry up the islands (a certain amount of alcohol made its way into Trukese hands illegally, and some islanders had learned how to manufacture fermented coconut toddy), alcohol consumption was more the exception than the rule during the rest of the Japanese colonial period (1914–1945). The American colonial regime following World War II continued the legal prohibition on islanders' use of imported beverage alcohol, although individuals were permitted to manufacture home brew "for their personal use in accordance with local customs and traditions . . . subject to community control" (U.S. Department of State 1956:91). The Americans governed under a U.N. Trusteeship administered first by the Department of the Navy and, after 1950, by the Department of the Interior. The worldwide process of decolonization during the 1950s influenced many events in Micronesia, including the right to drink. Legislative and administrative bodies from at least 1954 onward debated the question of giving islanders legal access to commercially manufactured alcoholic beverages.

Meller (1969:48) reports that soon after World War II the American administration created a "Truk atoll council" comprised of traditional leaders from all over Truk Lagoon who were to choose an "atoll chief." This artificial and alien political entity soon collapsed, and a "Truk advisory council" made up of the island chiefs and their assistants from around Truk Lagoon replaced it. The first all-Truk District magistrates' conference was convened in 1952, at which time a decision was made to establish a districtwide council of magistrates from all municipalities to meet annually. The magistrates' conference functioned as the closest thing Trukese had to a districtwide legislative body until the Truk Congress—elected by popular vote—first convened on November 4, 1957 (Ibid.:57). The Truk District Legislature supplanted the Truk Congress in 1963 (Ibid.:77), which became, in turn, the Truk State Legislature in 1979.

By the mid-1960s, the district legislature had full appropriating power over monies collected under its authority or allocated to the district by the Congress of Micronesia (established in summer 1965). Meller (1969:68) notes that district legislators were well aware that their financial powers were their greatest strength, "and undoubtedly the district-wide taxes originally imposed pursuant to district legislation and the continued expenditure of funds pursuant to district determination have given the present district legislatures their current political prominence." Indeed, as the district legislatures became more powerful during the 1960s and 1970s, municipal governments became relatively less important. The taxing powers of municipalities were curtailed, and they were forced to seek financial assistance from the district legislatures to provide accustomed municipal services (Ibid.:116).

DEPROHIBITION

The Third Annual Conference of Island Magistrates, held toward the end of 1954, considered the question, "Do the Trukese want to do anything further regarding permitting imported alcoholic beverages into the district?" (Truk District 1954:19). Several interesting points emerged from the magistrates' deliberations on this subject during a morning session on December 2. First, it was noted that homemade alcoholic beverages in Truk sometimes caused illness and blindness.[4] Second, local liquor production was prohibited without "specific permission from the island office," but illegal production took place nonetheless, with the islands of Dublon, Feefen, and Moen mentioned as cases in point. An argument for legalizing imported alcohol was that it would replace locally made "bad liquor." Third, the minutes of the Magistrates' Conference indicate Moen had a law permitting the consumption of local liquor with permission from the municipal office; hence passage of the proposed law "will not make any difference." A fourth point in the debate was that "Trukese drink only gives trouble," and that "no benefits derived" from alcohol. However, in response it was noted as a fifth point that imported alcohol would mean additional import tax revenues. Sixth, the minutes make clear that a de facto local option already operated in Truk District at this time: "At some islands drinking is completely prohibited but if the people of those islands should go to another island where drinking is allowed, the chiefs have no objection to their drinking" (Ibid.). The last point recorded from this meeting was an agreement on the need for a districtwide alcohol control law that would preserve the right of each island community to decide whether or not to allow drinking. At the end of the discussion the magistrates voted that each island should decide independently whether or not to permit imported liquor.

On the afternoon of December 2, responding to the results of the magistrates' deliberations that morning, the American district administrator agreed it was awkward that Americans were allowed to drink imported beer and liquor whereas Trukese were prevented from doing so. But he argued that Americans had more money and could afford to spend money on liquor, which Trukese could not. He feared money "which should be spent on food, house and other necessities" by Trukese would often be spent on liquor instead, and that access to alcohol would precipitate "fighting and some killing" (Ibid.:20). The district administrator also indicated he was not convinced the local option law would work, but ". . . if the Chiefs can formulate a policy and can convince him that it will work, he will be glad to approve it and send it to the High Commissioner" (Ibid.).

In the ensuing debate, Chief Enis Nedelec of Feefen led the proliquor magistrates in the discussion. He proposed the municipal offices (i.e., the magistrates) act as island liquor stores responsible for the beer supply and for determining who is allowed to drink and how much. Enis wanted to substitute imported, commercially produced alcoholic beverages for homemade brews, but failing this he was interested in the possibilities of manufacturing liquor locally and selling it on other islands. Chief Petrus Mailo pointed out that Trukese obtained alcohol not only by manufacturing it themselves, but also from Americans stationed there either as a gift or a theft. Later that afternoon a majority of the magistrates tabled the liquor issue because they could not come to agreement (Ibid.:20–22).

A year later, at the Fourth Annual Conference of Island Magistrates in January 1956, the liquor question came up again. When the issue was raised whether the Trukese people should be allowed to drink or not, 30 of the 36 magistrates present voted no (Truk District 1956:54). Immediately thereafter, the chiefs were asked to consider the possibility of a permit system allowing for drinking on special occasions; the vote was 10 for and 26 against. Despite these apparent antialcohol votes, the questions put to the district administrator essentially favored drinking—particularly legal access to commercially produced beer. The administrator left the door open to eventual deprohibition by stating, "I have already said that when you people agree to have it, I will agree to it and I think the High Commissioner will, but I want to have you think first about the whole District so we don't have the very difficult problem of keeping it off of islands where the majority doesn't want it" (Ibid.:55).

Two years later the Truk Congress finally appointed a Special Beer Committee "to study and make recommendations to the High Commissioner for the control of beer sales in the Truk District" (*Truk Review,* January, February, March 1959, p. 10).[5] Late in 1958, the Truk Congress voted 32–16 in favor of making beer available, citing the "unsanitary" nature of locally produced liquor (Truk District Legislature 1967: Public Law 2-1). The Congress charged the committee to investigate the problems of sales, controls, and taxes, and after examining the liquor laws of the Marshall Islands, Palau, Ponape, and Yap Districts, the committee drafted a District Order permitting the importation of beer commencing June 1, 1959 (*Truk Review,* May 1959, p. 2; Wolfe 1960:5), which the District Administrator signed on April 29 of that year. The deprohibition order emphasized municipal local option, set the district beer tax at 90 cents per case of twenty-four 12-ounce cans, and established the on-premises hours of sale as 4:30–10:00 P.M. Monday through Thursday with more liberal weekend hours (including noon to 10:00 P.M. on Sunday) (*Truk Review,* May 1959, pp. 2–3). For the first year or so only beer was allowed; in 1961, the law was modified to permit the importation, sale, and consumption of wines and distilled beverages (Mahoney 1974:12; Truk District Legislature 1967: Public Law 5-11).

Despite deprohibition, clearly not all of Truk's citizens were convinced of its desirability: One-third of the representatives to the Truk Congress in 1958 voted *against* liberalizing the liquor law. A referendum held in conjunction with the election of Feefen's representative to the Truk Congress in April 1959 also demonstrated antiliquor feeling. The vote was against beer, making "Fefan [Feefen] Island . . . the first Community to decide against the sale and drinking of beer since the approval of the congressional beer resolution by the High Commissioner" (*Truk Review,* April 1959, p. 5). Even in the heady days of release from colonially imposed prohibition, then, there was ambivalence and division of opinion in Truk over the use of beverage alcohol. This ambivalence was underscored further by Public Law 3-6 (Resolution 5-59) that the Truk Congress recommended in its Third Session held later in 1959. It "prohibited people from entering a beer hall with dangerous weapons such as knives, guns, fighting knuckles, broken bottles, or any objects used for fighting" (*Truk Review,* November 1959, p. 5).

DEPROHIBITION AND TAXES

Once importation of alcoholic beverages was legalized, taxes and license fees followed and quickly assumed a prominent position in the local budget. In the Truk Congress's Treasurer and Tax Collector report covering the first 10 months of 1959, more money was obtained from the beer tax than from all other import taxes combined, and this in only 5 months of beer sales![6] The largest single source of estimated income in the Moen Municipal budget for 1960 was money from beer licenses ($1,410 of $6,153), and the beer tax comprised 41 percent of the estimated revenue available to the Truk Congress in 1960 (Wolfe 1960:14, 17). This heavy reliance on taxes and fees from alcoholic beverages and tobacco products is commonplace in developing countries and has characterized the districts of the Trust Territory ever since legalization of drinking (Marshall 1981a:889–891; see also Chapter Six). Alcohol taxes and fees also figure importantly in the budgets of at least some Micronesian municipalities, for example, Darrit-Uliga-Delap on Majuro, Marshall Islands where in the early 1970s "almost all" of the annual budget was reported to come from these sources (*Micronitor,* January 25, 1972, p. 4).

In the fall of 1959, the Third Session of the Truk Congress established a Liquor Control Board to oversee matters relating to alcohol use in the district. The first Board was comprised of five members, two of whom had served on the Special Beer Committee (*Truk Review* November 1959, p. 5). Finally, during the Third Session, via Resolution 6-59, the Congress extended the hours of off-premises sale to 1:00–9:00 P.M., Monday through Friday (*Truk Review,* February 1960, p. 5).

The name of the Liquor Control Board was changed to Alcoholic Beverage Control Board in September 1963 with passage of Public Law No. 7-4 superseding previous alcohol legislation (Truk District Legislature 1967:65–71). This new law created a five-member board to be appointed by the district administrator for two-year terms, with the district sheriff and the district director of public health as ex officio members. Persons involved in businesses that imported, manufactured, or sold alcoholic beverages were explicitly disqualified from serving on the Board. The Board had the power to issue licenses to import, make, or sell alcohol; to make regulations consistent with Public Law No. 7-4; to stipulate how licensees kept records; and to maintain records of its own meetings and decisions.

DEPROHIBITION AND WOMEN

Given the striking attitudinal, gender-related differences toward alcohol and its use in Truk mentioned in Chapter One, we must note that at no point in the proceedings leading up to the legalization of drinking were Trukese women formally included in the decision-making process. There were no women magistrates nor, at that time, were there any women representatives to the Truk Congress. Women were not appointed to the Special Beer Committee, nor were they given a position on the Liquor Control Board. Although women *could* make their voices heard at the ballot box in local option elections, they were shut out of the official deliberations resulting in legal drinking.

As indicated in Chapter Two, the period from 1960–1977 was one of very rapid growth and development in Truk. The Kennedy administration greatly increased financial aid to Micronesia, contributing to a rapid expansion in government sector jobs. These funds also underwrote more schools, various social welfare programs, improved health care facilities, and, indirectly, growth of the private sector—principally in the merchandising of consumer goods. In 1970 a Micronesian counterpart replaced the last in a series of American district administrators in Truk, although Truk's first popularly elected governor and lieutenant governor were not sworn in for another eight years (*Micronesian Independent,* October 6–13, 1978, p. 8). Outer islanders migrated to the port towns in ever greater numbers to avail themselves of education, wage employment, and the amenities of town life. The legalization of drinking coincided with wrenching, irrevocable changes in the social, political, and economic life of Truk, and social problems associated with alcohol use were connected in complex ways to the modernization of Trukese society.

By the late 1960s a steady stream of newspaper articles appeared indicating that alcohol-related problems were proving costly for Truk. The press reported police chases involving drunken teenage drivers; accidents while driving under the influence of alcohol; men making New Year's resolutions wishing they could stop drinking; trouble and disruption in schools and in rural communities such as Toon; alcohol-related juvenile delinquency; and suicides and intercommunity fights linked to drinking

(*Met Poraus,* December 6, 1968, pp. 4 & 6; December 20, 1968, p. 17; January 10, 1969, p. 7; March 28, 1969, p. 9; November 13, 1970, p. 1; January 3, 1969, p. 11; January 10, 1969, p. 15; January 24, 1969, p. 12; January 17, 1969, pp. 12–15, 17; July 31, 1969, p. 5; October 29, 1970, pp. 5–6, 8; August 3, 1970, pp. 4–5; October 2, 1970, p. 1). Partially in response to these events, in 1968 the Catholic Mission began the *mwiichen asór* program in which drinkers pledged publicly in the presence of a priest and others to abstain for a specified period of time (*Met Poraus,* December 6, 1968, p. 8; Marshall 1979a:142–143); and a few local communities attempted to deal with alcohol-related juvenile delinquency (e.g., *Met Poraus,* March 14, 1969, pp. 12–13).

By the end of the 1960s and into the early 1970s these problems accelerated and others—breaking and entering to steal money for drink and, especially, trauma and homicide resulting from drunken brawls—increased (e.g., Falcam et al. 1978:2; Mahoney 1974; *Met Poraus,* January 3, 1969, p. 15; May 8, 1969, p. 6; October 2, 1970, pp. 1–2). In 1973, matters became sufficiently serious throughout the Trust Territory that the Community Development Division of the Trust Territory Government let a contract to a Washington, D.C., consulting firm to investigate alcohol abuse, particularly as it related to juvenile delinquency (*Micronitor,* August 6, 1973, p. 7). Late that year the Trust Territory Division of Mental Health sought public input for its announced intent to apply to the U.S. Government for funds to develop programs to combat alcohol abuse (*Micronitor,* November 19, 1973, p. 3; December 14, 1973, p. 2). This initiative eventually resulted in a grant from the U.S. Department of Health, Education, and Welfare "with which to mount a major program to counter alcohol abuse and alcoholism under the provisions of U.S. Public Law 91-616" (Mahoney 1974:2), and an Alcohol and Drug Abuse Plan for the Trust Territory of the Pacific Islands was produced (USTTPI 1975b).

In spite of mounting evidence that alcohol use was problematic, little was done in Truk to address the matter. A luxury tax took effect on November 1, 1969, that raised the price of alcoholic beverages and certain other commodities—beer was now taxed at the rate of 5 cents per 12 fluid ounces and distilled beverages at 30 cents per fifth (*Met Poraus,* September 25, 1969, pp. 1–3). Five years later the district tax on alcohol imports was raised yet again, but in each of these cases, the tax increase was instituted primarily to generate revenue and not as an alcohol control policy.

In a rather half-hearted gesture at control, in 1974 the legislature passed a law requiring an identification card (more popularly known as a drinking permit) (USTTPI 1974b), the application for which required information on mental competence, prior hospitalization for drug addiction or alcoholism, criminal conviction of offenses involving actual or attempted injury, or conviction of previous violation of the Truk liquor laws, along with routine biographical data. Like most alcohol control laws in Truk, this one was not well enforced and many drinkers ignored it. Moreover, less than a year later the legislature weakened this law significantly by reducing the fine for drinking without an identification card from $500 to $100 (USTTPI 1975a). At the next regular session of the Truk District Legislature the legal structure for alcohol control (which had never worked very well) was further undermined. The legislators usurped the Alcoholic Beverage Control Board's power to set hours of sale by repealing the relevant section of the Truk District Code and legislated more liberal hours of sale themselves (7:30 A.M.–10:30 P.M. for off-sale licenses). Although the district administrator (himself Trukese) disapproved this legislative action, on June 11, 1976, the legislature overrode his veto and the act became law (USTTPI 1976). Thus instead of greater control, Truk developed a well-deserved Micronesia-wide reputation for being "out of control"—for public drunkenness and violent disruption (see Marshall 1979a).

Finally, in 1976, Trukese church women and their male supporters, in an attempt to attack alcohol-related problems in their communities, managed to have two bills introduced in the Truk District Legislature. One (Bill No. 26-1-29) would have banned drinking throughout the district (see Appendix 1); the other would have eliminated all imported alcohol while permitting the manufacture and consumption of local brew. Bill No. 26-1-29 was assigned to the Political Committee, which held public hearings on the issue during the First Special Session of the legislature in June and July.[7] The Committee's report to the speaker of the legislature noted that hearings were attended by persons from both Protestant and Catholic churches (presumably including women), the four legislators who sponsored the bill, and other interested members of the general public. In support of the bill, it was argued that approximately one-third of all arrests and one-third of all suicides in Truk were alcohol related; that 40 percent of the patients in the hospital were sick from alcohol consumption; that 51 percent of homicides in the district were alcohol related; and that alcohol produced a net loss of $10 billion per year for businesses in Truk due to accidents, insurance claims, property damage, and loss of productivity (Truk District Legislature 1976a). The Political Committee forwarded Bill No. 26-1-29 to the full legislature for action on July 13, 1976. Instead of holding a general discussion on this bill, however, the legislature tabled it indefinitely (Truk District Legislature 1976b).

This, then, was the political state of affairs concerning alcoholic beverages at the time we undertook the 1976 research on alcohol use in Truk (Marshall 1979a). Antialcohol forces had begun to mobilize to stem the growing tide of family and community disruption that they saw linked clearly to drinking. Failing to gain cooperation from the legislature for stronger alcohol control policies, temperance advocates sought other means to attack what they viewed as the most pernicious social problem afflicting their island home. Quite surprisingly, given women's traditional lack of involvement in Trukese public life, women found the means to combat alcohol problems and provided the leadership to push for a municipal prohibition law in 1977. To understand why such public political action by women was so unusual, we turn next to a discussion of traditional women's roles and organizations in Truk and how they have altered in the modern era.

CHAPTER FOUR

Raa Feffeyittá: "Women Are Coming Up"

> . . . as yet woman has not sufficiently emancipated herself from the undue control her men folks have so long exercised over her thought. Taught from the outset of life that in matters outside a certain sphere it is her duty to leave thought and decision to her father or her husband, as the case may be, she has simply registerd [*sic*] his opinions (Quoted from *Vanguard,* November 7, 1908, p. 12 in Grigg 1983:157).

With the sweeping social and political changes in Truk during the past 30 years has come a shift from a subsistence economy based on gardening and fishing to one founded increasingly on wage employment. As discussed in Chapter Two, Moen's urban population has grown rapidly over this same 30-year period, Trukese students' opportunities for high-school and college education have increased, and an incipient class-based society has arisen in the islands. Amidst these radical economic, political, and social alterations, Trukese women have experienced profound changes in gender roles and in opportunities for advancement in careers outside the home. In this chapter we sketch the traditional roles women have played, discuss official government policy toward women post–World War II, assess the role of formal education in expanding women's options for wage employment, note women's involvement in various clubs and organizations, and finally describe women's engagement in politics and positions of leadership in Trukese society. This background helps us understand both the profundity and the possibility of women's involvement in Moen's prohibition movement during the past decade.

TRADITIONAL GENDER ROLES

Throughout Oceania a woman's life traditionally focused on home and family, largely as a result of her position as mother and family caretaker. These domestic roles continued after foreign contact, reinforced by nineteenth-century Christian missionaries who taught that "a woman's place is in the home," an idea that reflected Euroamerican biases of the day. These influences concentrated women's attention on the private, domestic sphere and discouraged attempts to take part in public affairs in the community at large.[1] However, the church did want women involved within its precincts in ways it prescribed (as discussed in Chapter Two; see also Chapter Five).

Only quite recently have some women begun to move in wider circles, consequent on access to higher education and wage employment. Even in the mid-1980s, the great majority of Pacific women remain firmly anchored to their homes and churches; the sophisticated, educated vanguard—the elite women mentioned in Chapter Two—are as yet relatively few in number and live in the towns. These modern, educated, elite women wield much influence among their peers, and provide important new models for what it means to be a woman in the contemporary Pacific.

All the traditional societies of Truk State made a clear distinction between male and female roles. Most behaviors and tasks were considered appropriate to one sex or the other, but not to both, although in a few areas gender did not seem to matter. Within this male-female division, a woman's place was associated closely with the home, tending to children and housework—laundry, dishwashing, housecleaning, sewing and weaving, and most food preparation and cooking. When women ventured beyond their homesteads to garden or to fish in the shallow waters close to shore, they usually did not travel far from home. All women were expected to marry and to bear children to perpetuate the matrilineage. Women and girls were at least nominally under the control of men, usually their male relatives. A girl was expected to obey all the males in her family, and a woman was expected to follow the orders of her brothers and her husband. A "good" woman would always do what her parents, older siblings (especially brothers), and other relatives asked of her without questioning their request or complaining about it. Stereotypically, women were considered intellectually inferior and physically weaker than men, although they were perceived to have the moral upper ground. "Women were humble, obedient, generous, and submissive. It has been like this for a long time, and it continues, in large measure, to be the same" (Kim 1981:4–5).

A Trukese woman is expected to be decorous in dress and behavior. Her clothing must not reveal her lower torso or thighs; her breasts, shoulders, and back should be covered in public (except when she is nursing an infant); and her hair, kept long, should be braided or held up with combs in a bun.[2] According to the canons of Trukese culture women might wear various perfumes and fragrant flower leis *(mwárámwár),* but make-up is inappropriate except for turmeric extracts employed as facial paint for traditional dances. Western-style social dancing (fast or slow) generally is looked upon as unacceptable behavior for Trukese women because it is believed to produce sexual temptation. Also,

> In the late fifties and early sixties, dancing was thought to be a money-making hobby for "bar girls" or cocktail waitresses. Therefore a lady who went to night clubs and danced was thought to be looking for easy money and would be labelled a "taxi" or an "U-drive", meaning any man can pick her up. A remnant of that idea still exists (Akapito 1982:4).

Persons of both sexes are enjoined to speak softly (one aspect of being *mósónósón,* or "humble"; see Marshall 1979a); however, this injunction falls more heavily on women. Finally, whereas males are *expected* to smoke and drink (Marshall 1979a), "good" women, who are "Christian," are not supposed to smoke tobacco or marijuana, let alone consume beverage alcohol. "Drinking of alcohol beverages is not only disrespectful but it is also degrading to the feminine image because it is considered a man's habit only" (Akapito 1982:5).

In sum, a traditional Trukese woman was supposed to be quiet and modest, adept at household management and domestic chores, submissive to her male kin and spouse, and to stay at or near home. These were "the characteristics of the traditionally 'proper' Trukese woman" (Kim 1981:5).

OFFICIAL POLICY TOWARD WOMEN

Ever since the U.S. Naval Administration of the Trust Territory was established shortly after the end of World War II, Micronesian women have had the right to vote in all elections, have been assured equal pay for equal work, and have not been discriminated against educationally or occupationally *at an official level.* Women were assured the same legal rights as men in everything from access to courts, to rights to own property and control earnings, to act as legal guardians, and to engage in business. Women also had all the rights that men had to hold public office and to exercise other public functions. By the early 1980s, the U.S. Department of State noted that Micronesian

> Women are running for elective office, holding managerial positions in important private businesses and, in general rising to the challenges of the modern world. Full political, economic and educational equality has not yet been achieved but, compared to just a few years ago, much progress has been made (1982:77).

The administering authority recognized "the equality of women in all matters" but made "no attempt to impose this arbitrarily" (U.S. Department of the Navy 1951:48), meaning there was no purposeful interference with local customs regarding appropriate male and female spheres.[3]

Although the official Trust Territory annual reports mention that the sexual division of labor in Micronesia involved "no implication of degradation" or threat to physical integrity, by Western standards Micronesian women were anything but liberated in their daily lives. This fact was underscored by the first delegate proposal tendered at the Micronesian Constitutional Convention (by Carl Heine of the Marshall Islands) convened on Saipan in 1975. As chairman of the Convention's Committee on Civil Liberties, Heine urged an end to all discrimination based upon sex and claimed that his proposal would bring sweeping changes to Micronesia's male-dominated society. In his view "Micronesia's customs and culture have kept women in a position of near-slavery and servitude for centuries, and . . . it is now time to elevate women to a position equal with men" (*Micronesian Independent,* July 25, 1975, p. 7). This goal has yet to be achieved.

EDUCATION: INCREASING WOMEN'S OPTIONS

At about the time the Trust Territory administration was transferred from the Navy to the Department of the Interior, PITTS was the only place where students could obtain education beyond intermediate school. In 1951, only 9 of 106 students (8 percent) enrolled at PITTS were female (U.S. Department of the Navy 1951:64). This gender discrepancy eventually came to the attention of a U.N. Visiting Mission in 1964 that then urged the U.S. administration to encourage girls to continue their schooling.

Although the proportion of girls to boys in Truk's general population was roughly equal, girls made up barely one-fifth of the Truk Intermediate School enrollment between 1959 and 1961 (see Table 4.1).[4] Prior to 1958, fewer than 10 girls attended Truk Intermediate School in any year, but the 1960 classes contained 45 girls (*Truk Review,* February 1960, p. 2; see Table 4.1). Nearly one-third of these girls were from Moen, and about one-fourth were from islands outside of Truk Lagoon. There were so few girl students primarily because of parental attitudes: " . . . They felt that sending girls to school wasn't worth as much as sending boys. . . . [and] They were afraid of sending their girls to Nantaku [Truk Intermediate School] because they considered it as a place where their girls might get into some kind of trouble" (Ibid.:3). The failure to provide many girls with intermediate or secondary education in the 1950s and early 1960s was still felt 20 years later. In 1978–1979, for example, women made up only about one-quarter of the indigenous elementary and secondary school teachers (public and private schools combined) in Truk (U.S. Department of State 1980:40).

Before 1965, fewer than 200 Trukese had completed high school (including PITTS and PICS), and only 13 percent (N=21) of them were female (Hezel 1979; Ilon 1978). However, Truk High began graduating students in 1965, and thereafter the number of Trukese with secondary education climbed steadily. By the end of the 1960s, Truk had 300 more high-school graduates, and their number grew even more rapidly during

TABLE 4.1 *Enrollment at Truk Intermediate School 1959–1961, by gender.*

YEAR	NO. MALES	NO. FEMALES	TOTAL	% FEMALE
1959	183	38	221	17
1960	175	45	220	20
1961	179	41	220	18.5
TOTAL	537	124	661	19

Sources: *Truk Review*, January, February, March 1959, p. 7; February 1960, p. 2; December–January 1961, p. 6.

the 1970s (Ibid.).[5] Significantly greater numbers of young women have completed high school in the years since 1970, but a marked gender discrepancy still exists, even though the gap between male and female high-school graduates began to close in 1975.

High-school or postsecondary education has played a key role in the development of Micronesia's incipient class system for women and men alike (see Chapter Two). Throughout the islands women have gained meaningful access to such education only in the last 20 years. Before 1970, only a minuscule number of women obtained high-school or advanced training, particularly relative to their representation in the total population. Many of Aames's (1976) female informants from the Trust Territory attending the University of Guam mentioned how their families (especially their parents) actively discouraged them from pursuing a college education, and of how obstacles were placed in their paths when they persisted. Parents feared ridicule if a daughter went away to school and returned home pregnant. They also worried over the loss of potential income a daughter might earn before marriage, which under Micronesian custom would go to her family.[6] One female student summed up the cultural and parental resistance to daughters going away to school by saying, "Men have wings, women only have feet," meaning men may be adventuresome and travel but women must stay at home and marry (Ibid.).

When we compare by sex the Micronesian students sent abroad for training beyond high school in the mid-to-late 1960s, women made up less than one-quarter of the total (336 of 1,624). At the University of Guam during spring term 1975, 12 percent of all students enrolled were from the Trust Territory, but just over one-quarter of these (N=98) were women (and only 13 of these women were from Truk District; Aames 1976). The underrepresentation of Micronesian women in postsecondary schooling reflects a general pattern that operated throughout most of the Trust Territory before 1970: The distribution of boys and girls in elementary schools was approximately equal; the number of girls who continued into junior high school declined; and the proportion of female high-school students was smaller still.

However, in the 1970s and 1980s education—especially postsecondary training—has provided women who work hard and prove themselves increased power and respect and, in many cases, entrance into the new middle class. In Truk, men and women alike argue that women who seek high position in the community should have the prerequisite education. Formal education beyond high school provides it, as well as training in speaking up, greater courage and self-confidence, more social skills, and new ideas—including the idea that women have potential and rights equal to men's. High-status Trukese women today have considerably more formal education than most women of their generation. Nowadays, some Trukese women continue their formal education beyond the A.A. or B.A. degree; a few take graduate work and a handful already have acquired Master's degrees. Formal education, and the access it provides to well-paid wage jobs, has been a major criterion for admission to the new elite in Truk.

Education has also been a key to a greater women's voice in community affairs throughout the postwar period. Elite women, including several leaders of Fin Anisi and Mwichen Maria, were among the special few in the 1950s and 1960s who received training as nurses and schoolteachers. Many of these women came from esteemed Trukese families and subsequently married elite men with important jobs. Their education prepared them for paid positions of considerable status in the emergent wage economy, gave them important skills and a measure of self-confidence, and helped them learn to read and write in English. Their schooling taught them how to organize schedules, prepare study plans, and prepare for future contingencies in ways alien to their mothers' or grandmothers' experiences. The few women who obtained more than an elementary education before 1970 were in their fifties and sixties by the time of the temperance movement, and their age and experience commanded respect.

For younger women who went to high school after 1970, and then went on for additional training, formal education frequently has played a more direct role in stimulating them to lead the women in their communities. Many of these younger women lived in the United States for several years while attending college or university, where they were exposed to the feminist movement via the media and through contacts with American women of approximately the same age. Some of these Trukese women encountered feminist activism more directly by enrolling in Women's Studies courses or by becoming involved in consciousness-raising groups. When they returned to Truk with a resolve to change the system, they found formidable obstacles in their way. Some subsequently fled Truk for the less constraining environments of Pohnpei, Guam, or the United States, but those who remain have worked slowly but surely to improve women's lot. The temperance movement of the 1970s and 1980s offered a focus for organization and an outlet for many of these latent feminist impulses (see Chapters Five and Seven).

WOMEN AND EMPLOYMENT

Throughout the Pacific region, elite women have begun to channel their resourcefulness into business ventures or wage employment as well as into traditional female concerns with family and community welfare (Ritterbush 1987). These successful women generally have better-than-average education, have lived or worked overseas, and have the active support of their husbands or other male relatives (who also typically are well-educated wage earners) (Ibid.). With rare exceptions, Pacific island women who have stepped outside traditional female roles live in the towns and urban areas where attitudes are more liberal and there are fewer social pressures to conform. Although some Pacific island women have made impressive economic contributions and developed highly successful commercial enterprises, all women in the region continue to face significant barriers on both local and national levels. Women frequently find male businessmen, financiers, and policymakers patronize their economic aspirations; find themselves relegated to or perceived as playing only a supporting role to men in the paid labor force; and find it much more difficult than men to acquire training, secure loans, and coordinate domestic responsibilities with those of the workplace (Ibid.).

In the Trust Territory in the early 1960s, the administering authority recorded that women were employed in nursing, education, communications, weather bureau, secretarial, and administrative work (U.S. Department of State 1962:97). Ten years later both the range and the diversity of employment options for women had expanded:

> Women operate a variety of businesses which include laundromats, beauty shops, bakeries, car rentals, handicraft cooperatives, retail stores, restaurants, commercial sewing shops, and performing local dances on a commercial basis for tourists.
>
> Salaried work for women includes positions such as court reporters, medical practitioners, nurses, medical record technicians, radio announcers, postmistress, policewomen, airline stewardesses, taxi drivers, gas station attendants, cooks, waitresses, secretaries, clerks and clerk-typists, tax collectors, teachers, and payroll clerks (U.S. Department of State 1972:101).

Relatively few Micronesian women held important wage jobs before the 1960s. In 1948, for example, the Navy reported that only about 20 percent of the Trust Territory's school teachers were women, the majority of whom obtained their training at PITTS (U.S. Department of the Navy 1948:42). In the early years of the U.S. administration most employed women came from the Palau and Marianas districts.

Between the late 1940s and the early 1970s in Truk a few women assumed highly visible positions. For example, in 1959, a young graduate of the Trust Territory School of Nursing "participated on an equal basis with the male members of an Administration team of sanitation, education, and public health workers carrying out a pilot health education project at an outlying island of Truk District" in what was labeled as "a notable excursion into an untried avenue" for a woman (U.S. Department of State 1959:79–80). Not until 1961 was a Trukese woman hired as a teacher at Truk Intermediate School (*Truk Review,* December–January 1961, p. 7). One woman, who earlier managed the Trukese Government Employees Credit Union, was hired as bookkeeper for the local Office of Economic Opportunity, where she was responsible for all expenditures and financial records (*Truk Tide,* August 11, 1967, p. 1). By 1968, Truk's local newspaper had a women's news editor and the statistics clerk at Truk Hospital was a woman (*Met Poraus,* October, 25, 1969, p. 5; December 13, 1968, p. 6). Fourteen years later a woman served as chief editor of the *Truk News Chronicle.*

Our informants indicated that it has become much more acceptable in recent years for Trukese women, whether married or single, to work outside the home. The earliest wage jobs open to women were as domestics during the Japanese period, although such positions were limited and few women on islands other than Dublon had access to them. Doubtless some exceptions existed, but most Trukese women in Japanese times were engaged in the traditional female tasks of fishing in the shallows, gardening, and taking care of home and family. Following World War II a few women became nurses and school teachers, and a number found work as domestics and nannies for American contract personnel and their families. In the past 15 to 20 years, as more women have completed trade school, high school, and college, Trukese of both sexes have become accustomed to women holding wage jobs. Indeed, the prospect today that a woman may obtain a lucrative wage job enhances her marriageability. Among the younger, educated elite in Truk it is no longer unheard of for a wife to bring home a larger paycheck than her husband, and this economic clout certainly strengthens women's authority in family decision making.

Logically, if a woman has more education, demonstrable skills, or knowledge than a man, she should get the superior position at work. In practice, however, this happens rarely in Truk, and most supervisors and senior administrators are men. A number of our informants pointed out that many Trukese women now find jobs, but very few hold high positions. They claim it is particularly difficult for women to become managers in the private sector. Most men remain unwilling to promote women to supervisory or managerial positions in either the private or the government sector in Truk. Men justify this slighting of talented women by assertions that women are innately unable to speak strongly to, argue with, or talk back to a man. In such circumstances, men say, customers or subordinates would simply take advantage of a woman.

Some younger women, frustrated by these cultural constraints, have left the system entirely by marrying a foreigner and living abroad, by finding a sympathetic Trukese spouse willing to migrate elsewhere for work, or by remaining single and searching for employment away from Truk (e.g., at

FSM headquarters on Pohnpei). Such opportunities for younger women have increased since the enactment of the Compact of Free Association, giving FSM citizens free rights of immigration to the United States.

INTERNATIONAL WOMEN'S MEETINGS

In 1928, the Pan-Pacific Union sponsored a conference in Hawaii on the status of women in the Pacific region. Two years later another Hawaii conference was held at which the Pan-Pacific Women's Association was formed. Its objectives were "to strengthen the bonds of peace among Pacific people by promoting a better understanding and friendship among the women of all Pacific countries" and "to initiate and promote cooperation among the women of the Pacific region for the study and betterment of existing social conditions" (Hooper 1976:371). The Pan-Pacific Women's Association was "the region's first independent international women's organization," although it has not been a significant force for change or for taking direct action in pursuit of its goals (Ibid.:367–368, 372–373). Despite the organization's limited contributions, it did formally establish organized women's activities in the Pacific Basin and, apparently, was "the first women's group *anywhere* to be founded upon transcultural premises" (Ibid.:367; emphasis added). Micronesian women attended meetings of the Pan-Pacific Women's Association in the 1950s and 1960s in Japan and Australia. In 1958, for example, three delegates from the Trust Territory attended, one of whom was a Trukese public health nurse (Pan-Pacific Women's Association 1958).

More recently, Micronesian women have attended other international meetings. In connection with the U.N. Decade for Women (1975–1985), representatives of the new elite from all six districts of the Trust Territory attended the International Women's Conference held in Houston, Texas, in November 1977. This gathering of about 11,000 women from all over the world received much publicity and concentrated attention on a host of feminist issues. Three Trukese women were among the 15 Micronesian delegates (*Micronesian Independent,* October 14, 1977, p. 4). For most women in the Micronesian delegation, this trip was their first to the U.S. mainland, and their conference role was primarily that of observers (although they did vote in favor of the Equal Rights Amendment to the U.S. Constitution; *Micronesian Independent,* December 9, 1977, p. 3). Before the Houston conference, Guam held an International Women's Year Conference in July 1977 (Poehlman 1979:119ff.), and the organizers of the International Women's Year in Micronesia put together a workshop on September 10 and 11 at the Truk District Legislature building. Workshop topics included education, wife beating and abuse, teenage pregnancy, strategies for change, health, and childcare (*Trade Wind,* September 26, 1977, p. 4). Although chaired by a woman, ironically, the Truk workshop's two major speakers were men.

The Congress of Micronesia was asked in early 1978 to appropriate $13,000 for a Micronesian Women's Conference that July, but the bill did not receive congressional support (*Micronesian Independent,* February 9, 1978, pp. 10–11). However, this proposal led one Micronesian male to pen a letter to the editor (requesting that his name not be used) railing against "this farce," and noting that the Micronesian women who attended the Houston conference "did nothing but pass the ERA (Equal Rights Amendment)." He went on to ask, "What is ERA in Micronesia? It is nothing but sin. Micronesia is not ready for ERA. Maybe in the next 200 years but not now" (Ibid.).

WOMEN'S CLUBS AND ORGANIZATIONS IN TRUK

Until the mid-1950s, the few women's organizations in the Trust Territory were religious in nature. During the period of U.S. administration after World War II, women's clubs took root, spread slowly, and eventually helped "to raise the standard of living, to arouse interest in adult education and . . . [to play] an ever increasing and important role in providing community leadership" (U.S. Department of State 1963:83). In 1954, mothers had organized themselves in female parent-teacher groups in a few communities of the Trust Territory (U.S. Department of State 1954:70), and by the following year "a few women's organizations [had] become active, particularly in the Palau and Ponape Districts, in promoting better child, home, and family care and in sponsoring community, social, and educational activities" (U.S. Department of State 1955:70). By 1962, the Trust Territory administration reported that "almost all districts now have local women's interests officers," although technically this was true for only three of the six districts, the others subsuming women's interests under the responsibilities of community development officers (U.S. Department of State 1962:91, 1963:77).[7] In Truk, for example, one of the first women graduates of Truk High School was sent to Hawaii for a six-month training program in commercial sewing at the Institute for Technical Interchange at the East-West Center, and upon her return to Truk she began working in the Community Development Office. Much of her advice to women's groups away from Moen consisted of teaching them "how to cook and how to sew," that is, in sharing her special training in home economics (Ibid.).[8] By 1967, more than 60 women's groups were organized in the Trust Territory, 5 in Truk District (U.S. Department of State 1967:91). Nearly all their activities were focused on women's traditional domestic and family caretaker roles. Clearly, the stereotypes surrounding women's roles in the United States at the time limited Trust Territory government efforts to cater to "women's interests."

During 1963–1964, a Women's Interest Coordinator was appointed in the Trust Territory Headquarters Community Development Office. Her duties were to promote and coordinate programs thought to be of interest to women, such as women's club activities, girl scouts, and training courses (U.S. Department of State 1964:89). After four years of activity, the position went unfilled unil mid-1970, by which time the job title had been changed to Women and Youth Programs Advisor (U.S. Department of State 1968:85, 1969:83, 1970:95).

In the mid-1960s, the Women's Interest Coordinator in cooperation with the Girl Scouts of America's field office ran a two-week training course in scouting for potential Girl-Scout leaders in the Trust Territory (U.S. Department of State 1964:96). More than 400 Micronesian Girl Scouts were registered by 1966, with troops in the Marianas, Marshall Islands, and Truk Districts (U.S. Department of State 1966:103).[9] In 1967, troops had been formed in Ponape District as well (U.S. Department of State 1967:92), and by the next year the Trust Territory boasted 30 Girl Scout troops enrolling 662 girls (U.S. Department of State 1968:85). Once again, these government efforts simply reinforced women's traditional association with home and family, and did little or nothing to expand women's horizons beyond the domestic sphere.

No overarching general membership women's organization had developed in Truk by 1985. More limited women's social organizations often start small, have a rather narrow membership and focus, and periodically die out, while new ones spring up as other women see new needs to be met. Many such organizations may exist only briefly. Perhaps women leaders are too few in number to meet the heavy demands of these clubs for time and energy, or when young women marry their husbands discourage them from involvement in club activities, or public gossip inhibits some women from continuing in social clubs. Who the officers are and whether or not one's friends go to meetings also are factors that influence attendance.

Micronesian and American business and professional women established the first formal women's club in Truk in 1960. The Trukese-American Women's Association (or TAWA) included government employees and women engaged in commercial activities (*Truk Review,* May–June 1960, p. 4; U.S. Department of State 1960:83). Among the 22 dues-paying members of this new club were women from all government departments and all major trading companies (*Truk Review,* May–June 1960, p. 4). The publicized purpose of this organization was modest indeed: "To gain a better understanding of one another and to provide an opportunity for social gatherings . . ." that occurred approximately once a month (Ibid.).

The Feefen Women's Handicraft Cooperative, which dealt primarily with handicraft marketing, was established in 1962–1963 (U.S. Department of State 1963:77). In subsequent years women's cooperatives also were begun on Dublon and Wuumaan, though by 1967 only those on Feefen and Dublon remained (U.S. Department of State 1964:96, 1967:91).

In April 1965, the Truk District Legislature allocated $5,000 to construct a Truk Women's Club House on Moen, and the High Commissioner approved this measure on June 30 of that year (Truk District Legislature 1967:94). Even so, apparently these funds were never released. Early in 1967 the legislators approved bills to purchase a new car for their official use, and to pay magistrates $5 per diem while they were on Moen conducting governmental business, but "Bill No. 21 which authorizes the construction of a TAWA Building was defeated" (*Truk Tide,* March 24, 1967, p. 1). Twelve years later, the district legislature again set aside $5,000 "for the purpose of rendering assistance to civic projects of the various Women's Associations and Organizations in Truk District" (USTTPI 1977c). This money was voted during a legislative session held when women were lobbying heavily in the community for the referendum in favor of prohibition on Moen (see Chapter Five). The act stipulated that beginning October 1, 1977, the district administrator would make grants to those women's organizations serving the public in the areas of social and economic development (Ibid.). During fiscal year 1978–1979, the Truk State Legislature designated $1,250 for a "Women Association Fund," but again these monies were not actually released. Men thus have used their control of public funds to constrain women's attempts to build women's organizations.

Beyond church women's groups, a number of other women's clubs existed in Truk in the mid-1980s. One—Club 20—was a latter-day version of the old TAWA organization. Club 20 was a multiethnic group of elite Trukese and foreign women who met in Moen restaurants on the 20th of each month and had a maximum membership of 20. According to their bylaws, the purpose of Club 20 was to further members' social and intellectual interests, and to cooperate with other organizations in advancing community welfare in the areas of beautification, sharing, and scholarships. Money for the scholarship fund was raised from white elephant, bazaar, and bake sales. In 1985, Club 20 had Trukese, Filipino, and American members, including local elite women who held government jobs or whose husbands were important government officials. The most recent attempt at a general organization linking various women's groups in Truk was the Truk Women's Association and its Planning Commission. Fin Anisi and Mwichen Maria women central to the temperance movement in Truk (see Chapter Five) established this organization and were the prime movers behind efforts to heighten women's involvement in the political arena.

Another important women's club, though one which includes men in some of its activities, is the Truk Red Cross. Koben Mori established the first Red Cross Chapter in Truk in the 1930s (Dolan 1974:59), but it was moribund during most of the American period. In 1984, the wife of one of Koben Mori's descendants revived the Red Cross organization in Truk to aid local relief efforts after a cholera epidemic. She also hoped the Red Cross would show women they could take care of others in their own communities without outside help. In 1985, recruiting meetings were held in villages throughout Truk State to explain the organization's goals to women in outlying areas. Essentially, the Truk Red Cross was organized as a private community charity because it was not chartered by either the American Red Cross or the International Red Cross. Truk Red Cross members often carried gifts of soap, towels, or clothing donated by businesses or wealthy Trukese to the elderly poor. In addition to caring for less fortunate people on Moen, Red Cross members have engaged in civic beautification projects—cleaning up rubbish around the airport and the boat pool and planting flowers in public places. The organization sponsored a nine-day-long health care training class in 1987, led by a Honolulu physician, which ended with official first-aid certification of 40 women (The Micronesia Institute 1987). A new building they erected in 1987 was destroyed by Typhoon Nina in November of that year and funds were being sought for its replacement (Ibid.).

Since at least 1981 a number of women's teams have been organized into the Truk Women's Softball League. This league had seven teams with more than 100 active players during the 1983 season (*Truk News Chronicle,* March 1983, p. 8). One softball club (Apwete) existed not only to promote women's sports, but also to sponsor entertainment for young adults, and it was involved in other community activities as well (Ibid.).

WOMEN IN POLITICS

Trukese politics are still largely those of kinship, and family ties are crucial, not only for getting elected, but also for getting things accomplished once in office. This is as true for women leaders as it is for men. Usually, large and important kin groups select only one of their number to run for office so that everyone will be able to rally around the candidate. When more than one person from such a kin group wants to run for the same office (or for one of a limited number of seats on a council), the relatives will decide collectively whom to support. The person with the least support is expected to withdraw from the race. This aspect of kin politics works strongly to the disadvantage of women candidates because men are viewed as more electable than women. Women *have* continued bids for office without the unified support of their relatives, to much criticism and significant social pressure not to split their family's vote.

A single woman may not be trusted to lead because it is thought she may use her position to grant favors to a lover. If she is married, a woman's followers at least feel that they know who will have special influence over her. Especially helpful to a woman's political ambitions is marriage to a clergyman or to a member of the political or business elite, although such a marriage is not mandatory if her kin group is behind her. As important as such marriages are, they also put women in a classic double-bind. To become a leader a woman must have her husband's support, and if he is a prominent person, he is likely to have political aspirations of his own.

Thus, a woman who marries well may find it awkward to run for office because she might be thrown into political competition with her own husband. In Truk, loyalty to relatives is assumed to transcend loyalty to a cause.

Having a sizable family (via matrilineal ties or through relations by marriage and adoption) assures a potential leader of votes and a reasonably reliable campaign staff. Of course, being from an elite family, wealthy, well-respected, and heir to traditional leadership positions outside of the introduced political system helps immensely. Campaigns have become very expensive in modern Truk, and an aspiring candidate must have access to financial resources. Wealthy persons also are more likely to have afforded the postsecondary education and foreign travel that exposes one to new ideas (for example, the notion of women leaders).

Few women have been prominent in the modern politics of Pacific island countries, and no nation in Oceania is led by a woman today. According to a recent study completed by the U.N. Economic and Social Commission for Asia and the Pacific (ESCAP), women's heavy underrepresentation in decision-making positions characterizes nearly the entire Asia and Pacific region (*Marianas Variety News & Views,* November 14, 1986, p. 25). In some Micronesian communities women occasionally assumed positions of political leadership (the exception rather than the rule). For example, in 1958 the woman who headed the highest-ranking clan on Ifaluk Atoll in Yap District assumed the role of atoll chief upon the death of her male predecessor and remained in this position until her own death in 1964 (U.S. Department of State 1964:103). Women served as traditional chiefs in the mid-1960s on Lamotrek and Wottagai in the outer islands of Yap District, and on Ailuk, Aur, Maloelap, Utirik, and Wotje in the Marshall Islands in the 1970s (U.S. Department of State 1966:102, 1971:104). The House of Iroij in the Marshall Islands Congress during 1951–1952 had five women members, but all were there by virtue of holding titles to traditional chieftainships and not because they were elected (Meller 1969:86; U.S. Department of State 1960:89).

In a pioneering move in Micronesian electoral politics, two women were elected to the Palau Congress in 1950 (Meller 1969:86). A Palauan woman was appointed to a vacancy in the Palau District Legislature in the mid-1960s, and two Trukese women won election to the Truk District Legislature in 1966 (U.S. Department of State 1955:80, 1964:104, 1966:102). Since then, women have run for positions in the Truk Legislature from time to time, but only one other woman has ever been elected, holding office as a senator from 1975 to 1986.[10] By 1968 in all six districts women had been elected or appointed to the governing bodies of the Territory's Community Action Agencies (U.S. Department of State 1968:84).

Early in the 1970s, several women announced their candidacies for the Congress of Micronesia or their respective district legislatures, prompting the authors of the Trust Territory's annual report to claim that "women are emerging into politics" (U.S. Department of State 1972:101).[11] This "emergence" fizzled, however, since none of the women was elected (U.S. Department of State 1973:105). Nevertheless, their campaigns *did* represent an important first in women's political visibility in Micronesia and produced rhetoric reminiscent of the women's movement in the United States. For example, a woman running for a Congress of Micronesia Senate seat from Pohnpei tweaked her male opponents, saying, "They think women are just low people, and not fit for this job. I'm sure a woman can do much better than a man" (*Micronitor,* January 25, 1972, p. 1). In this same news story the candidate said she hoped for women voters' support, although she was unsure whether it would materialize. She also noted that women's demonstrations a month before to keep Pohnpei's bars closed offered "a sign that women were starting to take some action" (Ibid.; see Chapter Eight). Even though women candidates were unsuccessful in electoral politics in 1972, women were appointed by this time to numerous territorial boards, committees, and councils—for example, the Personnel Board, Health Planning Council, Scholarship Committee, district boards of education, and the Congress of Micronesia Political Education Committee (Ibid.). Finally, in 1974, the first woman (Carmen Milne Bigler of the Marshall Islands) was elected to the Congress of Micronesia as a member of the House of Representatives.

Trukese women had not been elected to positions on the Moen Municipal Council as of 1985. Women leaders of the prohibition movement recognized that having female supporters on the municipal council would allow them to assume a watchdog role over any future Council attempts to overturn the Moen Ordinance (see Chapter Five), but instead, have had to rely on the good offices of male church leaders on the Council to alert them to political machinations regarding the prohibition law.

Women have fared little better in obtaining appointive positions in local and state government in Truk. A major woman leader served as a member of the State Alcoholic Beverage Control Board in 1985, but that body never met as a committee of the whole. In frustration at women's continued exclusion from appointive positions as recently as 1983, the female editor of the *Truk News Chronicle* had this to say:

> I am writing this article not to criticize the government, but out of wonderment. As I listen to the appointments to the different department heads or board members or commissions I ask myself these questions: Why are all these appointments males? What's wrong with the Trukese females? Are the females in Truk State so stupid and unqualified that they cannot hold any responsibility? Other states are a mixture of males and females holding high positions. Women make up half if not more than half of the population of Truk, and I think women have rights in the government too. There are some qualified women on our islands who are able to serve on the governmental boards and commissions and would serve more ably than some of the males. There

> are qualified women who are not being used to their fullest. I hope in the future there will be some women on boards and different commissions. I am hoping that Trukese men will stop their discriminatory attitude towards women (*Truk News Chronicle,* March 1983, p. 6).

Shortly before the above editorial was written, another well-educated Trukese woman concluded that, despite strong desire and interest on their part, "there is no real opportunity for Trukese college-educated women to be active contributors in community or state affairs" (Kim 1981:14).

In the precolonial political systems of Micronesia, women had a significant voice in collective decisions although they seldom occupied positions with authority over the entire society. Margold and Bellorado (1985) argued that hard work, contribution to customs that bring prestige, and a certain autonomy were the bases of women's power in Belau, whereas they described the status of women in Pohnpei as far more ambiguous, suggesting that matriliny and matrilineal land inheritance may be the key to women's political role there. In the Trukic-speaking societies found in Truk State, the outer islands of Yap State, and on Tobi, Sonsorol, and Pulo Anna in the Republic of Belau, women exercised considerable behind-the-scenes political influence in the traditional system. On Ulithi, for example, the eldest woman in the district chief's matrilineage led the women, who acted as a group. In this accepted collective fashion women could influence the district chief's decisions both by making their requests known and by presenting him with gifts (Figirliyong 1976:17). In Ulithi's contemporary political system, women continue to influence the district chief's decisions, especially on matters such as drinking rules and general community activities (Ibid.:35). In Truk, church women's groups serve as modern-day equivalents to this aspect of traditional Carolinian social organization, playing a very similar political role in representing women's voice to male political leaders and in influencing the decisions men make (see Chapter Five).

LEADERSHIP IN TRUK

Ideally, Trukese leaders—whether women or men—should possess certain characteristics. A leader must solve problems effectively and creatively. Formal education and foreign travel (which provides a source of new ideas to draw upon in solving problems) would seem essential in leadership development. Also a leader ought to be a hard worker, one who follows through on her or his proposals. In the Trukese view a person who merely suggests what to do but is unwilling or unable to organize and press ideas into action is not a true leader.

Leaders also must have specific social skills before others will take them seriously and, potentially, follow them. Chief among these skills is public speaking—an ability to speak out politely but forcefully and a willingness to take a public stand in a firm and appropriate manner no matter who might be in the audience. Fluent English is a helpful adjunct to public speaking but not an essential requirement for many leadership positions in Truk. [12]. A good leader must mingle well in the community and in a variety of social groups. Leaders should be able to organize other people and get them to accept the leader's direction in the process of getting things done.

To be a leader, a Trukese also must personify a set of desirable personal qualities; among them are honesty, kindness, generosity, humility, maturity and self-control, a willingness to listen to people, and political independence. Aspiring leaders must not have a quick temper, be obnoxiously loud, or react hastily before they have thought matters through.

Women who wish to lead must possess all of the above characteristics and qualities plus a few more specific to females. Women must be gentle in manner, must demonstrate that they care for others rather than themselves, and should pay special attention to generally accepted canons of dress and behavior. Women convince others they can lead by their ability to chair a meeting, speak out in public meetings, and speak up even when men are present. Of course, being outspoken does not make a woman a leader in and of itself; occasionally a woman may become recognized by others as a strong leader in spite of reticence to make public speeches. To be effective, speaking out must be accompanied by tact, by having something worth saying, and by knowing how to say it firmly but gently. Women who wish to lead also must be able to speak informally with small groups and more formally in front of large audiences. This kind of politicking is very important and requires a willingness to meet different people, even those one does not know well. A woman leader should be able to talk with all sorts of people, from the uneducated villager to the sophisticated, college-educated elite. She should have the capacity to listen, to communicate her commitment and concern, and to show self-confidence. But although this second kind of speaking is important, perhaps more than any other single characteristic, a woman who would lead must show that she is not afraid to speak up in public. Often on this basis alone the Trukese assess a woman's leadership potential. Ironically, this exactly opposes what women are taught as appropriate traditional behavior.

An aspiring woman leader will gradually acquire the respect of her community if she regularly displays the above-mentioned characteristics and behaviors in public. Fortunately, public life has been less restricted for women in the past decade, providing them more ways to demonstrate leadership potential in the community, particularly in wage employment and involvement in church or community service clubs.[13] At present, two occupations have provided Trukese women with opportunities to widely demonstrate their social skills, personal attributes, capacities for problem solving, and ability to care for others effectively: school teaching and nursing. In clerical work, by contrast, a woman has less public exposure;

and, in the business world, women have been kept from holding positions of much responsibility.

Participation in church activities and her religious belief may give a woman the social support and spiritual strength to pursue a public life. A church women's group provides opportunities for her to actually practice leadership skills, show she is morally upright, and attract a loyal following. By drawing on new ideas obtained from modern churches elsewhere (for example, Hawaii or Guam) and church-sponsored regional workshops, ambitious women find an avenue through which to initiate and forge change in their society. Ideas derived from mainstream Western religious institutions carry great moral and political weight in Truk and are difficult to oppose. Thus, island women's long-standing position as pillars of the faith gives them access to a particularly potent means for affecting public opinion.

In Truk's political climate, formal education has become a very important qualification for political leadership. If young persons excel in school today, older family members may begin to think of them as possible future standard-bearers for their collective interests, as well as future moneymakers for the kin group. In the past quarter century, the attainment of formal education has allowed women leaders to gain a hearing and to claim legitimacy for their opinions. During the 1950s and 1960s the small number of women who graduated from nursing school, PITTS, or Truk High School included the first Trukese females who tried to combine formal education with other characteristics and behaviors necessary to lead in Truk. Greater access to education in the 1970s and 1980s has created a pool of talented, well-trained elite women; it remains for them to become old enough and well enough established in their employment and family roles to challenge successfully for communitywide positions of leadership in their islands.

SUMMARY

Since the end of World War II, the position of women in Trukese society has altered significantly. Formal education—particularly access to high school and college from the late 1960s onward—has increased women's opportunities for gainful employment in the wage economy. Such employment, and the responsibilities and income it has provided, have emboldened some women leaders to speak out on public affairs and matters of community welfare. The most prominent of these women have become widely recognized public figures in Truk's modern port town; of them, it has been said, "*Siya rong iiter iyeey,* 'Now we hear their names'."

For those women leaders who have taken an active part in contemporary public affairs in Truk, church women's groups—more than other women's organizations—have provided the base for reaching out to the whole community. Temperance activities orchestrated through Fin Anisi and Mwichen Maria groups have offered women leaders a way to demonstrate that their concern and caring for family and community were more powerful than their traditional shyness and embarrassment at speaking out in public. Many actions temperance women took to address what had become a major home and community problem were based on new ideas derived from reputable Christian sources abroad. And these were ideas that *worked*! The temperance-prohibition movement has offered middle-class Trukese women a perfect vehicle to demonstrate that they could provide leadership in the society at large and not just within their own traditionally accepted spheres. We turn next to a chronicle of that movement.

CHAPTER FIVE

"Never Underestimate the Power of a Christian Woman"[1]

> . . . . the husbands and fathers of the land are being stricken down on every side by this vile traffic against which we wage war, and . . . the sons of the land are so beset by temptation that very many of them fall early into a drunkard's grave, and many more who live on, but live to disappoint the fond hopes which are centered in them, and which, but for this fell destroyer, they might fulfill. These evils . . . are not in far-off lands, but at our own doors . . . (Helen Sparrow, spokeswoman for the Portland, Oregon Woman's Crusade, quoted in Blocker 1985b:95).

During the first 25 years of Congregationalist (ABCFM) activity in Hawaii the missionaries became increasingly disturbed over what they viewed as the damaging effects of alcohol and tobacco on the Hawaiian people. The Reverend Samuel C. Damon agitated tirelessly with Kamehameha III to impose total abstinence in the Hawaiian kingdom, and by the 1840s he and his fellow clergy had convinced the king to officially prohibit islanders from using intoxicating liquors. Unfortunately for the missionaries' efforts, this declaration did not apply to foreigners, and so the law proved unenforceable. In a continued crusade to dry up Honolulu, Lahaina, and other Hawaiian communities, Damon founded an influential temperance newspaper, *The Friend,* in January 1843, that he used to pursue the mission's antialcohol goals. By the mid-nineteenth century, abstinence had become a sign of Christian respectability in Hawaii, and the ABCFM faithful carried this strong antialcohol attitude with them to the Marshall, Gilbert, and Eastern Caroline Islands when the Micronesian Mission was launched. From the very beginning of Congregationalist proselytization, then, alcohol use was marked as a highly charged symbol for separating Christians from nonbelievers (Marshall and Marshall 1976).

Following their successes in the Hawaiian Islands, the Congregationalist missionaries of the ABCFM created the Hawaiian Missionary Society in 1850 to recruit and train Hawaiian converts to carry the word of God to other Pacific islanders. Under auspices of the Hawaiian Missionary Society, American and Hawaiian evangelists first visited the islands of Eastern Micronesia in 1852, with initial attention concentrated on the mountainous volcanic islands of Pohnpei and Kosrae (Crawford and Crawford 1967;

Loomis 1970). The first American missionaries to reside in Truk, Robert W. and Mary Logan, made preparations to leave for Micronesia between autumn 1873 and May 1874, at precisely the time that the Woman's Crusade against alcohol was grabbing headlines all over the United States (see Chapter Seven). The Logans arrived on Pohnpei in 1874, moved to Oneop in the Mortlocks in 1879, and eventually settled at a site they named Anapauo on Moen Island, Truk in 1884 (Aberley 1975). Earlier in the 1870s, Pohnpeian converts established the first ABCFM mission stations on the atolls of the Mortlock Islands, southeast of Truk Lagoon; however, not until December 1879 did American ABCFM missionaries and their Pohnpeian converts contact directly the high islands of Truk proper.

The ABCFM gained a firm foothold in Truk during the 1880s at a time when temperance, led by women, had become the dominant social reform movement in the United States. With the Woman's Christian Temperance Union (WCTU) in the ascendant back home, and with the visit of a representative of the World's WCTU to Hawaii in 1883, the link between alcohol use and social problems became a central concern for Protestant missionaries to Micronesia, of which the ABCFM translation of the WCTU's Primary Temperance Catechism into Marshallese is one illustration (Pease and Pease 1894).

Christianity preceded the arrival of beverage alcohol in Truk. The letters of the ABCFM missionaries living among the Trukese documented a total lack of alcoholic beverages there as late as 1888 (*Missionary Herald* 1881:209, 1886:18, 1888:325). A reasonable assumption then is that the staunch ABCFM antialcohol position shaped overall Trukese attitudes toward liquor when they eventually did encounter it toward the end of the nineteenth century. In addition, the American women's temperance movement, filtered through the ABCFM missionaries, influenced Trukese women's attitudes toward drinking and drunkenness. The Liebenzeller Mission that supplanted the ABCFM in Truk in 1907 reinforced the temperance legacy (Kohl 1971). In this century the position of Protestant Christianity toward alcoholic beverage use in Truk has not altered, which may account for the considerable ambivalence Trukese display toward alcohol today.

The ABCFM mission experience in Hawaii provided a blueprint for organizing mission activities in Micronesia beginning in the 1850s. Many techniques developed for working with Hawaiian women were employed later in Micronesia. For example, male clergy generally preached and taught the men whereas missionary women taught children and worked with female adults (Grimshaw 1985:76). This division of labor, reflecting contemporary American gender roles, proved fortuitous for the involvement of Hawaiian women (and, later, Micronesian women) in the organizational and educational work of the church. The separation of islander men and women "gave the mission women a full opportunity to read scripture, pray, and " 'conveniently to give sisterly and maternal counsel to multitudes of their own sex' . . . The separation similarly gave more scope for 'the awakened native talent and zeal' of the Hawaiian women as well as men in church work" (Ibid.:77). One upshot of the involvement of island women in church activities, such as teaching, preparing parish functions, and leading prayer groups was that it "not only offered women alternative occupations, *but pointed them in the path of an effective community activism* which could be reconciled with deference to the dominant sex" (Ibid.:87; emphasis added). As part of the ABCFM's efforts to transform Hawaiian women and to promote women's "effective community activism," the Woman's Board of Missions for the Pacific Islands (WBMPI) was founded in Honolulu in 1871. This organization continues as a vehicle for women's involvement in Christian social reform. From its inception, the WBMPI was responsible for a wider mission field than Hawaii alone, and in 1884 it sponsored its first missionary to Micronesia, Annette Palmer, who served for 22 years on Pohnpei and Kosrae (WBMPI 1976, 1984).

Most Micronesian women are extremely pious; they attend church regularly, if not daily, and are heavily involved in religious affairs through church women's groups. Both the Catholic Mwichen Maria and the Protestant Fin Anisi are very active on Truk. Historically, the minister's wife headed the Fin Anisi group. The various ministers' wives, in turn, met annually as a supervisory committee in advance of the annual meeting of all Fin Anisi. Essentially, they did everything for the Fin Anisi: They ran the meetings, did the public speaking, and taught the lay women. Because they were married to ministers, none of whom drank liquor, alcohol was not a personal problem for them and they never addressed it formally. If a woman in the congregation had an alcohol-related problem in her family, she spoke privately with her minister's wife, who would then pray for her. Fin Anisi groups practiced the more genteel Christian virtues—going to the hospital to sing and pray for the sick and to give the patients small gifts such as bars of soap; however, these lay women never assembled in groups to talk about their own shared problems.

In the early 1970s, the young wife of the minister of one of Truk's more important Protestant churches suggested to other ministers' wives that they not preside over the Fin Anisi groups. Her experiences abroad where she learned that women's fellowships in many South Pacific countries governed themselves and were no longer headed by ministers' wives emboldened her. When the ministers' wives dismissed her idea, she fell into the respectful silence Trukese expect of younger persons interacting with their elders. After a while, though, she raised the idea again, arguing that Fin Anisi was a lay organization and lay women the group elected ought to govern it. After much controversy and some acrimony these ideas held sway, and at the 1975 annual meeting the ministers' wives decided to turn the Fin Anisi groups over to lay leadership.

Ironically, lay women were reluctant to accept this reform, maintaining that they did not know how to do the job right. The idea's sponsor again jumped into the breach, exhorting them that they were quite capable of speaking in front of a group and acting as leaders in the church—that they could do anything if they tried. Using herself as an example of one who had overcome these fears, she argued that many Fin Anisi were more capable than she was, and she pointed out one elite woman in particular whose ideas she felt were superior to her own. This woman subsequently was elected the first lay president of the Moen Fin Anisi.

The new president, and those who successively replaced her, viewed Fin Anisi as a forum in which women of all classes could talk together openly, discuss common problems, and cooperate to seek solutions. Fin Anisi's lay leaders wedded Christian concern for one's fellow human being, and the search for peace and harmony, to the long-standing Trukese notion of women as caretakers of home and community. Alcohol's disruptive effects on family and community life soon became a central issue in Fin Anisi meetings. When alcohol abuse and its related issues in Truk reached a flash point in the mid-1970s, the church women's fellowships responded collectively.

In 1976, approximately when Trukese women took the first steps toward stemming the growth of alcohol-related problems in the port town on Moen (see Chapter Three), Fin Anisi leaders were completing arrangements to affiliate formally with the WBMPI. During early March, a delegation of 12 women, 4 men, and a child from Moen visited Hawaii to renew historic ties with the Woman's Board, to share common concerns, and to explore possible future relationships. At the beginning of April, the President of Fin Anisi formally applied on behalf of her organization for affiliate status with the WBMPI. The Woman's Board Annual Oahu "Country Meeting" approved this request on April 22. In late May and early June, the WBMPI president in Honolulu traveled to Majuro, Kwajalein-Ebeye, Truk, and Pohnpei to meet with church women and make final official arrangements for these groups to affiliate with the Woman's Board (WBMPI 1976:4). On June 14, 1976, at the 105th Annual Meeting of the Woman's Board in historic Kawaihao Church in Honolulu, the Moen Women's Fellowship was received as an official member organization. Prophetically, the final resolution in the certificate of membership read, "We seek ways in which we may encourage, inspire and cooperate with one another—in great tasks if God calls us to any; in small ones if it be His will." Just five months after this new relationship began, the Woman's Board sponsored an alcohol conference in Honolulu with temperance and prohibition on the agenda as important social causes for Micronesian women to pursue in their communities. Ideas from this conference had a direct bearing on events that unfolded in Truk soon thereafter.

THE HONOLULU CONFERENCE: "CHRISTIANS CONCERNED ABOUT ALCOHOL"

Protestant church women from the Marshall Islands requested a conference on alcohol in the Pacific islands. It was held at Hawaii Loa College in Kaneohe on Oahu, from November 13–20, 1976. The conference idea arose during July 1975, when a delegation of Marshallese women visited Hawaii for the previous year's annual women's conference and raised the problem of alcohol abuse in their communities. On her spring 1976 trip through Micronesia, the WBMPI president heard inquiries from women's groups in all districts about the possibility of an alcohol workshop. After further consideration and a year of planning, the "Christians Concerned About Alcohol" conference convened. Fifty-three Micronesian delegates attended, the great majority of whom were women from Majuro and Kwajalein-Ebeye in the Marshall Islands. Three delegates were from Pohnpei and four—two women accompanied by two church men—represented Truk.

Although sponsored by a Protestant religious group, the conference was not moralistic and the material presented was action oriented. Conference organizers developed a varied program involving a mix of formal presentations led by experts in alcoholism treatment and prevention, group discussions and exercises, field trips to different drinking spots in Honolulu to observe places and people, and the use of assorted printed materials. Representatives from the Alcohol Education Program at the University of Hawaii, the State Substance Abuse Agency, the Salvation Army Detoxification Center, the Hawaii Committee on Alcoholism, the Hawaii Council on Alcohol, and the Office of Human Resources for the City and County of Honolulu were among the speakers. The field trips were to Waikiki on one day and to the Hotel Street-Fort Street Mall-A'ala Park area on another. Micronesian students attending schools in Hawaii were invited to the conference one evening to discuss who drank, why they did so, what happened afterward, and who paid for the alcohol (and the fines, if any). A representative from the Young Men's Christian Association led discussions of alternatives to youthful drinking, and participants visited a special program called TEEN CHALLENGE set up to help Hawaii's youth "who were aimless and adrift in life." Home visits were arranged for the delegates to watch two hours of television with special attention to alcohol advertisements and the depiction of drinking in television programs. The 1975 Alcohol and Drug Abuse Plan of the U.S. Trust Territory of the Pacific Islands formed the basis for small group conversations one day, and the conference schedule involved regular think tank discussions in which delegates considered how to apply what they were learning when they went home. Each participant's registration packet included a variety of pamphlets from such agencies as the National Institute on Alcohol Abuse and Alcoholism (NIAAA), the Distilled Spirits Council of the United States (DISCUS), the American Council on Alcohol Problems (ACAP), the American Medical Association (AMA), the Alcohol and Drug Abuse Branch of Hawaii's State Department of Health (ADAB), and Alcoholics Anonymous (AA).[2] Finally, every conference participant was issued two pins similar to campaign buttons worn during American elections. The first pin read, "Go Into All the Future"; the second had "Christians Concerned About CH_3CH_2OH" printed on it (see Figure 5.1).

FIGURE 5.1 *Pins distributed to participants in the Honolulu conference, "Christians Concerned About Alcohol," November 1976.*

Two conference handouts staff at the Woman's Board prepared are of particular interest here: A copy of the Cold Water Army temperance pledge from nineteenth-century America that captures the overall tenor of the meeting and demonstrates the direct inspiration derived from America's earlier temperance movement (see Appendix Four), and a sheet entitled, "Summary of Approaches to Dealing with Alcohol Abuse in Your District." In this latter document, presumably drawn up toward the end of the conference as a result of group discussions, three primary approaches were listed:

1. Abolish importation and sale of all beverage alcohol into the district or municipality (i.e., prohibition);
2. Limit or control sale or use of beverage alcohol by changing present laws and/or by persuading and helping people not to use or abuse alcohol (i.e., temperance);
3. Provide special services for victims of alcohol abuse, for example, counseling, self-help groups like Alcoholics Anonymous, and the like (that is, treatment and prevention).

In addition to these three approaches, the Hawaii women sought to support, embolden, and empower their Micronesian counterparts to speak out publicly and take direct action on the alcohol issue. One important message was, "Not all problems can be solved, but no problem can be solved unless first of all it is faced." Conference leaders taught the Micronesian women how to organize and run a demonstration and suggested they march on their legislatures and lobby with legislators to achieve their goals. The power of petition drives in support of prohibition, temperance, treatment, and prevention was discussed, along with how to undertake such a drive. The Micronesian women also were encouraged to plan and hold workshops on the alcohol issue, both as a means of public education and to gain support for their antialcohol position. Last, but by no means least, American church women at the conference were strong, assertive, and unafraid to speak out for what they believed; they were women willing to work hard to improve the quality of life in their communities. They stood as powerful and significant role models for the Micronesians attending the conference. Significantly, they claimed to derive their strength from their Christian beliefs and from prayer, a faith the Micronesian women shared fervently. The message was, "As Christians, we don't only have things happen, but we *make* things happen." The Micronesian women were encouraged to be self-reliant—to not depend on anyone but themselves—if they wanted to protect their homes and their communities.

WE PRAYED, WE PLANNED, WE PICKETED

Although the stimulus for the Christians Concerned About Alcohol Conference came from Marshallese women, Trukese and Pohnpeian women faced equally daunting alcohol-related problems in their communities. In fact, Truk was where the lessons learned at the Honolulu conference first bore fruit. It was in Truk, as one woman leader put it, that "First we prayed, then we planned, then we picketed."

Upon their return from Hawaii, the two Trukese women delegates, both of whom were important Fin Anisi leaders, shared what they had learned with other church women at their regular meetings.[3] Initially, some male ministers and deacons sat in on these meetings offering advice and urging the women to be strong in their resolve. Eventually, as antialcohol ideas took hold among the Fin Anisi rank and file, the deacons and ministers began to stay away from these meetings (though they were not requested to). During this period, some ministers spoke out against alcohol regularly and forcefully in their sermons. Meanwhile, the two women delegates continued to talk with different Fin Anisi groups. They emphasized the need for self-reliance and courage in the face of opposition, and they stressed that women had the right to hold political demonstrations to achieve their goals of protecting the people and peace in their communities. Of course women continued to pray for an end to alcohol-related violence in Truk, and for the strength to sway public opinion on this matter, but although prayer was important, they believed, they repeated the lesson learned in Hawaii that prayer was not enough. Prayer had to lead to action.

As the delegates met and prayed with different groups of Protestant church women, spreading the message of hope that women, together, could make a difference on the alcohol issue, they encouraged the women to take some kind of political action. At first there was reticence because public political protest was not only foreign to Trukese mores, but also completely at odds with traditional expectations of appropriate female behavior. Some older women who never had left Truk recoiled at the idea of a demonstration. But as discussions and prayers continued, even most of these women were won over to the new ideas. They were desperate for a solution to the death and disturbance they attributed to alcohol, and they related finally what was being advocated to their own personal situations. That these ideas came from the church, wrapped in the rhetoric of Christian caring, made them infinitely more acceptable than had they been introduced in a secular context. Fin Anisi, reaching out to Catholic women through the Mwichen Maria organization, began to plan for action.

Since alcohol consumption had been legalized in Truk in 1959, disruptive public drunkenness had grown steadily. As in Pohnpei and the Marshalls, beverage alcohol consumption was primarily a male pastime, and most women saw little benefit from drinking. Instead, women viewed male drinking very negatively for numerous reasons. They associated it with criminal activities, with violent assaults and homicides, with general community disruption, with domestic violence such as wife-beating, with the destruction of property, with arguments among kin that sometimes led young men to suicide after they had been drinking, and with a waste of money that could have been used otherwise to benefit the entire family. Women were opposed to the public violence that increasingly was the order of the day in their communities. Women were opposed to having their husbands come home dirty after drinking, without money to run the household until the next paycheck, or to having them gone for several nights while on a drinking binge. Women were tired of being berated or beaten by their husbands after the men had been out drinking. Women were categorically opposed to the deaths resulting directly or indirectly from drinking via homicide, suicide, drunk driving crashes, drownings, and alcohol-related illnesses (including ethanol overdose). Women were unwilling to see their children abused by their drunken fathers. These were the reasons women were against alcohol. In taking a stand against drink women saw themselves as speaking out for the old people and the children, as well as for themselves. Their feeling was that the tax money earned from beverage alcohol was of no use if people were not happy and at peace. Alcohol made families *wosukosuk* "pressed," "stressed," and women and children were *riyáffëw fáán iten ewe sakaw* "distressed because of booze." Something had to be done.

By the mid-1970s, alcohol use in Truk was associated with a variety and increasing number of serious social problems (see Chapter Three). Laws meant to control drinking excesses and drunken violence either were unenforced or enforced weakly and intermittently; drinking was essentially an "open-go" situation and drunks ruled the streets. Men benefited most from drinking in Truk; relaxation, male camaraderie, a culturally acceptable means for expressing aggression, and substantial tax revenue for the legislature's coffers, were enjoyed or controlled primarily by men. Women and children bore disproportionately the costs of alcohol abuse. Clearly, the stage was set for a major disagreement between men and women over the place of alcohol in Truk.[4]

WHEN PUSH CAME TO SHOVE

By mid-1976, six bars operated on Moen, most major stores sold alcoholic beverages imported primarily from the United States, and fortnightly pay weekends were marred by drunken violence, especially in and around downtown bars. Fights occurred, weapons were used, injuries were common, and homicide was an ever-present risk (see Marshall 1979a for a detailed discussion; cf. Mahoney 1974; Hezel 1981). Drunk driving crashes were more likely on pay weekends, adding another source of injury and occasional death (see Figure 5.2).

Moen had become a battlefield for men from all over Truk. Those involved in bar fights usually were from different communities or islands in Truk State, and an altercation often would lead to reprisals against any male known to be from the opponent's community. The violence peaked during early 1977 with a string of serious stabbings, some resulting in death, followed by a fight at Happy Landings Bar (next to the airport runway) between a young man from Dublon and his opponent from Wonei. The day after this fight, approximately 60 men armed with knives, machetes, spears, and rifles sailed to Moen from Wonei, anchored in the

FIGURE 5.2 *Drunk driving wreck on Moen, July 1985.*

vicinity of the boat pool, and sent a message ashore that in two days (on a pay Friday) they would make war against Dublon. To underscore their seriousness they fired rifles from their motorboats into the air. At this point the district administrator was called. He immediately ordered a temporary closing of all bars on Moen (Falcam et al. 1978:2), and after considerable effort, brought the magistrates of Wonei and Dublon together to enact a formal apology ritual. A similar ritual was then conducted between the principals to the bar fight and a truce achieved without bloodshed.

Following this serious threat to public order in Truk, the district administrator, himself a lay minister, called other Protestant ministers together to discuss the matter. Their consensus was that alcohol had caused the recent troubles on Moen and that something would have to be done to control drunken violence. The ministers conferred with the leaders of Fin Anisi, including the two women who had attended the alcohol conference in Hawaii a few months before, and these women urged a petition drive among Moen Municipality voters to ask the Moen Municipal Council to hold a referendum on the question of total prohibition.[5] Several council members who were serious drinkers balked at taking any action that might lead to enactment of prohibition. Some of their female constituents reminded them of their elected responsibility to serve the people and work for the common good. To ensure that these members did not sway the opinion of others on the council, women and some Protestant ministers attended the meeting at which planning of the referendum was discussed. Their presence shamed the councilmen who were drinkers into silence, and those on the council who favored the dry law set the local option process in motion. Fortuitously, the groundwork temperance women had laid through their Fin Anisi organizations coincided with a pressing community need for some kind of strong action on the liquor question.

Officially, Truk had possessed a local option system—whereby each municipality could establish legal prohibition within its jurisdiction—ever since drinking was legalized in 1959. The procedure in force in 1977 for deciding the liquor question in a municipality, which took effect on April 27, 1967 (Truk District Government 1970), was very simple. If two-thirds of the registered voters of any municipality submitted a petition to the municipal clerk requesting a referendum on the liquor question, the municipal magistrate[6] was obliged to call an election within 90 days of the filing. If a majority of the voters approved the referendum, the municipal council was required to prepare and adopt an ordinance in accordance with the election mandate. In spite of this straightforward process, local political intrigue and competition often intervened and derailed efforts at prohibition (e.g., Marshall 1975a).

Church women's fellowship leaders and sympathetic members of the Moen Council circulated petitions throughout Moen during late spring 1977. More than two-thirds of the registered voters in Moen Municipality signed these petitions, and public meetings were held around the island at which the advantages and disadvantages of the proposed liquor ban were discussed. Women temperance leaders spoke out publicly at these meetings, an action quite out of keeping with the traditional political role of Trukese women (see Chapter Four; cf. Tiffany 1987). Millay (1987a) reports that many male Protestant ministers supported temperance women by sermonizing on the evils of drink during the weeks leading up to the vote, and that women undertook "a great deal of low-key activity" in order "to insure a maximum turnout of registered female voters." In the midst of all this activity, the legislature appropriated $500 from the General Fund for the chief of police to underwrite the expenses of the alcoholic beverage consumption identification card program for another year (USTTPI 1977a). Finally, on July 2, a formal referendum was held on the question: "Should the sale or consumption of intoxicating beverages in Moen Municipality be prohibited? Yes or no?" Of 2,163 votes cast 93 percent (2,014) favored prohibition (*Marianas Variety News & Views,* July 28, 1977, p. 14; *Trust Territory Highlights,* August 1, 1977, p. 2).[7]

This overwhelming vote left the Council with no choice but to draft Municipal Ordinance No. 5-77 banning the sale or consumption of alcoholic beverages (see Appendix 2). However, because Moen is the only port of entry for Truk State, provision was made in the ordinance for licensed importers to legally store alcoholic beverages for transshipment to wet municipalities elsewhere in the state. Since there has been at least one wet municipality continuously from 1977 to the present, this provision produced a loophole that has led to a thriving black market in alcohol on Moen (see Chapter Six). The district administrator signed the Moen ordinance on October 25, 1977, and it took effect January 15, 1978. Chief among the numerous responses to this act was that "Protestant Church groups wrote and extended congratulations to the Administration for its wise decision" (Falcam et al. 1978:4).

The petition drive in favor of prohibition found a strong supporter in Moen's mayor,[8] who turned the drink issue to his advantage while campaigning for reelection that year. The petition drive also attracted support from a majority of the Moen councilmen, in part because of an unresolved dispute with the district legislature that had festered for several years over sharing alcohol revenues. During 1977 legislators representing Moen initiated a revenue-sharing plan between the district legislature and the Moen municipal government, but other legislators would not support the proposal. Taxes and fees from alcoholic beverages were the largest single source of district revenues, accounting for 49 percent of the 1977 annual budget (Millay 1987a:175), and the legislators were reluctant to share this money with the Moen Municipal Council. Many councilmen felt this was grossly unfair because Moen bore the brunt of alcohol-related problems in the district. The prohibition movement provided them with a significant political threat in their power struggle with the district legisla-

FIGURE 5.3 *Cartoonist's view of the competition over liquor tax revenues among the local, state, and national governments* (Truk Chronicle, *November 30, 1979, p.6).*

ture. Some Moen councilmen hoped the anticipated loss of income due to prohibition would convince the legislature to share alcohol-generated revenues with them, at which point the Council could then repeal the prohibition law.

IN THE AFTERMATH OF PROHIBITION

The year 1978 was quiet and peaceful on Moen. As part of a U.S. federally funded Justice Improvement Commission program Trust Territory Headquarters initiated "to revitalize law enforcement in Micronesia" (*Micronesian Independent,* August 31, 1979, p. 6), a new chief of police and police captain were hired in late 1977. These men, and their counterparts in Pohnpei, Yap, and Belau, were expected to combat the growing public violence in Micronesia, to bolster police morale, and to institute training procedures to improve police efficiency in each of these districts. The new chief and captain arrived in Truk shortly before the Moen ordinance took effect, and they and their men assiduously prosecuted infractions of the prohibition law once it was in place. The chief, especially, was a proverbial "tough cop," a fearless, young Hawaiian-Portuguese man of imposing stature and great physical strength. Soon after his arrival, he sought out the biggest and toughest drunken troublemakers on Moen and challenged them to fight. Those who accepted lost the fight; those who declined lost face. His exploits became legendary and remain so even since his departure. Without question, Trukese drunks were afraid of him and so kept a low public profile.

Also, during 1978 the black market was just getting established. Initially, alcohol brought in and sold on the black market was very expensive (e.g., $20–$25 per fifth of hard liquor), and the high price curtailed the amount of illegal drinking, although locally produced distilled spirits *(chooriyú)* made a comeback at this time.

If 1978 was uneventful, 1979 was not. By then the state legislature was in a serious financial pinch brought on by lost alcohol-generated revenues that plummeted from $441,605 in calendar year 1977 (Millay 1987a:175) to only $403 in the first full fiscal year (1978–1979) following imposition of prohibition (Truk State Legislature 1980a). Rather than work out a "share the wealth" arrangement with the Moen Council, the legislators planned to override the Moen ordinance on grounds that state government had ultimate jurisdiction over such matters.[9] They also began to cast about for other revenue sources and increased the state tax on tobacco and cigarettes during their March 1979 session (FSM 1979a).

Early in 1979, via an elite woman with important government connections, Fin Anisi leaders learned of the legislature's plan to void the Moen ordinance, and they immediately went into action. Following meetings that included other important women, they circulated petitions urging statewide prohibition throughout all 39 municipalities of Truk State. A joint committee of Fin Anisi and Mwichen Maria officers wrote the petition (see Appendix 3). If they succeeded in obtaining the necessary signatures, they hoped to pressure the legislature into eliminating the transshipment loophole in the prohibition law because there would no longer be any wet municipalities in the state.

On Moen, women traveled to every house in every village with copies of the petition in hand. Because the gubernatorial election was at hand, many thought initially that the women were visiting their communities as campaign workers. Once their true purpose became known, however, they received a mixed reaction. Drinkers laughed or swore at them and taunted them with statements such as, "Oh, those ladies are trying to practice women's leadership." Nondrinkers were happy to see them, though, and women and old people encouraged their efforts. Working through church fellowship networks, women also circulated the petition to every community in Truk Lagoon. Trusted women traveling on government ships carried copies of the petition to the outer islands, and within a couple of months it had reached every outer island community. No effort was made to restrict the signers to registered voters: Signatures were accepted from women, men, and children alike. By March 1979, although it was not yet completed, this petition drive had proven very successful.[10] It was then that women learned of the legislators' intent to move ahead rapidly to legalize drinking again on Moen.

At least one bill was introduced to create a state liquor store that would have monopolized legal sales of alcohol in Truk (*Truk Chronicle,* April 6, 1979, p. 3). Numerous commentaries and discussions were held on Truk's radio station, many of which expressed strong opposition to any legislative effort to change the dry law. At the same time near-weekly debates on the liquor question went on in the legislative chambers, and a variety of persons from businessmen to clergy testified. Not surprisingly, given traditional Trukese male prejudice against women's involvement in public matters, no woman received an invitation to present women's concerns to the legislators.

On March 28, 1979, the Truk State Legislature established a Special Committee on Alcoholic Beverage Control to review the alcohol issue and present recommendations to the full legislature by May 1979 (Truk State Law No. 1-1-3, 1979, signed by the Governor on April 2, 1979; *Truk Chronicle,* April 20, 1979, p. 7).[11] This move prompted one woman to pen a letter to the editor of Moen's newspaper stating:

> I know that the Truk Legislature is going to make drinking legal again and I don't like it. Last year they asked my people from Moen if we want drinking and we voted that we don't want it. Now it seems like they don't care what we want, they only care about getting money for their pay. I hope they won't bring back drinking because I don't want any more fighting and drunk people around my house (*Truk Chronicle,* April 6, 1979, p. 6).

The women knew they had the tacit support of a powerful and crucial ally in the person of the mayor. Appointment of the Special Committee stimulated two women leaders to speak with the lieutenant governor and the governor, seeking support to prevent the legislature from overturning the Moen ordinance. Both officials agreed to help the women, and a delegation was sent to the legislature to request that the women be given an opportunity to present their case. This overture was rebuffed on grounds that the executive was interfering in the legislative process. In the face of this response leaders of Protestant church women's groups, together with their Catholic counterparts and other concerned women, organized a protest demonstration—something theretofore unheard of in Truk. This idea (including the concepts of marching, picketing with signs, and sit-ins) was taught to the participants in the Christians Concerned About Alcohol Conference in November 1976, and had been thoroughly

FIGURE 5.4 *Logan Memorial Church, Mwáán village, Moen, Truk.*

discussed by members of Fin Anisi groups. As will be described in Chapter Seven, women in the temperance Crusades of 1873–1874 in the United States also successfully used protest marches and picketing (Blocker 1985b:43, 48).

In preparation for the Moen demonstration the organizers recruited participants. Fin Anisi leaders wrote to women on other islands in Truk Lagoon, informing them of the date and time of the protest, and asking them to join. When the demonstration took place, a number of women from other islands came to Moen and stayed with relatives so that they could participate. All Fin Anisi groups on Moen, plus Catholic women from the Mwichen Maria, were contacted personally and invited to march. Radio announcements urged women to assemble at the Logan Memorial Church to discuss strategy. On the appointed day women arrived at the Logan Church (see Figure 5.4), many with signs they had made earlier. Some signs were mounted on sticks; others were just carried. The signs, written in English and Trukese, proclaimed: "Alcohol causes problems in families"; "Alcohol causes harm to many people"; "Alcohol creates problems for our elected officials"; and "Alcohol can break a marriage."[12] Some women walked or rode to the Moen Municipal Council offices in Mwáán Village; others assembled at the Micronesian Legal Services office in the downtown area.

The actual march was from the Hotel Maramar where the women assembled to the Truk State Legislature Building (see Figure 5.5).[13] The chief of police, who strongly supported the women on this issue, drove the fire engine,[14] on which a number of the women rode while others marched on foot. When the march began, approximately 200 protesters proceeded to the legislature building, waving signs amid shouts and

FIGURE 5.5 *Truk State Legislature Building, Moen.*

occasional blasts from the fire engine's siren. Protesters surrounded the building and, at the request of its lone female member, the legislature recessed so that its members could read the signs. The women sat outside on the lawn and on the veranda every day for close to a week before the Speaker finally invited a group of 8 to 10 of them in to present their case.[15] These women presented to the Speaker the signed petitions against alcohol that had circulated throughout the state. They also spoke quietly but firmly their strong opposition to any attempt to make Truk wet again. In the words of one woman leader, "We were carrying out the wishes of the people and encouraging the senators to give the people peace and not destruction."

During the women's demonstration and sit-in, the legislators avoided talking about the liquor law, and instead convened special evening committee meetings about which the women were not informed. Some legislators were completely taken aback by the women's demonstration—which they viewed as a brazen, wholly inappropriate action. Their first reaction to this perceived threat to their dignity and authority was to conduct business on the liquor law behind closed doors; however, one consequence of the demonstration was that selected women's leaders were invited to testify before legislative committees. Yet the Special Committee appointed in March later disbanded and never produced a full report.

In response to an official query from the state legislature, the courts upheld the jurisdiction of municipalities over local option liquor laws. This opinion, combined with the women's active protest, deflated the legislators' drive to override the Moen ordinance. Women, organized and mobilized, beat back the first attempt to abolish Moen's prohibition law.

Unable to eliminate prohibition, the legislature passed Truk State Law 1-1-13 establishing an alcoholic beverage possession tax, which was signed into law on April 27 (FSM 1979b). They hoped this new tax would partially recoup lost alcohol revenues by effectively taxing the black market. The possession tax increased the levy on beer by 5 cents per 12-ounce container, but it nearly trebled the fee per gallon for distilled beverages (from $2.50 to $7), perhaps in recognition that *wiisiki* had become the mainstay of the black market (see Chapter Six). In addition, another bill established legal penalties for disturbing legislature business (FSM 1980)—a bill approved on July 16 and clearly aimed at preventing a repeat of the women's protest demonstration. The governor vetoed it on July 24, 1979. When the legislature reconvened in September, it overrode the veto, and the bill became Truk State Law 2-1-2, although in the years since it has not been effectively enforced.[16]

A number of other important events related to alcohol in Truk also took place in 1979. Toward the end of April, the chief of police completed his tour of duty and returned to Honolulu, and was replaced by another American (*Truk Chronicle,* May 4, 1979, p. 1; *Micronesian Independent,* August 31, 1979, p. 6). But shortly before his departure, the state police confiscated nearly 300 cases of contraband liquor on Moen, reportedly worth over $30,000 on the black market at then-current prices (*Truk Chronicle,* April 20, 1979, p. 1). Some of this illegal liquor arrived in two air freight shipments on Air Micronesia (in Foremost dairy products boxes), whereas the remainder came in by ship (Ibid.). These shipments were addressed to two state legislators, one of whom then served as chairperson of the Special Committee on Alcoholic Beverage Control (Ibid.:4). Complaining of a lack of space in the Public Safety building to store "all this stuff," the chief of police was quoted with characteristic candor as saying; "I am mad at these smugglers and sellers. If I could break their heads, I would do it. It's unfortunate that the bad guys are getting richer, while the government and good citizens are getting poorer" (Ibid.). Perhaps not coincidentally, in June *after* the chief left Truk, the two state legislators obtained liquor licenses to sell alcohol in their home municipality (Wonei), which had just passed a "wet" law (*Truk Chronicle,* June 29, 1979, p. 3). The governor approved these licenses over the negative recommendation of the state's Alcoholic Beverage Control Board, which reportedly turned down the applications "based on our investigations, current public interest, and the petition submitted by the Women's Group" (Ibid.). The governor's action prompted at least one public criticism in a society where such criticism is rarely voiced (*Truk Chronicle,* August 10, 1979, p. 6).

In September and October a further major dispute developed surrounding prohibition. In an executive order dated September 28, the lieutenant governor, serving as acting governor while the governor was away on business, revoked the Moen ordinance as of October 20 (*Truk Chronicle,* October 5, 1979, pp. 1 & 5), purely, he claimed, for economic reasons (Ibid.). He drew his authority for overriding a municipal ordinance from a section of the Trust Territory Code that permitted a governor to intervene in this way with "good cause"—that being in this instance the economic hardship wrought on the state via lost taxes and other revenues from alcohol sales. Although this executive action was announced widely (e.g., *Truk Chronicle,* October 5, 1979, pp. 1 & 5; *Micronesian Independent,* October 25, 1979, p. 6), it was soon retracted. Unbeknownst to the acting governor, the section of the Trust Territory Code from which he drew his authority had been repealed on July 2, 1979, a fact gleefully pointed out to him by Moen's mayor (*Truk Chronicle,* November 2, 1979, p. 6).

On November 29, 1979, The Truk State High Court reached a landmark decision with respect to liquor legislation. Representing two young men from Wuumaan Island, the Public Defender challenged the validity of Wuumaan's local prohibition law (Uman [Wuumaan] Municipal Ordinance No. 1-77) on grounds that it did not comply with the legal steps set out in the Truk District Code. In Case 7-79, the High Court overturned Wuumaan's prohibition ordinance, stating that:

> Counsel have stipulated that there was no petition calling for an election, and that neither the question of prohibition generally, nor Ordinance No. 1-77 specifically, was ever placed before the voters of Uman. It follows that the Municipal Court acted without authority in the matter [in trying the defendants] and that Uman Ordinance No. 1-77 must be, and is, declared invalid (USTTPI 1979:2).

The immediate effect of this decision was to clarify that only 2 of Truk's 39 municipalities—Moen and Oneop—were legally dry since they were the only communities to have followed proper procedures in enacting local ordinances to prohibit alcohol consumption and sale as provided for in state law. From a practical standpoint the High Court's decision strengthened the position of liquor importers: It in effect reinvigorated the transshipment loophole; importers could again stockpile large quantities of alcohol on Moen for shipment to most of the rest of the state.

Following up actions from the previous April, a draft bill concerning alcohol control in Truk State was submitted to the legislature for discussion in December 1979 (*Truk Chronicle,* December 14, 1979, pp. 1 & 4). An American serving as the legislature's economic advisor prepared this draft that was based in part on recommendations from the Special Committee on Alcoholic Beverage Control established in late March. The gist of the proposal was to have a single state liquor store serve as the only legal importer and wholesale outlet for alcoholic beverage sales in Truk. The draft proposal noted that prohibition had been fairly successful in reducing alcohol-related violence, but that it created problems of its own, notably the black market, loss of government revenues, and a drop in the tourist business. Its author believed his proposal would solve these new problems while further decreasing violence (Ibid.). Although the press reported a revised bill based on the draft might be taken up at a special legislative session in January 1980 or in the regular session in May (*Marianas Variety News & Views,* December 11, 1979, p. 1), the legislature never acted on this proposal.

The next two years were comparatively quiet on the alcohol front. The black market was well established by this time and much drinking took place (Millay 1987b). With the bars shut down and drinkers still afraid of arrest and prosecution, *public* drunkenness and violence were minimal. Most drinkers stayed in their houses or hid in the bush. A brief furor attended a Filipino ship captain accused of possible liquor smuggling (*Truk Chronicle,* November 16, 1979, p. 1; January 11, 1980, pp. 1, 3, 5), but little came of that. During this period the Moen Municipal Council decided to consider repeal of the prohibition law on grounds that it was unenforceable and that too much government revenue was being lost, with profits from the liquor trade instead lining the pockets of those with black-market outlets.

When women heard of this proposal, they mobilized and sat outside the council chambers daily while the council was in session.[17] Once again the mayor supported temperance women. He pointed out to the councilmen that the women had assembled outside in opposition to repeal, reminded council members of women's voting power, and then recited a legend. In olden times in Truk, before colonial control, warriors were enjoined to respect women. If men from different communities or islands were fighting and a woman appeared on the battlefield, the fighting was supposed to cease immediately. By their very presence women could halt men's destructive acts. The mayor then noted the analogy to women's presence outside in opposition to alcohol. In drawing on this legend the mayor shrewdly, creatively employed his own cultural repertoire to deal with contemporary political events.

Although they did not speak up publicly to the council as a body, women reminded individual councilmen who entered and left the chamber of their unalterable opposition to repeal. The women also commented that they would watch how each councilman voted. This mix of moral force (councilmen were said to be "ashamed" to vote against prohibition with their mothers, sisters, and wives present), veiled political threat (women made it clear that anyone who voted for repeal would have difficulty being reelected), and the mayor's support proved successful and prohibition remained in force. Once again, organized groups of women were victorious on the liquor question.

The temperance forces, both men and women, were further encouraged when Ta Municipality in the Mortlocks went through all the proper legal procedures for enacting prohibition. The governor signed into law Ta Municipal Ordinance No. 2-81 on February 2, 1981. This victory was an especially heartening and symbolic one for temperance advocates because when the Moen ordinance was drawn up in 1977, Ta was the only other wet municipality, and on its account the transshipment loophole had to be included in Moen's dry law.

There was considerable confusion on the part of most Trukese, including legislators and other government officials, about which municipalities were legally wet and which were legally dry. In fact, as a result of the Truk

State High Court ruling noted above, only five municipalities had met the letter of the law in enacting local option prohibition as of August 1, 1985: Moen, Oneop, Ta, Ulul, and Wonei. Nevertheless, numerous other municipalities operated as essentially dry communities because strong municipal leaders and public opinion were against alcohol.

In 1983, proliquor forces mounted a third attempt to repeal the Moen ordinance—this time as a second effort from within the Moen Council. Approximately one-quarter of the councilmen voted against prohibition back in 1977, and opposition on the council rose in the years following. Significantly, though, Moen's mayor remained a public supporter of prohibition, and his opinion carried considerable weight. Around March 1983, a group of Moen businessmen petitioned the Council to lift prohibition. As might be expected, they cited economic considerations, notably, the alleged negative impact the dry law had on tourism and the loss of government taxes.[18] The businessmen proposed alcohol distribution be controlled by issuing licenses only to such businesses as hotels and entertainment spots (*Truk News Chronicle,* April 1983, pp. 1 & 8). Of course, hotel bars and "entertainment spots" had always been the major locations of fights and disruption in the years leading up to prohibition. Once again the call went out to Moen's temperance women.

On this occasion the women had very little time to organize because they learned the council planned to discuss repeal only two days before the meeting was to take place. Consequently, instead of extending personal invitations to all the different Fin Anisi and Mwichen Maria groups, the UCC Fin Anisi who first learned of this matter announced on WSZC that women interested in opposing this possible council action should convene the next day at the Logan Church. About 50 UCC women showed up, prepared signs, planned what they would do, and agreed to return to the church in the morning. When they reconvened, they picked up their signs and marched from the church to the council chambers in a single long line.[19] Later in the week some women from the Nómwoneyas Fin Anisi groups and some Catholic women joined the demonstration.

This time the women did not sit quietly by, chatting with the councilmen as they went in and out of the council building. Instead, they mounted a public demonstration somewhat on the model of the 1979 protest at the state legislature building. In all, about 80 women jointly representing Protestant and Catholic church women's groups began demonstrating on April 18, and they continued to do so over the next week whenever the council met (see Figure 5.6). Their opposition was very clear, and very verbal. They carried hand-lettered signs bearing such statements as, "Love your Mother; Don't permit drinking on Moen"; "Money brings about the trouble of our island and family. Please bring about *peace* [that] there will be no liquor"; "Don't kill/injure my children"; and "We do not want money—we want peace." If the council was in session, women protesters were outside and in the wings reminding them of their intense opposition to a return to legal drinking. When the matter came to a vote on April 25, the proposal to repeal prohibition lost 13-7.[20] Temperance women won once again.

The several efforts of male politicians (both state and municipal) to rescind the Moen ordinance convinced women of the need for constant vigilance on the matter. This necessity had a historical precedent in the nineteenth-century United States where "the liquor business [also] proved a resilient foe, as one new dealer after another attempted to move into the vacuum created by the Crusaders' successes. Again and again the women remobilized their forces to march upon a new opponent" (Blocker 1985b:192). The major difference between the situation in Truk and that in America was that the Trukese women did not march on the black market liquor outlets that sprang up in the aftermath of prohibition, reserving their protests instead for the state legislature and the municipal council.

Following five years of prohibition, and three unsuccessful attempts to get rid of the Moen ordinance, the state legislature, desperate over lost liquor tax revenues, enacted on November 20, over the governor's veto, the State Tax Act of 1984 (FSM 1984), an act first introduced during summer 1983 (*Truk News Chronicle,* July–August 1983, p. 1). Among other provisions, this law levied an excise tax on alcoholic beverages at the port

FIGURE 5.6 *Women's 1983 protest demonstration outside the Moen Municipal Council Chambers.*

of entry *in addition to* the alcoholic beverage possession tax passed five years before. This excise tax amounted to 30 cents per 12-fluid ounces of beer and $10.50 per gallon of distilled beverages, a sixfold and a sevenfold increase over the alcohol sales taxes enacted in 1969. The new law also taxed cigarettes and other tobacco products, and put a 3 percent ad valorem tax on all other imports. This last provision, in particular, was extremely unpopular with the business community and led to organized noncompliance while the issue of its legality was pursued in the courts. Members of the Truk Chamber of Commerce refused to pay the sales tax and held it in escrow at the Moen branch of the Bank of Guam while they challenged the act's legality. They did so because of a self-serving legislative decision: At about the time the legislators passed the State Tax Act of 1984, they tripled their own tax-free individual yearly allowance (from $5,000 to $15,000), on top of an already substantial salary of $12,000 per year. This dispute was not resolved until 1986 when the Chamber finally transferred the accumulated sales tax from the escrow account to the state's general fund because the state government was in financial difficulty (Martin 1986a:12)

By August 1985, enforcement of the antialcohol ordinance had become fairly lax on Moen. A new chief of police from Hawaii began his duties in June 1982, and he viewed prohibition as unenforceable and felt the black market mocked the law. Consequently, he instructed his men to leave drinkers alone unless drunks wandered into public places, whereupon they would be arrested and jailed. By summer 1985, at least four clandestine bars (speakeasies) operated more or less openly on Moen. Two of them favored Moen's monied elite, catering only to those they knew would not be disruptive drinkers; these bars also ran gambling operations on the side and enforced a dress code. Essentially, the police tolerated drinking so long as it was done in private and drinkers created no public disturbance.

Women seemed reasonably content with this situation since they had won the moral victory, and since they had sustained prohibition three times when challenged. Moreover, small but significant signs showed the protemperance tide still ran strong in Truk State: Abiding by all necessary legal steps, Ulul Municipality became officially dry on October 29, 1984, and the citizens of Wonei Municipality (which turned wet in 1979; see above) enacted a prohibition law effective July 31, 1985. The local option process was begun in Nomwin Municipality during 1985, but it failed when the antialcohol faction was unable to get the signatures of two-thirds of the registered voters. At the time of our research in 1985, a petition circulated in support of prohibition in Parem Municipality, and later that year a dry law apparently passed there (Francis X. Hezel, personal communication). Most recently, Paata Municipality's ordinance against the sale and consumption of alcoholic drinks was signed into law by the governor on September 21, 1987.

RECENT EVENTS

In March 1986, Truk held a general election for governor, lieutenant governor, and representatives to the state legislature.[21] Five candidates filed for the gubernatorial race, and it required a runoff election, held April 29, 1986. The victor, with 55 percent of the vote, was sworn into office on May 8 (*The National Union,* May 1986, p. 6). Moen's mayor supported his candidacy in part at least because he promised to enforce Moen's liquor law if elected. Clearly, prohibition remained an important public issue. One letter to the editor of the *Truk Chronicle* prior to the election asked why the Speaker of the legislature could not control other legislators who were selling liquor illegally and thus disrupting the community (*Truk Chronicle,* February 8–21, 1986, p. 6).

Shortly after the new governor was elected, he made it known that state police would enforce the Moen ordinance, which meant tightening up controls over public drunkenness, and going after black market outlets and the speakeasies. Soon thereafter, the police chief was fired, not surprisingly since he and the mayor of Moen had been political opponents for a number of years, and because he had been notoriously lax in enforcing the Moen ordinance. Following his departure, the police raided a number of illegal liquor outlets and confiscated their supplies as a warning that the new administration was serious about its publicized hard line on drinking.

That fall, the governor issued a memorandum to all state departments stipulating that government personnel caught drinking on Moen would be fired. Whether any government workers were actually removed from their jobs as a result is not clear, but the memo recreated an atmosphere of caution around drinking that had begun to dissipate. By October 1986, some black market outlets folded in the face of the new governor's get tough policy, although drunks reportedly still roamed about town and imported beer continued to arrive by ship "for Truk's wet municipalities." Just before Christmas the police cracked down again. One particular liquor outlet was raided, and police confiscated about 1,000 cases of beer and 50 cases of liquor.[22] Also in December, police arrested a number of salesgirls for selling alcohol at businesses licensed only to legally store it for transshipment elsewhere in Truk State.

The new administration tightened up enforcement considerably over that of the preceding few years. The American chief of police was replaced by another American who promised to step up actions against those found in violation of the Moen liquor law. With a single possible exception, the five speakeasies in operation during summer 1985 were shut down by the beginning of 1987 (although some apparently had reopened by August 1988; Francis X. Hezel, personal communication). Although the black market in alcohol continued to thrive, sales were made much more discreetly than before, and those black market dealers still in business took the precaution of obtaining an import license to avoid having the police confiscate their goods. The police department again emphasized the sale of drinking permits for $10 a year, technically required of anyone who consumed alcoholic beverages in any of Truk State's wet municipalities.[23] In effect, anyone the police caught with liquor on his breath and without a drinking permit was arrested. Those with permits, on the other hand, were much less likely to be taken in because the police rationalized they might have been drinking in Fano Municipality (which is "wet"; see Figure 2.1) or out in a boat on Truk Lagoon. By the summer of 1988, however, Moen municipal authorities adopted a much more aggressive policy of arresting anyone who smelled of alcohol, regardless of whether he was actually causing trouble. Clearly, the degree to which the prohibition ordinance is enforced (and by whom—state police or municipal authorities) shifts with the political currents of the day.

What changed between the summer of 1985 and the end of 1988 was the atmosphere surrounding alcohol use. Stricter prohibition enforcement did not stop drinking, but it drove drinkers underground again at a time when they had become bolder about appearing in public. It also made purveyors of illegal alcohol a great deal more cautious about whom they sold to and how sales were transacted. In a brief article in *Pacific Magazine,* in October 1986, Petrus Martin commented that "It does look like Truk State is in for another dry spell," although he went on to note that "no one can really say that alcohol consumption and sales have come to a standstill" (1986b:26). Martin also mentioned that municipal fines for violation of the Moen ordinance had recently been raised. In spite of this general tightening up of the drinking climate, one of Truk's more sensitive and knowledgeable observers had the following to say about the situation:

> . . . . in my rounds of the hospital I see plenty of evidence that drunken fighting is alive and well in Truk. Perhaps one difference, but one that I can't give numerical evidence for, is that many of the stabbings and beatings nowadays seem to be administered by close friends or even family of the unfortunate young man (Francis X. Hezel, personal correspondence).

Support for prohibition apparently continued through 1988. For example, the Truk State Legislature adjourned its Fourth Special Session on March 17 "without taking further action on a proposed bill . . . intended to designate certain areas on . . . Moen to serve [alcoholic] beverages, to reestablish and enforce the drinking ID card and to prohibit off selling of alcoholic beverages in other areas" (*The National Union,* March 1988, p. 3). Clearly, the antialcohol law, championed by women a decade before, continued to enjoy substantial community and official government support in Truk, even though it had not entirely eliminated alcohol use and alcohol-related problems. We next examine the impact of the Moen ordinance on the economic and social life of the community.

CHAPTER SIX

What Prohibition Hath Wrought

> One of the most important developments in the field [of social and epidemiologic research on alcohol] is a new emphasis on change. Twenty years ago, drinking habits were seen as relatively permanent characteristics and there was a tendency to overlook or deny the phenomenon of change. . . . Now it is clearly recognized that major changes occur, in whole populations as well as in individual lives, and a beginning has been made on understanding the processes behind these changes (Institute of Medicine 1987:107).

In this chapter we will document and assess the general economic, social, and political effects of prohibition on Trukese society and culture from January 1978 to August 1985. What forces maintained Moen's prohibition in the face of powerful opposition? What were the benefits and drawbacks of this rather draconian method of alcohol control in Truk? How did prohibition affect patterns of alcohol use? Has prohibition contributed to increased use of other substances such as marijuana? Prior to the present study, two brief investigations were made of the impact of prohibition in Truk (Falcam et al. 1978; Millay 1987a, 1987b). In discussing the changes the Moen ordinance brought about, we draw on these articles and on ethnographic information contained in a community study of drinking and drunkenness on Moen in 1976 (Marshall 1979a).

THE CONTEXT OF DRINKING

For someone returning to Truk right after prohibition was enacted, perhaps its most noticeable effect was that drinking had been driven underground. Most of the showier aspects of public drunkenness—men staggering through the village, beer can in hand, fighting with other young men, stopping vehicles on the road, and destroying family property with kung fu kicks (described in detail in *Weekend Warriors*)—had ceased. Closure of the public bars removed a primary setting for public intoxication and fighting, and because the police would usually arrest anyone found drunk on a public thoroughfare, prohibition significantly altered the context of alcohol use in Truk. In the years since passage of the Moen ordinance, most drinkers have stayed in their homes or hidden in the bush without venturing into town, village, or public streets as they would have done before. The dramatic performance aspect of drunken comportment no longer adequately describes intoxicated behavior in Truk.

Now the Trukese say the stricter enforcement, in particular, has made drinkers *nuwokkus,* "afraid" or "scared," to be caught in public. But it appears closure of Moen's public bars made the greatest difference in reducing public acts of alcohol-related violence. Bar fights usually involved combatants from different communities who often did not know each other, and frequently ended in tragedy. Drunken men spilled out of the bars onto the streets to accost innocent bystanders, and many people were afraid to walk on the roads alone or at night. Intoxicated young men lurched along the roadsides, shouting indiscriminately or unleashing a distinctive Trukese yell associated with drunkenness (see Marshall 1979a, 1990).

By mid-1985, it was rare to see a drunk in public. Many men drank more moderately or at least exercised more control over their behavior after consuming alcohol. To be sure, *fitikooko,* "trouble," was still associated with Trukese drinking, but public violence involving strangers was much less common than before as drinkers hid from the police. Most disturbances now occurred in social settings where others present (kin and friends) were likely to intervene before someone was seriously hurt or killed. A widespread public perception existed in 1985 that Moen's prohibition law had reduced the incidence of alcohol-related fights, homicides, and suicides, even if the facts suggested otherwise. This shared public fiction is critically important for understanding what Millay (1987b) calls the symbolic value of the prohibition law.

Following Gusfield's (1963) lead that the very existence of a law symbolizes public affirmation of the ideals it embodies, Millay argued that the Moen ordinance served "the important symbolic function of affirming Christian temperance values held by older males and many women and denigrating the more permissive values of younger male drinkers in Truk" (1987b:190–191). This idea seems plausible, but it does not begin to exhaust the symbolism of Moen's dry law. The dry law also stood for women's organized public involvement in and impact on a major social policy issue in Truk, representing a political clout that they did not have before. In 1976, women provided the impetus for attempts at more stringent alcohol control policies through a few sympathetic legislators. In 1977, elite women planted the idea of a petition drive in support of prohibition on Moen with the district administrator, mayor, and other leaders, and women carried the petitions around to Moen's various communities. In 1979, and twice thereafter, women organized through their church groups demonstrated at the legislature and the municipal council building, and remonstrated with male politicians to defeat three different attempts at repeal. Primarily because of women's public protests over alcohol abuses, male politicians voted to remain dry; it was said that the politicians *nuweyiti aramas,* "were afraid of the people." "The people" were incarnate in groups of chanting, placard-waving, hymn-singing Trukese women.

Moen's dry law also symbolized something less tangible than raw political power. It stood for a state of *kinamwmwe,* "peacefulness" or "harmony," replacing a previous state of *fitikooko,* "trouble" or "disturbance." In effect, the law was a statement that a majority of the citizens of Moen Municipality had had enough, that public alcohol use had become abuse, and needed to be reined in. As we've already noted, the law accomplished this by moving drinking "backstage"—into the bush or people's homes. Drunken violence continued into 1985, but it usually occurred outside the public arena, and it no longer commanded the attentive and appreciative audience it once had (see Marshall 1979a). *Public* life, therefore, *was* more peaceful after the law took effect, and this fact may account for the widely shared perception that things were better, safer under prohibition, even though the ordinance failed to eliminate drinking.

Several highly placed Trukese elites told us they believed Trukese drinkers had become *sineenap* about drinking, that they had "learned to handle it." The point was made in a news account that postprohibition "those who drink haven't reduced the amount they drink, they just show their drunkenness less" (*Truk Chronicle,* April 6, 1979, p. 3). Some persons we interviewed asserted that people no longer *ingeyiti,* "admired" or paid attention to, drunks seeking to demonstrate their *pwara,* "bravery"; by 1985, it was said, the audience to drunkenness *opwut,* "disliked" or "hated" such behavior. Public drunkenness had been redefined as something *assááw* "shameful." Whether these comments are accurate for all Trukese or not is immaterial. What *is* important is that they reflect the altered social climate—the changed set of public attitudes—surrounding drinking in Truk in the prohibition era.

The law does not deal with everyone equally in Truk, anymore than in the United States, and being a member of the elite has its privileges. In keeping with the more hidden settings in which drinking occurred, some elites regularly served alcohol at private parties, secure in the fact that the police would not arrest them. Elite party-givers promised to control their guests, and the police sometimes were told about the party in advance and asked to stay away. In fact, most such gatherings were quiet, and any guest who became too drunk was kept overnight until he had recovered. Similarly, managers of some of the speakeasies that had opened by summer 1985 were *nefinifin,* "discriminating," in whom they admitted or how much they were willing to serve to their guests. Known troublemakers and poor people typically were excluded from the better establishments, although there were at least two speakeasies where anyone with the money could buy a drink.

An interesting anthropological issue arises here concerning perceptions of changes in alcohol use in Truk: Previously published writings about Trukese drinking may have shaped people's views of the problem in 1985. Most Trukese under age 50 can read English, as can a few persons older than that. A majority of today's elite is fluent in both written and spoken English, and many have read *Weekend Warriors,* published approximately a year and a half after prohibition began. Although a number of copies were sent to persons in Truk shortly after the book appeared in 1979, most Trukese who read it did so while working on college credits as part of the EOSC extension program in Truk that began in 1980. Over the years, several different EOSC instructors assigned the book in "social problems" classes, including one held during summer 1985, with the result that many copies circulate in Truk. Some Trukese students on Guam or in the United States also used *Weekend Warriors* to prepare research papers for college classes there. The book's high visibility in Truk may have influenced Trukese elites' perceptions of the place of alcohol and drunkenness in their society so much that they may have offered spuriously similar information on the topic in 1985 (see Marshall 1989). How much the ideas in *Weekend Warriors* may have contributed to the altered circumstances surrounding alcohol use in Truk in 1985 cannot be known, but the book clearly is part of the overall context in which changes vis-à-vis alcohol have taken place.

DOMESTIC LIFE

Enactment of Moen's prohibition law may have improved family life in Truk, an area that constituted one of women's major concerns in launching their attack on alcohol. Prior to the law, some husbands, after drinking, frightened and sometimes beat their wives and children. Physically abusive drunken fathers or husbands were not discussed in *Weekend Warriors.*[1] Yet based on data gathered in 1985, it seems domestic abuse was a considerable problem " intimately connected in the community's mind with the evils of drink" (Hezel 1985:13, 15). Women also worried when their brothers, husbands, or sons were out drinking and did not return home at night, never knowing whether the man was injured or even dead. Spouses argued over money squandered on bar drinking, the husband buying rounds for his friends or for everyone in the house, and leaving little or nothing with which to pay for food, clothes, taxi fare, school fees, and other household expenses. Divorce was often the net result of such behaviors before prohibition. The domestic concerns Trukese women expressed in 1985 were remarkably akin to statements women Crusaders made in the United States in the 1870s that "emphasized threats to women as family members: pain, shame, and economic loss. They drew upon an image of women faithfully performing their duties in the home while men neglected their obligation to protect women from the world outside" (Blocker 1985b:96; see Chapter Seven). Some elite women we interviewed stated that alcohol-related family violence had decreased markedly since 1978, that there were fewer arguments over money spent on alcohol, and that problem drinking was much less frequently a cause for divorce. They claimed these positive changes derived from the Moen ordinance.

Of course, the law has not completely eliminated family problems linked to alcohol. Some respondents mentioned problems have continued in families with young adult males. These young men, when drinking around the homestead, often argued with other family members, and sometimes beat up their fathers or struck other relatives. They also yelled, cried, threw things, and occasionally destroyed property when inebriated (cf. Marshall 1979a:70–72, 74). Drunk driving was also a problem in such families. Not only did these young men endanger themselves and their passengers when driving while drunk, they also threatened other drivers and pedestrians—especially children playing on the roads. Women also noted drinkers frequently misbehaved at home—talking too much or too loudly, violating speech taboos in the presence of certain relatives (e.g., sisters; see Marshall 1981b), using foul language with women around, sleeping in the nude, or having sex with female kin. Misuse of family money on alcoholic beverages also continued in some homes. Given the much higher cost of black market alcohol, a man drinking heavily in 1985 spent an even greater proportion of the family income on his habit. Despite the Moen ordinance, drinking in Truk continued to be accompanied by a variety of normally inappropriate or forbidden behaviors.

To the extent that prohibition reduced the number of regular drinkers on Moen, or the frequency with which men drank, it had a positive effect on a continuing social problem with implications for domestic welfare, namely, job absenteeism (*Truk Chronicle,* April 6, 1979, p. 3). Not unusually, men showed up several hours late for work the day after a drinking bout, if they showed up at all. Specifically, on at least two occasions during summer 1985, the Truk State Legislature was without a quorum because members were hungover and absent. Job supervisors rarely punished workers on such occasions.

PROHIBITION, CRIME, AND VIOLENCE

One major stimulus to the prohibition movement, as it gained strength in 1976 and 1977, was the perceived increase in crime and violent behavior attributed to alcohol abuse. In the mid-1970s in Truk, alcohol was looked upon as the root cause of most of society's ills (see, e.g., Mahoney 1974). For instance, Falcam et al. (1978:3–4) wrote that "Moen residents had begun to understand that trouble couldn't be controlled if drinking was not stopped," and that "they believed that these crimes were all caused by people who were drunk and could not control themselves. Many felt the ban would put an end to all these problems, and so they supported it." Likewise, Millay (1987b:198) summarized his interview data by stating that "the most often mentioned 'benefit' that Trukese people hope to gain from prohibition is a reduction in alcohol-related crime and violence." Those Trukese concerned over the direction in which their society seemed to be moving thought eliminating alcohol would radically reduce crime, especially violent crime.

A little over a year after the Moen ordinance took effect, the chief of the Trust Territory's Mental Health Branch assessed the effects of prohibition on violence in Truk by examining Truk Hospital emergency room records for trauma for the year before and the year after the alcohol ban (Dale 1979). He compared figures for automobile accidents, knife wounds, injuries inflicted with stones, gunshot wounds, and "other injuries," and found that in every category except gunshot wounds "the amount of trauma . . . has been substantially reduced by a factor of three to four" (Ibid.). Dale's study was publicized in the popular press (*Marianas Variety News & Views,* March 30, 1979, p. 5) and gave the impression that prohibition had dramatically lowered alcohol-related injuries in Truk.

A major difficulty with any such research in a developing country like Micronesia is that recordkeeping is desultory at best. Information often simply is not recorded at all, or if it is, it is recorded inaccurately or incompletely; so subsequent use of the data is problematic. Staffing is a problem in the records room of Truk Hospital as well as in the outpatient clinic. If the hospital is busy, patients often are treated and released without record, particularly if the patient did not require prescription medications. Even if reasonably good records *are* made at the time of, for example, a hospital emergency room admission, proper storage and record maintenance is not always performed. Hence, records studies in Micronesia should be approached with caution.

Dale's (1979) data show an apparent, interesting, and encouraging downward trend in the number of trauma cases reported in Truk Hospital records for the year immediately following passage of the Moen ordinance, but the trend does not prove prohibition alone caused the decline. Another difficulty, particularly given the small number of cases involved (total N=63 for 1977 and N=20 for 1978) is that one cannot determine what the normal year-to-year fluctuation in reported trauma was over a period of several years. Possibly, the reduction during 1978 fell within typical patterns of variance from one year to the next. Dale also mistakenly assumed that most alcohol-related injuries in Truk were brought to the hospital emergency room for treatment. In 1976, at least, informants indicated a great many such injuries were self-treated, treated in municipal dispensaries, or treated by traditional medical practitioners; indeed, with the advent of legal prohibition the number of alcohol-related injuries treated in the hospital may have diminished out of fear that the resultant records would draw attention to unauthorized drinking and lead to arrest (cf. Marshall 1979a:77).[2]

In 1981, Millay visited Truk Hospital to check the same emergency room records Dale had investigated, except he obtained data from 1976 through 1979 in an effort to examine year-to-year fluctuations. To his surprise, not only did he find substantial variation in categories of trauma from one year to the next, but he also obtained different numbers of cases for 1977 and 1978 than Dale had (N=33 and N=32 respectively). From his own work, Millay concluded that "a detailed coding and analysis of all cases recorded in the emergency room log book from 1976 through 1979 does not substantiate Dale's findings and conclusions. Rather, the pattern of trauma cases is largely unchanged when comparing the two years before and the two years after prohibition" (1987b:204).

By summer 1985, recordkeeping and maintenance at Truk Hospital had so degenerated that it proved impossible to reexamine the cases Dale and Millay studied or to extend the analysis beyond the end of 1979. But from the evidence presented above, the records available to Dale and Millay do not support a conclusion that the Moen ordinance produced a notable reduction in traumatic injuries resulting from alcohol-related violence in Truk.

A public perception arose rather quickly during the first year of prohibition that this new legal measure significantly curtailed crime (Falcam et al. 1978; Millay 1987b; *Truk Chronicle,* April 6, 1979, p. 3). From all accounts there *was* such a reduction during the first year or so of the ban, owing mainly to the lack of a well-organized black market, to stringent law enforcement, and to a very real concern on the part of drinkers about prosecution should they be caught. But as the black market got going, and a widely understood modus operandi developed between drinkers and police about "permissible" drinking behavior, alcohol-related crime statistics crept back up. Millay (1987b) demonstrated this trend using material on the caseload per year in the Truk District Court. If treated cautiously, arrest records the Truk State Clerk of Court kept can provide a crude measure of alcohol use's continued relation to crime. Our own data suggest that by 1983, if not before, approximately two-thirds of all arrests were alcohol-related and remain so (see Table 6.1).

Unfortunately, these arrest records do not extend to a time before prohibition, which means a before-and-after comparison is impossible. What they do show, however, is that alcohol still figured importantly in public disruption, driving arrests, and interpersonal violence. In aggregate, the number of alcohol-related arrests has remained constant at approximately two-thirds of all arrests per year, over a period of almost five years.

"Alcohol-related arrests" is a composite category that includes several different offenses. By far the most common of these is Drunk and Disorderly Conduct. In addition, the following legal offenses also are included in this category: Illegal Possession of Alcoholic Beverages, Illegal Sale of Alcoholic Beverages, Driving Under the Influence of Alcoholic Beverages, Assault, Assault and Battery, and Disturbing the Peace. Based on information the Truk State Police provided, the Drunk and Disorderly

TABLE 6.1 *Alcohol-related arrests, Truk State, September 20, 1980–August 1, 1985.*

TIME PERIOD	TOTAL ARRESTS	ALCOHOL-RELATED	% OF TOTAL
9/20/80–12/31/80	63	53	84
1/1/81–12/31/81	210	119	57
1/1/82–12/31/82	151	87	58
1/1/83–12/31/83	396	256	65
1/1/84–12/31/84	391	258	66
1/1/85–8/1/85	141	89	63
TOTAL	1,352	862	64

Source: Records of memoranda from the Department of Public Safety (police) to the State Clerk of Court, Moen, Truk, regarding cash bail posted at the police station for all arrests. [records on file in Truk State Court offices.]

Conduct charge is brought against those arrested in public places; Disturbing the Peace is the charge used when the behavior has occurred on private property and there has been a formal complaint. The chief and deputy chief of police estimated that more than 90 percent of all Assault and Assault and Battery charges were alcohol-related; knowing this, we included *all* cases of Assault and Assault and Battery in Table 6.1, even though doing so might have slightly inflated the percentage of alcohol-related arrests. But we did so because there was no way to identify the small number of assaults that did not involve alcohol.

News accounts do not provide a systematic sample, but they do offer information on the occurrence of certain alcohol-related crimes, particularly the more visible ones such as homicide. As such, they provide some additional documentation of drunken behavior in Truk since prohibition. The news accounts since 1978 record a continuation of drunken homicide (e.g., *Truk News Chronicle,* January 1983, pp. 1 & 8; July/August 1983, p. 6), persons becoming so physically ill they required hospitalization (e.g., *Truk News Chronicle,* April 1983, p. 3), and deaths resulting from drunk driving crashes (e.g., *Truk News Chronicle,* July/August 1983, p. 6).[3]

With the paving of Moen's main roads, drunk driving has increased and inevitably led to new hazards: single or multiple vehicle traffic accidents and risks to pedestrians who walk along the roadside because there are no sidewalks in Truk. So too, persons who have been drinking, especially at night, sometimes venture onto the road, staggering or lurching about, and run the risk of being hit by cars whether the driver is drunk or sober.

Suicide among young men in Truk is another serious problem that has developed in recent years (Hezel 1984, 1987a; Rubinstein 1983, 1987). Although we cannot say being drunk causes young men to take their own lives in Truk, nevertheless, most such suicides are drunk at the time of the act. Sometimes, as well, the apparent precipitating incident leading a young man to suicide involves an issue around alcohol. For example, a suicide may have just been scolded by a close relative for drinking or for misdeeds committed while drunk or he may have been refused money with which to purchase more liquor. No evidence exists that prohibition has had any direct influence on this particular kind of violent behavior in Truk.

The prohibition law seemed to have a calming effect on *public* drunkenness in Truk. Prohibition altered significantly the places where drinking occurred and the public nature of drunken behavior. But prohibition apparently did not change the amount of drunken violence among young men (the fighting simply seems to have shifted from a public forum to private settings), nor did it notably affect the association between drinking and crime in Truk. However, although it was not public behavior, women reported that the incidence of domestic violence was less after the law came into effect.

As we've already noted, prohibition altered the drinking pattern in Truk. Drinking went underground. And the sheer amount of drinking that took place in the first year or two after prohibition was reduced via a combination of limited supply, high price, and industrious policing. However, as drinkers adjusted to the new circumstances, and as the black market got well established, supplies increased, prices came down, and the amount of drinking in the community appears to have returned to preprohibition levels. But unlike the days before the Moen ordinance, the likelihood a drunk might accost one on a public thoroughfare was almost nil, and drunken young men no longer disrupted community life on a daily basis. Prohibition had brought at least the illusion of "peacefulness."

ENFORCEMENT

Enforcement is a significant political development that has grown up around Moen's prohibition law. Initially, the police enforced the law zealously. Black markets were raided and supplies confiscated. Illegal imports were intercepted and the importers fined. When drunks were encountered, in public or in private, they were arrested regardless of their social position. The law applied equally to all. Under these circumstances alcohol consumption declined precipitously during 1978 and those who drank "lay low." Then the chief of police from 1977–1979 completed his duty assignment and returned to Hawaii. In the years following his departure, enforcement of the Moen ordinance became a major political squabble.

All three chiefs of the Truk State Police who served between 1979 and the time of our research were much less interested in and effective at enforcing the dry law than their predecessor. They all looked upon the black market as a form of victimless crime. The police chief from 1982–1986 denigrated the prohibition law, viewing it as "asinine" and "unenforceable," particularly when a person could legally go out and drink in a motorboat just beyond the jurisdiction of Moen Municipality. As word of his attitude circulated around Moen, black markets began to operate more openly and drinkers became somewhat less cautious about hiding from the police. As enforcement declined, an important policy question arose: Whose responsibility was it to enforce the prohibition law?

The Moen ordinance is a *municipal* law, not a state law, and recent chiefs of the state police have reasoned that municipal police should enforce municipal laws. Moen had 13 municipal police in July 1985, 2 of whom were women, and most of whom were mayoral appointees with little or no training in police work. Given their other duties, their numbers were woefully inadequate to enforce prohibition. When they arrested persons for drinking violations, they took them to the state police's jail because the municipal jail was closed at the governor's request and for financial reasons. However, the state police often simply released the offenders whether or not they posted bail or paid a fine. By 1985, so much animosity existed between the state and municipal police forces (played out through the persons of the state chief of police and the Moen mayor) that these two groups of law enforcement officers rarely cooperated. As a consequence the Moen Municipal government collected very little income from alcohol-related fines; the mayor reported this sum to be about $1,000 per year, even though a single offense could net a fine of up to $100.

A more serious enforcement problem concerned the drinking habits of the police themselves—both state and municipal. Many policemen drank in 1985, a fact widely known in the community. A number of police were involved in the black market trade or confiscated alcohol in exchange for not arresting someone caught drinking. Public knowledge that the police were routinely breaking the law in a cavalier fashion seriously undercut respect for both the law and its enforcers. The administration that took office in May 1986 took steps to strengthen enforcement and reverse the erosion of public trust in the state police force, but we do not know how effective these measures have been.

REEFER MADNESS

One enduring legacy of the Peace Corps to Micronesia was the introduction of *Cannabis sativa* in the late 1960s, along with information on how to smoke its leaves. Marijuana grows prolifically in Truk's lush tropical environment and is now ubiquitous on the islands in Truk Lagoon. It does not thrive on the low, coral, outer island atolls of Truk State, so much of the marijuana consumed there is imported from Truk at a price of $2–$4 per joint (double or quadruple the going price on Moen).

Even though the plant was brought to Truk in the late 1960s, Trukese young adults did not use it much until the mid-1970s when significant numbers of them left for college in Hawaii and on the U.S. mainland. At that time marijuana use was popular on American college campuses, and Trukese students learned the proper rules for smoking behavior and acquired such paraphernalia as roach clips and belt buckles with removable pot pipes. As these students returned home for visits or for good, many brought marijuana seeds with them to plant. For at least the past decade, then, marijuana has taken root in Truk both agriculturally and socially.

Marijuana is classified as a controlled substance in the FSM although this classification has had negligible impact on its use and spread (FSM 1982:265–266). Millay (1987b) comments that few arrests are made in Truk for possession of marijuana, a fact our own examination of arrest records confirmed. Millay also notes that some people attributed the increase in marijuana use in Truk to the expensive price of black market alcohol, "but it is difficult to document any precise cause and effect relationship between the prohibition ordinance and the increased use of marijuana" (Ibid.:197).

Data from our general population survey suggest that very few Trukese have *substituted* marijuana for alcohol although we cannot prove this assertion. The survey results show that those who drink alcohol are very likely to use other substances as well. When male drinkers are contrasted with male nondrinkers in terms of marijuana and tobacco use, the smoking of either substance highly correlates with alcohol use. In summer 1985 more than two-thirds of the 208 persons in our sample who reported ever using marijuana also said they currently drank. These findings suggest marijuana use has not replaced alcohol use in Truk, but rather that its use is additive. Moreover, we cannot argue that marijuana has provided a substitute for alcohol because Trukese drunken behavior and stoned behavior are radically different (Larson 1987; Marshall 1979a). But perhaps Trukese young men seek a "high" regardless of how they get to that state.

Numerous Trukese parents would rather their children used marijuana than alcohol simply because pot smokers do not become violent and create a public disturbance in the way drunks often do. Instead, after "blowing grass" young men become withdrawn, introspective, and quiet. Even so, many Trukese are ambivalent about marijuana. They know it is illegal, and many have heard it can be physically harmful (although similar information about the negative health consequences of tobacco and alcohol use have certainly not stopped Trukese from using these drugs). There is a set of young men, mostly in their twenties, reputed to be "crazy" from smoking too much marijuana. Whether these persons suffer from mental illness unrelated to pot smoking, or whether heavy marijuana use has exacerbated or potentiated a preexisting emotional disorder, is unknown. Nonetheless, a folklore exists on Truk that overuse of marijuana can make you crazy.

THE BLACK MARKET

An obvious change prohibition triggered was in the marketing of alcoholic beverages. Alcohol is big business in Truk. During 1976, prior to prohibition, Truk Trading Company (TTC)—Moen's largest commercial enterprise—"sold a mind-boggling $300,000 worth of cigarettes and $250,000 worth of beer and liquor" (Kiener 1977:36). Four other package stores also sold alcoholic beverages at that time, not to mention the half-dozen bars and hotels then in operation where one could drink. Carry-out beer cost about 50 cents per can in 1976, although it was 75 cents per can on licensed premises. In that same year the average price of a fifth of liquor ranged from $4.67 for vodka and rum to $6.56 for Scotch; mixed drinks in the bars cost $1.00–$1.50. Because of the transshipment loophole in Moen's prohibition ordinance, necessitated by Truk's municipal local option law and the fact that there had been at least one legally wet municipality continuously since 1959, inevitably one effect of the Moen ordinance was creation of a black market in alcoholic beverages.

At first, prohibition cut deeply into alcohol distribution, but as the black market got established, profits from selling beverage alcohol grew exponentially. During the first year of the Moen ordinance relatively few alcoholic beverages were legally imported or smuggled into Truk. It took most of that year for black marketers to get organized, and because the police diligently enforced the prohibition law, the risks of illegal sales were considered high. Some commercially manufactured beer and liquor got through, of course, but only the elite could afford it on anything like a regular basis. Quite a bit of home brew also was produced during this period in the form of "yeast" and especially "moonshine," *chooriyú,* a beverage Trukese had almost ceased to make when they could buy commerically manufactured liquor. A year after prohibition, however, the black market had expanded to meet Moen's continued high demand for beverage alcohol and to take advantage of the substantial profit that could be made by engaging illegally in the liquor trade. Fifteen months after prohibition took effect, Truk's local newspaper reported a prospering black market in illegal alcohol with estimates of transactions ranging from $5,000 to $13,000 per week (*Truk Chronicle,* April 6, 1979, p. 1). Most contraband liquor was brought in as air freight, with one Air Micronesia employee estimating that about 20 cases of liquor arrived per week on their flights (Ibid.). Five years after the ban began, a representative of a Guam-based liquor distributor was quoted as saying that "his business was selling more liquor to Truk now than before the prohibition" (*Marianas Variety News & Views,* May 20, 1983, p. 7).

Profits were even greater because smugglers paid no liquor taxes, because some black market operatives did not purchase import licenses,[4] and because black market prices were much higher than preprohibition store prices. Soon after the Moen ordinance took effect in 1978, for example, a fifth of liquor typically cost $20–$25. This had dropped to $15 by April 1979 (*Truk Chronicle,* April 6, 1979, p. 1), to between $10 and $20 by summer 1982 (Millay 1987b), and to an average of $10 per bottle by summer 1985, a price still well above the preprohibition level.[5] Beer cost $20 a case in summer 1982, and still sold for anywhere from $18–$24 a case of twenty-four 12-ounce cans in 1985. Its price has not declined significantly on the black market because demand for it is probably higher (see below), and because cases of beer are more difficult to store and hide in an illegal operation than are bottles of liquor. In any event, seven-and-a-half years after prohibition began on Moen, alcoholic beverages were roughly twice as expensive as they were in 1976 before the dry law took effect. The black market also thrived because once the alcohol was acquired very little work or risk was involved in selling it.

Even allowing for inflation, the profit margin on liquor in 1985 was greater than before the dry law. One source reported, for example, that the wholesale cost of importing beer to Truk was between $8.50 and $9.00 per case. In June 1985, on Guam, American beer (Old Milwaukee) sold for as little as $6.95 a case, Scotch whiskey was $5.99 per 750 mL, and bourbon cost $6.95 for a 740-mL bottle (*Pacific Daily News,* June 28, 1985, pp. 10, 20, 37). Between May and July 1985, advertisements in the *Marianas Variety News & Views* indicated that U.S. beer (Budweiser, Lowenbrau, Schlitz, Strohs) sold for about $12.50 per case on Saipan, with 750-mL bottles of liquor ranging from $5.45 for Crown Czar vodka to $11.09 for Old Parr Scotch. In August 1985, the wholesale price of a carton of Budweiser via a major dealer on Guam, not counting shipping charges to the Trust Territory, was $7.90 (Ambros, Inc. 1984).[6] Since transportation costs from the United States to Guam and Saipan are quite similar to Truk's, these comparative prices indicate how much money can be made in black market alcohol on Moen.[7]

At the beginning of prohibition there were few illegal sellers and little alcohol was imported even by those who could legally do so by virtue of possessing an import license. As it became clear that huge profits could be made on the black market, though, the number of illegal outlets multiplied to meet demand. In summer 1982, for example, Millay documented the existence of 12 black market outlets on Moen, and had reports of nearly 40 others elsewhere in Truk State (1987b). Persons with import licenses ran some, but smugglers and illicit manufacturers of locally produced liquor ran the others. Three years later the number of black markets on Moen had more than doubled: Twenty-eight such outlets operated quite openly on Moen at the time of our research. Nearly everyone on Truk knew the locations of at least some of these operations, along with what they had for sale and what the going prices were. Three of the 28 outlets had established themselves as speakeasies—small cafes that surreptitiously served beer to customers who asked for it. Beer was sold only by the glass, which was brought to the drinker wrapped in a paper napkin to disguise its contents. As with Moen's population, most black markets were located in or near the downtown area, but outlets also were to be found in Iras, Mechchitiw, Mwáán, Peniya, Sópwúúk, and Tunnuuk (see Figure 2.5). A glance at the map shows this distribution effectively covered the island, making it convenient for anyone who wished to buy alcohol to do so.

From the beginning, prosecuting black market dealers, most of whom were "respected men in respectable positions. . . . [who] know they can get away with it because of their positions" (*Truk Chronicle,* April 6, 1979, p. 3), was a politically sensitive issue. Based upon his research in 1981 and 1982, Millay (1987b) also noted that most black market owners were among Truk's elite—merchants duly licensed to import alcoholic beverages for transshipment. These same "duly licensed merchants" were often locally powerful businessmen, politicians, and government employees, including members of the state legislature and the Moen Municipal Council. Hence, some in the power elite exploited their fellow citizens and grew richer at their expense by providing an illegal product. In effect, prohibition produced an income transfer from poorer people to those elites involved in the black markets. Not only did this situation make for a wry cynicism among Moen's populace regarding the likelihood that the police would ever prosecute black marketeers, but it also meant some of the elite had a vested interest in *maintaining* prohibition, not for moralistic reasons or for reasons of public health and safety, but for their own financial gain (cf. Millay 1987b). This shabby state of affairs is strongly reminiscent of "Rum Power" in the United States in the nineteenth century, which Dannenbaum has described as "implacable in its greed, powerful in its wealth and political influence, respectable in social standing, and, above all, protected by the law" (1984:85).

Quite a few black markets were set up as family businesses, often adjunct to a small store selling bread, canned foods, cigarettes, kerosene, instant coffee, and so on. Some black marketeers hired kin to run their liquor outlet while they themselves continued to work at a well-paid office job in the town center. Other owners simply had their wives or children sell the illegal alcohol whenever a customer appeared, so that children as young as 11 or 12 were sometimes in charge of black market outlets, with brothers and sisters as young as 6 fetching the customer's purchase from the back room where it was stored. Few elite women had husbands engaged in black market sales, and most elite women in the temperance movement had their husbands' support in their struggle against Demon Rum. However, we were aware of at least two cases in which a Fin Anisi leader worked for prohibition even as her close male kin (brother, son) or husband grew wealthy from illegal liquor sales. There was no hypocrisy here; the women detested alcohol, spoke out strongly against it in the family, but could not control the actions of their menfolk. Many black market dealers in alcohol also sold marijuana by the joint (at $1 per reefer). In effect, Moen's black markets had become drug emporia where customers could buy their drugs of choice: ethanol, nicotine, caffeine, or THC.[8]

Because of the higher price of alcohol on the black market, another apparent consequence of prohibition in Truk has been to shift drinkers' preferences from beer to distilled liquor, something particularly true of younger drinkers. Observational and other qualitative data from the 1976 ethnographic investigation of alcohol in Truk suggested beer was far and away the most popular drink at that time, which, indeed, conformed to a pan-Pacific preference for beer over other kinds of beverage alcohol (Marshall 1987b). But when we asked drinkers in the 1985 survey what beverage they usually drank, 59 percent answered whiskey (meaning distilled spirits of any sort), 38 percent answered beer, and just over 2 percent chose yeast. Of course, in Truk as in the United States 100 years before, black market dealers in spirits may have "looked upon the [prohibition] movement as a boon, since they believed the closing of the saloons boosted demand for their more easily transported and more readily concealed product" (Blocker 1985b:216). Thus, the rise in distilled liquor as a beverage of choice may have been partially a function of availability.

A number of important differences existed between whiskey drinkers and beer drinkers in 1985 (see Table 6.2). Whiskey drinkers were younger as a group, more likely to be unmarried and unemployed in the wage economy, and much less likely to have any college education. A substantially higher percentage of whiskey drinkers began drinking before age 15 and were more prone to smoke marijuana. And although they seldom consumed more than seven drinks per drinking bout, much higher percentages of these men reported getting so drunk they passed out and getting so sick they could not walk by themselves. (Obviously, number of drinks consumed is less significant than alcohol content.) These differences, in aggregate, suggest a class difference in alcoholic beverage preference under prohibition. Millay (1987b) also suggested that the higher cost of black market alcohol "affected the consumption levels of the poor more than the rich," but he seemed to have assumed that poorer persons would drink less. In fact, what appears to have happened is that less affluent drinkers have switched from the prestige beverage—beer—to stronger drink that is cheaper per unit of ethanol. Beer drinkers are more likely to be among the married, monied elite, with wage jobs and better education, who can afford the high price of beer on the black market. Whiskey drinkers, by contrast, typically pool their meager cash resources to buy black market alcohol. These young men usually buy whiskey because it gives them "more bang for the buck." Several commented they

TABLE 6.2 *Selected comparisons between whiskey drinkers (N=132) and beer drinkers (N=85).*[a]

SURVEY ITEM COMPARED	% WHISKEY DRINKERS	% BEER DRINKERS
Age = less than 25 years	49	29
Marital status = single	69	34
Education = some college or college graduate	7	27
Unemployed for wages	79	53
Began drinking before age 15	14	7
Usually drinks less than seven drinks per sitting	49	23
"I got so sick I couldn't walk by myself."	82	51
"I got so drunk I passed out."	78	55
Currently smoke marijuana	61	40

[a]*Determined by responses to the question, "What do you usually drink?"*

like 151 proof rum (75 percent ethanol) because a bottle purchased for $10 and mixed with soft drinks or water yields three bottles of approximately 25 percent ethanol, enough to get everyone in the peer group drunk.

Clearly, stronger forms of alcohol have become more popular—a significant negative consequence of prohibition. Given the basic Trukese drinking pattern ("drink everything available until it's gone"), this trend may lead to serious personal and public health problems. Accidents resulting from severe intoxication, deaths from alcohol overdose, and physical illnesses known to be linked to long-term heavy drinking (e.g., cancer of the upper respiratory and upper gastrointestinal tracts and cirrhosis of the liver) may all become more common in Truk following this shift to stronger drink.

BEER MONEY

During the fiscal year preceding and including the start of prohibition (1977–1978), 49 percent of state-generated revenues in Truk came from alcohol taxes, amounting to over $440,000 (Table 6.3).[9] This sum plummeted in the first full fiscal year after the dry law took effect to one-tenth of 1 percent of Truk's state-produced income—a paltry $403 (Truk State

TABLE 6.3 *State-generated revenues from alcoholic beverages and tobacco products, Truk State, 1977–1983.*[a]

FISCAL YEAR	ALCOHOL REVENUE		TOBACCO REVENUE		% OF TOTAL REVENUE
	AMOUNT	% OF TOTAL	AMOUNT	% OF TOTAL	
1977–1978	$441,605	49	?	?	?
1978–1979[b]	403	0.1	88,457	22	22.1
1979–1980	90,177	16	168,562	29	45
1980–1981	193,808	28	137,133	20	48
1981–1982	124,299	22.5	79,417	14	36.5
1982–1983	236,065	38	55,065	9	47

[a]*Because of the legal controversy between the Truk Chamber of Commerce and the Truk State Legislature over the State Tax Act of 1984, financial data for the period after the 1982–1983 fiscal year were unavailable during the period of data collection. As of this writing, information on revenues the state collected after June 30, 1983, had not yet been published.*
[b]*The figures from 1978–1979 onward differ from those Millay (1987b) reported in two ways. Millay relied on data provided by Joseph Walther, the Assistant Tax Collector for Truk State, who calculated revenues for 1979, 1980, and 1981 on a calendar year basis, and who produced a calendar-1982 estimate based on receipts from the first six months of that year. Data presented here from 1978 through 1983 were taken from the official financial statements and auditor's reports prepared for the Truk State Legislature, and these are reported on a fiscal year rather than a calendar year basis.*

Sources: For 1977–1978: Walther (1982); for subsequent years: Truk State Legislature (1980a, 1980b, 1981, 1983, 1984).

Legislature 1980a). Essentially, prohibition led to a loss of *half* of the state government's annual revenue in the first full fiscal year after the law took effect! Although Millay (1987b:194) asserted that "prohibition has given the Moen Municipal Government a lucrative new source of revenue from the collection of ordinance violation fines," and that "the Moen Municipal Government has profited at the expense of the Truk State Government . . . ," we found no evidence that this was, in fact, the case. Given the rather lax enforcement of the ban after the first year or so and the tendency not to convict violators of the law even when they were arrested (Ibid.), relatively few fines were collected for the municipal government's coffers.

Passage of the alcoholic beverage possession tax in spring 1979 partially recovered lost alcohol tax income in the 1979–1980 fiscal year (Table 6.3), and although this recovery has continued, income in 1985 from alcoholic beverage taxes remained well below the dollar amount the legislature obtained from this source before prohibition was declared. Even as a percentage of state-produced revenue, alcohol-generated taxes had not returned to the 1977–1978 level five years later. Antiprohibition forces have rallied around the loss of economic revenue for the state government, more than any other single issue.

Economic reasons for repealing prohibition have been argued in many different ways in Truk, none perhaps more novel than the suggestion that beer be brewed as a cottage industry, bottled, taxed, and sold as a way for Truk to "have its own industry, generate money here and most important, keep it here" (*Truk Chronicle,* April 20, 1979, p. 11). And though the closure of Moen's six bars in January 1978 led to the lay-off of approximately 40 workers (Falcam et al. 1978:7), it is likely an equivalent number of wage-compensated jobs were created in the black market distribution system. In the Falcam et al. study it appeared the ban might have had a small negative effect on the number of tourists who visited Truk during the first year of prohibition. When Millay reexamined this matter in 1982, however, he concluded that "overall, the evidence does not support claims that prohibition had a crippling effect on tourism in Truk" (1987b:196). In the mid-1980s members of the business community asserted strongly that Moen's dry law kept tourists away, but (as noted in Chapter Five) a cholera epidemic in 1982 and 1983 that received wide publicity in the international media probably had much more to do with any decline in tourism at that time.

The tax levied on alcoholic beverages by the Truk District (and now the Truk State) government has increased markedly in 25 years (Table 6.4). The excise tax remained constant at $.0375 per 12-ounce bottle of beer for a decade. In 1969, a new luxury tax was applied to beer (among other commodities) that brought the total tax levy on 12 ounces of beer to $.0875. Five years later the legislature raised the excise tax to 15 cents, increasing the total tax per can/bottle to $.20. The two new taxes added since 1974, instituted to recoup lost revenue from alcohol imports, have steeply increased the overall tax on those beverages legally brought in for transshipment. Addition of the possession tax in 1979 boosted the total tax per 12 ounces of beer to 40 cents, and the 1984 sales tax hiked the total state tax on a bottle or can of beer to 70 cents.[10] So the tax on beer more than doubled in 1969 and 1974; in 1979 it doubled; and in 1984 it increased by another 75 percent.

Table 6.4 also records the rise in district or state taxes assessed per gallon of distilled liquor over the period such beverages have been legal in Truk. The rate rose by 50 percent in 1964 and again in 1969 where it stood at $4.50 per gallon with the addition of the luxury tax. In 1974, the excise rate was actually *reduced* slightly, dropping the overall tax per gallon to $4. Following prohibition, however, new taxes on distilled beverages drastically increased the cost of legally importing liquor. In 1979, the total tax burden per gallon was raised by 175 percent to $11; in 1984, the rate was nearly doubled again to $21.50 per gallon.

These figures show the percentage rate of tax increase per unit grew more rapidly for beer than for distilled spirits from 1959 to 1974, but since that time the rate of increase has been higher for liquor. Clearly, in an environment in which many Trukese ignore the liquor laws or work

TABLE 6.4 *Truk District/Truk State taxes on alcoholic beverages, 1959–1984.*

YEAR	TAX TYPE	LEVY ON BEER (PER 12 OZ.)	LEVY ON DISTILLED BEVERAGES (PER GALLON)
1959	excise	$.0375	none[a]
1962[b]	excise	$.0375	$2.00
1964	excise	$.0375	$3.00
1969[c]	luxury	$.05	$1.50
1974	excise	$.15	$2.50[d]
1979[c]	possession	$.20[d]	$7.00
1984[c]	sales	$.30	$10.50

[a]*Distilled beverages were not legally allowed in Truk until 1961.*
[b]*This tax was later superseded by Congress of Micronesia legislation.*
[c]*These taxes were added on to whatever excise tax was levied at the time.*
[d]*Levied on the stated amount or any fraction thereof.*

Sources: For 1959, *Truk Review,* May 1959, pp. 2–3; for 1962 and 1964, Truk District Legislature 1967; for 1969, *Met Poraus,* September 25, 1969, pp. 1–3; for 1974, USTTPI 1974a; for 1979, FSM 1979b; for 1984, *Truk News Chronicle,* July–August 1983, p. 1.

assiduously to get around them, these major tax increases have encouraged smuggling by black marketers to hold down costs and increase profits.

The FSM national government, first elected and installed in 1979, levies an import duty on a variety of commodities, among which are alcoholic beverages (FSM 1985).[11] Some of this money is apportioned among the four state governments of Kosrae, Pohnpei, Truk, and Yap. The FSM import tax on beer in 1985 was 4 cents per 12 ounces or less, and liquor was taxed at a rate of $7 per gallon. Although Truk State receives a portion of the import tax on alcohol (and tobacco) the FSM government collects, factoring out the specific income Truk obtains in this way is impossible because the overall national import tax data are not disaggregated by commodity. Thus, figures showing alcohol's specific contribution to the total funds involved in revenue sharing are unavailable.

Most alcoholic beverages are price elastic, meaning that as price goes up, purchases go down, at least to a certain point. Wagenaar (1982:3) notes that controversy surrounds the degree of price elasticity of beer although "the weight of the evidence indicates an inverse relationship between price of beer and quantity purchased/consumed." Thus, government can use price as one method of alcohol control. Although clearly not a conscious government policy, we can assume that the rise of Truk's black market, with the very sudden and dramatic increase in price soon after prohibition took effect (Millay 1987b), lowered consumption significantly—many people simply could not afford to drink. Room (1978:287) has noted that "a major shift in the distribution of consumption between the social classes" appears to have been a consequence of the higher price of alcoholic beverages in the United States during Prohibition, with working-class consumption declining while that of the business, professional, and salaried class was relatively unaffected. In Truk, as the black market expanded and competition ensued, the price of beer and liquor came down to what the trade would bear. As price declined, we can assume consumption went up, possibly even to preprohibition levels, a fact reflected partially in the revenue figures in Table 6.3.

SUMMARY

Prohibition has produced numerous economic, social, and political effects on Trukese life, some short-term and others of more lasting consequence. Perhaps prohibition's most pronounced effect has been to alter the context of drinking from bars and village areas to more private settings in people's homes or in the bush. Preprohibition, drunks roamed Truk's public thoroughfares with impunity; after the Moen ordinance it was rare to see a drunken man in public. This change also meant drunks no longer accosted innocent bystanders in town and no longer attracted an appreciative audience as they once did. Indeed, drunkenness was redefined in the public view as something to be looked down upon and despised. To a remarkable degree, then, prohibition brought relative peacefulness to life on Moen.

Another major long-term effect of the antiliquor law was to radically reduce the locally generated revenues available to the Truk State Legislature. Despite the addition of various new taxes, and despite what amounts to a tax on the black market (the possession tax), Truk State Legislature revenues remained lower in 1985 than they were preprohibition.

Although they do not constitute a single uniform voting bloc, Trukese women gained a measure of political respect by championing the Moen ordinance and then upholding it in the face of three repeal attempts. Although divisions within the Protestant churches in Truk State have weakened the Fin Anisi organization, women leaders have created other outlets for group political action (e.g., Planning Committee, Red Cross). So far, though, nothing approaching the U.S. women's movement in the late 1800s has yet emerged from Truk's temperance activism (see Chapter Seven).

Women with whom we spoke unanimously agreed that prohibition had improved domestic life and reduced domestic violence. We have no way to verify these assertions and can only take the women at their word.

Concerning the impact of prohibition on crime and public violence, we can speak with greater authority. In the face of strong enforcement and a very limited supply of bootlegged liquor, alcohol-related arrests *may* have declined in the first year or two after the law began. But by 1980 such arrests again made up a substantial majority of all arrests, and they remained steadily at that level through early August 1985 (Table 6.1). Violence linked to drinking (drunk driving crashes, homicide, suicide, trauma) did not decline significantly postprohibition, but—importantly—a strong public perception exists that it did. Perhaps this perception occurs because much less alcohol-related violence happens in public than before the law.

Prohibition has led to a measure of political cynicism on the part of many citizens, consequent on lax and selective enforcement and the burgeoning of the black market. Young men, especially, resent that the police hassle or arrest them for drinking and generally leave senior public servants and politicians alone. That many police officers drink, sometimes using liquor they confiscate, adds to the antagonism. Many residents of Moen—women and men alike—are indignant at the huge financial profits some elites reap from illegal liquor sales.

Prohibition has *not* led drinkers to shift to marijuana as a substitute. But the higher price of alcohol on the black market seems to have contributed to a notable switch in beverage preference for many drinkers from beer to distilled spirits. This switch, in turn, may harbor serious long-term negative health consequences for Trukese people.

Thus, prohibition in Truk has been a mixed blessing. It *did* reduce levels of public drunken disruption and apparently produced beneficial effects on family life. It also contributed to new patterns of consumption and new perceptions of drunkenness. The dire economic consequence for state government of major revenue loss was tied to the equally undesirable "rich get richer" syndrome of a few unscrupulous elites prospering from black market sales. The Moen ordinance has had little effect on violence, crime, public health, and personal risks of illness or accident related to drinking.

The available data allow a very tentative estimate of what happened to the overall level of consumption of alcoholic beverages in Truk following prohibition. TTC, one of six licensed liquor outlets in 1976, had retail sales of beer worth $250,000 in that year (Kiener 1977:36). If we accept that TTC sold approximately one-third of all beer marketed on Moen in 1976, total retail beer sales would be estimated at $750,000. Since beer cost 50 cents per can back then, this dollar amount translates into 1.5 million cans of beer. Another estimate, based upon interview and observational data from the 1976 study in Peniyesene, is that beer made up about two-thirds of all alcohol consumed and distilled beverages the other third. Distilled alcoholic beverages cost an average of $5.35 per fifth in 1976 (Marshall 1979a:52–53). One-third of total 1976 consumption equals $375,000, or roughly 70,000 fifths of distilled liquor. So total estimated 1976 consumption of commercially produced alcohol for Truk is 1.5 million cans of beer and 70,000 bottles of "whiskey."

Comparing the above estimates with postprohibition figures is difficult, but we will venture a few guesses nonetheless. In 1979 it was estimated that illegal sales of alcohol on Moen amounted to between $5,000 and $13,000 worth of alcohol per week (*Truk Chronicle,* April 6, 1979, p. 1). At an average then of $9,000 per week, black market sales were $468,000 per annum. If the shift we recorded in beverage preferences in summer 1985 began to occur in 1979, as seems likely, and if we estimate that half of the annual consumption was beer and half distilled beverages, we can estimate the number of cans and bottles that were drunk in that year. Beer has consistently cost about $20 per case of twenty-four 12-ounce bottles since prohibition began; "whiskey" sold for about $15 per bottle on the black market in April 1979 (Ibid.). Using these prices we end up with 1979 consumption of 280,800 cans of beer and 15,600 fifths of distilled liquor. Admittedly these figures are guesswork, but it seems reasonable to conclude that three years after prohibition began it had radically reduced overall consumption of commercially manufactured alcoholic beverages in Truk.[12] What is not figured in here, of course, is consumption of home-brewed *yiis* and *chooriyú* at that time.

Despite the perhaps more numerous negative consequences of prohibition, ranging from a damaging loss of state revenues to political cynicism, the Moen ordinance continued to enjoy strong community support in 1985, from drinkers as well as nondrinkers, and from most men as well as nearly all women. Ninety percent of the 958 respondents to our survey question, "Is this a good law or a bad law?" indicated that the law was good. More than two-thirds of those who answered this question, and who reported themselves to be current drinkers in 1985, thought that it was a good law. Although a higher proportion of women than men believed the Moen ordinance to be a good law (97 percent versus 84 percent), the degree of male support was striking. In championing the prohibition law as a way to protect their communities, their families, and themselves, Trukese women of the 1970s and 1980s bore a notable resemblance to temperance women in the United States a hundred years before. We examine this resemblance in the next chapter.

CHAPTER SEVEN

Exorcising the Evil Spirits:[1] "The Whirlwind of the Lord"

> At all times the Temperance movement in America has drawn its membership, its energies, and its moral code from organized religion. In the final quarter of the nineteenth century, when Temperance was again a significant social and political activity, much of its tone was permeated by the spirit of Christian concern for humanitarian justice and sympathy. Intemperance was part and cause of a complex of evils which the social Christian sought to eradicate (Gusfield 1963:72).

During the 1830s and 1840s, the temperance movement in the United States directly influenced the creation of comparable movements in Finland, Norway, and Sweden (Hauge 1978; McMillin 1973; Wuorinen 1931). In like fashion, prohibition in Truk in the 1970s and 1980s bore marked resemblances to American temperance and prohibition movements during the second half of the nineteenth century. The most striking similarity involved the role of women and Protestant church women's groups as seedbeds for discussion, mobilization, and action on "the liquor problem."

The influence of the American temperance movement on Trukese women's attitudes toward alcohol began in the nineteenth century via the WBMPI. The New England missionary women of the ABCFM, who eventually established the Woman's Board in 1871, began to instruct Hawaiian females in "the cult of true womanhood" (piety, purity, submissiveness, and domesticity) and in other nineteenth-century American notions of femininity soon after they arrived in Hawaii in 1820 (Grimshaw 1985). Reform attempts were concentrated on Hawaiian family life in the hope that the missionaries might have an impact on the entire social system. To this end ABCFM mission women involved their Hawaiian female charges in the organizational and educational work of the church, formed Maternal Associations at each mission station, and established special schools for girls such as the Wailuku Girls' Seminary (Ibid.). ABCFM missionary women who helped carry Congregationalism to Truk in the 1880s undertook similar activities and programs. Prominent among mission attitudes taught to Hawaiian and Trukese women alike was a profound abhorrence of Demon Rum.

A case was made in Chapter Five that the Protestant legacy of America's nineteenth-century women's temperance movement—in the form of the Honolulu alcohol conference the WBMPI sponsored—helped shape Truk's recent prohibition movement. In this chapter we will demonstrate the many parallels between women's temperance and prohibition activities in Truk and those in the United States a century before. Of necessity we must provide information on American women's role in the nineteenth-century temperance movement. This involvement is sketched below, and pertinent events are related to comparable developments in Truk between 1959 and 1985. Circumstances similar to those surrounding temperance in the United States during the 1800s—political inequality between the sexes, women's limited public political participation, differences between men and women in regard to alcohol consumption and with respect to temperance activities—were all present in Truk in the period 1959–1985. Like their American counterparts in an earlier era, Trukese women used temperance to criticize and control men's behavior and, in order to do so, developed a collective political response where none had existed before.

WOMEN, PROHIBITION, AND EVANGELICAL PROTESTANTISM

Perhaps the clearest parallel between the situation in Truk preprohibition and that of the nineteenth-century United States exists in the position of women in these two societies. Traditionally, Trukese women were identified mainly with hearth and home (see Chapter Four). Women were not to take an active role in public political affairs and were not to speak out at public gatherings.[2] Women in Truk and elsewhere in the Caroline Islands were expected to remain in the village areas under most circumstances. They are associated symbolically with the land whereas men are linked to the sea (Alkire 1968, 1989). Women were gardeners and homebodies; men were voyagers and explorers. Throughout the nineteenth century, American women were closely identified with home and family—this was women's sphere and they were not to venture beyond it into the male, public political domain. The number of women organized in support of temperance, and the fervor with which they pursued their goal, grew as alcohol was increasingly seen as a threat to home and family. This intense concern to protect the domestic realm from the destructive consequences of drink also animated Trukese women as they girded themselves to battle Demon Rum in the 1970s.

Writing about nineteenth-century American temperance women, several different historians have noted women's greater participation in temperance activities, beginning in the 1840s, provided not only a means for economic self-defense, but also a vehicle for shaping their own consciousness and aspirations (Blocker 1985b; Bordin 1981; Epstein 1981; Tyrrell

1982). Typically, this took the form of some kind of women's organization, whether through a religious body or via one of the secular temperance societies that sprang up at this time, such as the Daughters of Temperance or the Martha Washington Society. In Truk, Protestant church women's fellowships have existed since the late nineteenth century as an outgrowth of ABCFM mission activity; and when Catholicism became established in Truk, Catholic women's groups also were begun. These organizations were important as one of the few venues where Trukese women could gather to discuss matters of mutual concern without men's interference. (Via church groups women also have bettered their communities in activities ranging from visiting the sick to civic beautification projects.) In the absence of widely subscribed secular women's clubs, church women's fellowships provided the obvious means for organizing a campaign to achieve a public political goal the vast majority of Trukese women held: to control alcohol-related problems in their homes and communities.

As with American women who opposed alcohol, Trukese women used Protestant church groups both as a leadership training ground and as a preexisting network through which to organize and express a public protest (Bordin 1981). Like their American counterpart in the 1870s, Trukese women's temperance movement was "religiously and morally inspired social reform . . . [which] had its base in the Protestant churches," especially among "Congregationalists or their descendants" (Epstein 1981:89). In Truk, as in the small towns of nineteenth-century midwestern America, women temperance crusaders had to enlist other women and secure general community support, initially in both places by soliciting endorsements of the movement from ministers and other local leaders. Numerous public meetings were held to build community support: "Initially, their meetings were attended by various sympathetic clergymen, but gradually the sessions developed into gatherings for women only" (Blocker 1985b:32). In Truk, as in Ohio and similar locations, women often deployed throughout the community after a meeting to solicit signatures on pledges or petitions demanding that local government councils enforce existing laws or enact restrictive or prohibitory ordinances.

Nineteenth-century American women used similar tactics. For example, in Rochester, New York, between 114 and 350 women attended daily hearings of the Board of Excise Commissioners to demand that liquor licenses not be issued and to exert moral pressure on the Board by their presence (Blocker 1985b:39). So too, Trukese women dealt with the Moen Municipal Council when it considered repealing prohibition (see Chapter Five).

It appears that the Hawaii alcohol conference in 1976 affected Trukese women much like the Ohio Crusade convention during the early 1870s affected women of its day: "For the first time in their lives they could feel themselves to be part of a women's mass movement. Conducted with efficiency and dispatch, the convention probably had a strong impact on its participants. Many of them returned home to organize new Crusades or to invigorate ongoing ones" (Ibid.:17). Many of the events surrounding prohibition on Moen, and its maintenance via women's continued watchfulness, might have occurred in the absence of the Hawaii alcohol conference. But the ways women activists organized the prohibition battle in Truk were influenced profoundly by ideas they encountered in Hawaii in 1976.

Working for the public political goal of prohibition through their church fellowships, Trukese women resembled their nineteenth-century American counterparts in several significant ways. They utilized the traditional rhetoric of the "helper," or the person who cares for others (Tyrrell 1982:144). Like nineteenth-century Crusaders, Trukese women recognized that a plea for community support of their antialcohol views would be effective only if they behaved in a manner that emphasized community interests and well-being (cf. Blocker 1985b:47). Women found this behavior easy since it was in keeping with their traditional roles. This public-mindedness greatly aided their efforts to garner community support and harness it to their goal. The prohibition battle stimulated a few women leaders to question the political and social fetters with which Trukese women had to contend. This questioning process set a small but influential minority of elite Trukese women on the road to political activism and support for other social causes. Women in Truk pursued "temperance," namely, a reduction in habitual drunkenness or regular heavy drinking, as a way to ameliorate other social problems such as crime, violence, individual failure, family dissolution, poverty, and illness (Levine 1985:103), just as nineteenth-century and progressive-era reformers had in the United States. Under the circumstances in 1977, prohibition seemed the best way to achieve "temperance" in this sense. Prohibition women in Truk also resembled their American predecessors in that they took control of the social movement to ban liquor, which led, as it had with their American sisters of the 1850s, to significantly greater access to the public platform.

THE RISE OF TEMPERANCE IN THE NINETEENTH-CENTURY UNITED STATES

Levine (1978) contends that between 1785 and 1835 a transformation occurred in social thought and in the structure of American society that involved a weakening of many of the social and political structures of colonial society in which numerous traditional forms of social control no longer worked. These changes were accompanied by the rise of the cities, the increased centrality of the market in economic life, and the development of an urban middle class. Dannenbaum (1984) describes the social and economic problems of the late 1840s as "new and frightening," observing that the pace of change steadily quickened and that its effects were often deleterious—particularly so because of the large-scale immigration from Germany and Ireland by the end of the decade. At mid-nineteenth century many American communities were beset with "widespread social disorder" in the form of "burgeoning slums, growing numbers of impoverished residents, marked increases in crime, and frightening epidemics of disease, as well as more frequent incidents of Sabbath-breaking, rowdiness, and disturbances of the peace" (Ibid.:70). This actual and perceived state of social disorder injected a sense of extreme urgency into the temperance movement. Temperance advocates believed that only all-encompassing temperance reform offered any possibility for "stability, morality, safety, and a truly humane society" (Ibid.:85). Many transformations that took place in the United States during the first half of the nineteenth century are similar to changes that occurred in Truk between 1945 and 1975 in the period leading up to the temperance movement there.

New England clergymen formed the earliest American temperance organizations during the first decade of the nineteenth century. Epstein (1981) claims that Protestant men, especially members of Congregationalist churches, provided the network of organizations that launched the temperance movement. The enthusiastic participation of Congregationalist clergy in establishing many of the early temperance organizations in the United States is particularly relevant when we view the ABCFM's orientation toward beverage alcohol in Hawaii and Eastern Micronesia as they spread the gospel to the islands during the nineteenth century.[3] The advent of the ABCFM mission to Hawaii in 1820 coincided with the rise of a nationwide temperance movement in the United States, and the Hawaii missionaries received much support and encouragement for their antialcohol efforts from their parent organization.

Women played an active role in the national temperance movement in the United States beginning in the 1820s, although generally they did not hold office, vote, or speak at meetings where men were present (Dannenbaum 1984). Tyrrell (1982) notes that temperance and church missionary activities were closely related between 1826 and 1840 and that temperance "was able to involve pious evangelical women without appearing to strain too far the conventional limits on female decorum" (Ibid.:130). Under church auspices, which had allowed them to meet, discuss, organize, and participate to some degree in reform activities, American women "began to reach out from the isolation of their homes" (Knight 1976:201).

In 1840, a significant new development occurred in the temperance movement—the formation of self-help groups like the Washington Society (Tyrrell 1982), which was the first temperance group to seek self-reformation of inebriates on a large scale. Accompanying the rapid growth of the Washington Society, and similar organizations like the Good Templars, the Rechabites, and the Sons of Temperance in the 1840s and 1850s, women's involvement shifted to women's auxiliaries, such as the Martha

Washington Society and the Daughters of Temperance (Epstein 1981). During this time, temperance activities were popularized via fiction, drama, music, parades, and outdoor meetings replete with flags and banners. One of the more vivid examples of this mass emotional appeal was the development of a *children's* group known as the Cold Water Army that through songs, parades, and demonstrations publicly proclaimed the advantages of water over the evils of drink (Gusfield 1963). Delegates to the Honolulu alcohol conference in 1976 received a copy of the Cold Water Army pledge in their conference packet and discussed the Army's public demonstration tactics in their meetings (see Appendix Four).

By the early 1850s, further changes took place in the temperance movement. Perhaps most significant was Maine's passage of the nation's first prohibition law on June 2, 1851. This law made it an offense to manufacture or sell any intoxicating liquor within the confines of the state, authorized search and seizure, and encouraged enforcement by allowing prosecuting officers to retain all fines they collected (Dannenbaum 1984). In the years before the Civil War, 12 other states (plus the Territory of Minnesota) passed prohibition laws patterned after Maine's, although many of these were repealed by the early 1860s due to enforcement problems. Only 5 of the 13 states with prohibition in 1855 remained dry in 1863 (Aaron and Musto 1981).

A second important change in the temperance movement by mid-century was that links were forged with the nascent women's rights movement (Tyrrell 1982). This linkage occurred especially through the Woman's New York State Temperance Society among whose leaders were Elizabeth Cady Stanton, Amelia Bloomer, Susan B. Anthony, and Mary C. Vaughan (Ibid.). By this time a small but influential minority of women were becoming politicized and advocating feminist issues along with temperance, as evidenced by the founding of the woman's suffrage movement at the Seneca Falls convention in 1848 (Epstein 1981; Tyrrell 1982). During this period some temperance women began to demand the right to speak in public, to participate equally with men in the movement, and to press for full membership in men's temperance organizations (Dannenbaum 1981). Tyrrell (1982) notes a trend by the early 1850s toward politicization of women's temperance and that temperance women supported feminist issues even though only a small minority completed the transition from temperance to feminism at that time.

A third change in the temperance movement around mid-century was the mounting of direct action against the liquor business by bands of female vigilantes. Women adopted these tactics because moral persuasion had been discredited and political efforts to effect change were beyond direct female influence because women lacked the vote. In a number of communities across the country, small groups of women took the extralegal, militant action of destroying the liquor stock of local drinking establishments (Dannenbaum 1984).[4] These actions against the liquor trade, along with confrontations of saloon keepers by nonviolent bands of praying women, were carried on intermittently throughout the 1860s and early 1870s. A surprising amount of middle-class male support for the female vigilantes of the 1850s existed. Dannenbaum (1981:243) suggests that men saw the "indecorous, illegal, and violent saloon destruction" as "essentially domestic in nature"; women were perceived "to be protecting their homes and families."

In the tumultuous decade of the 1850s, then, American women found their own special temperance perspective, began to speak out publicly on the issue, and occasionally directly battled the liquor trade. Such acts not only changed the course of temperance reform, but also gained women much wider access to public speaking platforms via their demands from within the temperance movement, access which worked to the benefit of the fledgling women's rights effort (Dannenbaum 1981). By the mid-1850s, however, the temperance movement became fragmented and regionalized; temperance societies in the North were militantly antislavery and their members "inundated subscribers to southern temperance journals with abolitionist literature" (Aaron and Musto 1981:147). At about this time temperance reform experienced a reversal of fortunes after nearly half a century of continued successes. Drinking regained some respectability and popularity during the 1850s, and the liquor industry grew stronger politically and economically. Women looked upon all these changes "as immensely threatening to the security of their families" (Dannenbaum 1984:182).

By the early 1870s, drinking was thought of primarily as a male activity and women increasingly saw drunken violence as a threat to their homes, families, persons, and pocketbooks. This perceived threat, coupled with the existence of women's organizations and missionary societies in several Protestant denominations, catalyzed what Dannenbaum has called "the spectacular phenomenon of the Woman's Crusade in 1873–1874" (1981:236). As discussed in Chapter Five, a similar phenomenon arose in Truk just over a century later.

THE WOMAN'S CRUSADE

In many respects, the Woman's Crusade was the single most dramatic episode in the long history of the U.S. temperance movement. Led and staffed almost entirely by women, it directly involved between 57,000 and 143,000 demonstrators (Blocker 1985b; Bordin 1980). The sudden emergence of the Woman's Crusade created the impression that it appeared from nowhere, when, in fact, it is best viewed as the culmination of the "female-dominated confrontational temperance" that started with the episodes of saloon destruction in the 1850s. Dannenbaum documents the Crusade's direct links to antiliquor events that occurred in Ohio during the 1860s, and indicates that by 1873, "women across the country were demonstrably ready to fight the saloons for what they saw as the safety of their families" (1984:204).

The Crusade's distinctiveness was that it—like its Trukese counterpart—was a grass-roots effort on the part of Protestant Christian women who, to protect their homes and families, tried to rid their communities of liquor outlets, particularly saloons. The participants emphasized religion and morality. Crusading women saw themselves as forces of good and their opponents as evil (Epstein 1981); similarly, Trukese women visualized themselves as caring for their community and set against the pro-liquor forces who would destroy it.

Blocker (1985a:461) calls the Crusade "the largest nineteenth-century protest movement by women"; Bordin (1978:402) sees it as equivalent to a conversion experience that moved women toward feminist principles "even if they did not recognize them as such"; Epstein (1981:90) refers to the Woman's Crusade as "a mass female assault on the saloons of Ohio and surrounding areas"; and Dannenbaum (1984:219) looks upon it as "a public theater of propaganda aimed at stripping social drinking of its growing respectability within the middle class." The Crusade marked a significant transition in which women took over leadership of the temperance movement and developed "a sense of collective purpose and solidarity,"—a "moral comradeship" (Aaron and Musto 1981)—with important repercussions for women's reform movements and the women's rights movement over the next half century. Until the Crusade of 1873–1874, women's role in the temperance movement had been relatively minor and passive for all but a handful of women. Although the evangelical fervor fueling the Crusade was spent in less than a year, the Crusade altered the face of temperance reform, involved great numbers of women in a public program of militant action—protests Bordin (1980:22) calls "almost a holy war"—and gave birth in 1874 to the largest and most significant women's organization of nineteenth-century America, the Woman's Christian Temperance Union. For the next quarter century, until the advent of the Anti-Saloon League in 1896, women were the major and most creative source of leadership for the temperance movement (Bordin 1978; Kerr 1985).

The Woman's Crusade began on December 24, 1873, in Hillsboro, Ohio, and spread quickly throughout Ohio and other parts of the country, especially to small midwestern towns. (Blocker 1985b). Hillsboro was then a town of 5,000 people with 13 saloons and 18 hotels and drugstores selling liquor (Knight 1976:202). Its economic prosperity depended heavily on the liquor traffic, and this dependency was one of several factors that inhibited the Crusade's long-term success (Isetts 1979). The precipitating event of the Hillsboro Crusade was a speech by Diocletian Lewis, a Harvard-educated homeopathic physician and professional lecturer on the temperance circuit. Lewis had a set speech in which he urged women to act against the liquor trade in their communities by actually entering saloons and praying for their closure. Lewis's speech had inspired 50 women to march praying into the saloons of Dixon, Illinois, as early as 1858 (Bordin 1978). Although Lewis had delivered the speech many times prior to that fateful Christmas Eve in 1873, its results had always been temporary, local, lacking momentum—as women's vigilante attacks on saloons in the years preceding the Crusade had been (Dannenbaum 1984). The Crusade was different. It developed rapidly as a grass-roots movement when women in a cluster of communities in southwestern Ohio produced prayer bands all at once. Their activities were discussed widely and broadcast through newspaper accounts. This media attention further invigorated the Crusade, and praying bands were formed elsewhere in Ohio and beyond (Ibid.; Blocker 1985b).

But the crusading women did not depend on the vagaries of newspaper articles alone to spread the movement. The women of Hillsboro assembled and sent out a Crusade organizing kit that "included a circular describing the origins, tactics, and progress of their movement; copies of their pledges; the appeal to liquor sellers used in Washington Court House [Ohio]; a petition to the Ohio constitutional convention then in session; and an adapted version of an appeal to local women for support" (Blocker 1985b:15). In addition, an Ohio Crusade Convention met in Columbus on February 24, 1874. This meeting likely had a strong impact on its participants and stimulated many of them to return home to organize new crusades or to invigorate ones already under way. Finally, a good deal of personal contact among Crusaders via emissaries or visitors occurred, and Blocker considers that to have been the key factor in diffusing the Crusade during its first nine weeks.

In November 1976, two of Truk's most prominent Protestant church women's leaders returned from the Christians Concerned About Alcohol Conference in Hawaii. The conference provided each participant with a kit containing information about alcohol, alcoholism, and various actions that might be instigated in the control, prevention, and treatment of alcohol-related problems. These materials may have served much the same purpose for Trukese women as the Hillsboro Crusaders' "Crusade organizing kit" did for women in other Ohio communities early in 1874. The materials offered information and ideas on how women might unite to fight the problems men's drinking caused in their communities. The WBMPI's Alcohol Conference in Hawaii likewise is analogous to the Ohio Crusade Convention. Each meeting made a strong impression on its participants, and each appears to have stimulated some of the women in attendance to help organize against alcohol once they returned home.

Typically, a Crusade began with a group of well-to-do, middle-class, white, Protestant women meeting in a local church and resolving to take on the liquor traders in their community. During the organizational meetings some men might be present, especially Protestant clergy, but as the Crusade developed men usually were excluded from subsequent meetings. The Crusade organizers appealed to other women in the community to join them, prepared pledges for saloon keepers to sign indicating they would forswear the liquor trade, and discussed which methods of persuasion to use. This planning and organizing was accompanied by group.

praying and hymn singing, and by exhortations from the Crusade's leaders. Once all was ready, the women marched from the church single file or two abreast, voices raised in song. They entered a saloon, knelt at the bar, singing all the while, and endeavored to get the owner to sign a pledge to abandon his business. If they were refused admittance or forced from the premises, they might congregate outside and pray for the owner's soul and those of his clientele.

The Crusade was unique, according to Mitchinson (1981), because in it women refused to restrict their prayers to the sanctity of the church; they prayed and demonstrated against liquor in the bar itself. They sometimes encountered their sons or husbands in the saloons, which was a source of great embarrassment to the men. Although many Crusade confrontations in saloons and other liquor outlets were peaceful, not all owners and patrons eschewed violence, and women were sometimes threatened with weapons, spit upon, or doused with stale beer. Marchers also were subject to verbal abuse and occasional physical harassment from men in the streets, though this was more likely to occur in big cities like Cincinnati than in small towns where the majority of the Crusades took place. Marching bands of praying women kept up the pressure until the owners of licensed premises eventually succumbed. When a saloon keeper finally signed a pledge, there was great rejoicing, and church bells often were rung to commemorate the event. Frequently, the Crusaders rolled the saloon's kegs of beer and barrels of whiskey into the street and smashed them, creating further spectacle.

Leaders and major activists in Truk's women's prohibition movement of the 1970s and 1980s resembled the American women who enrolled in the temperance cause for the first time during the late nineteenth century: They were an educated group of urban, middle-class women who had gained experience and organizational skills through Protestant church groups. Isetts (1979:106, 108) characterized the Crusaders of Hillsboro, Ohio, as "the social elite" and "the upper crust of their society," and to a significant extent this may be said of the Moen women who worked actively for prohibition and participated in the demonstrations against repeal. Blocker (1985b) observed that often leaders of the Crusade already had been active in women's organizational work; such was definitely the case in Truk. Although Trukese women did not march on bars and saloons like their American sisters had a century before, they picketed the municipal council meetings and orchestrated a public protest outside the legislature building as part of their antialcohol campaign (cf. Blocker 1985b:48). As with the Woman's Crusade, these demonstrations were the largest public women's movement mounted in Truk to that time. And the issues the women's prohibition movement in Truk raised in the 1970s—liquor control, protection of home and family, political action, and gender roles—were those the temperance forces in America raised in the second half of the nineteenth century (Ibid.:65).

As a result of the Crusades, by April 1874 more than a thousand saloons were closed at least temporarily (Epstein 1981). In the short-term, a majority of the Crusades successfully shut down all the local saloons or had a local prohibitory ordinance enacted (Blocker 1985b), and temporarily the sale of alcohol dropped dramatically (Epstein 1981). But these immediate victories were all short-lived. Almost as soon as the Crusaders ceased their marches and sit-ins, saloons reopened; within a few months it was difficult to find evidence that the Crusades had ever taken place. The central importance of the Crusades, in the long run, was their effect on the women who participated in them rather than their impact on the saloons (Epstein 1981:100; cf. Bordin 1980:23). The Crusades expanded the horizons of their participants and allowed them to begin to feel their collective power. The rather amorphous set of moral values that informed the Crusades "began to take shape as a social outlook and a guide to women's action" (Epstein 1981:114).

Again, the parallel with Truk is striking. As a result of women's push for use of the petition and referendum procedure, a local prohibition law was enacted on Moen, and all of the bars in the port town were closed. Unlike the American communities in which Crusades occurred, where the saloons reopened shortly after the women ceased marching, the bars on Moen remained closed 10 years later. As with the Crusaders, antialcohol activism also expanded the horizons of Trukese women, indicating to them that by planning and working together they *could* effect change on public policy issues.

In the Crusade, midwestern Protestant women took politics into their own hands in an effort to shut down the saloons. They did so in the belief that saloons threatened the religious and moral standards with which women identified. Bordin (1980:23) refers to the "essential feminism" of this movement, which she sees as "not just a campaign against intemperance, but at least unconsciously an assertion of feminist principles." Whereas Epstein (1981) believes the Crusaders marched because of a threat to religious and moral standards, Blocker takes the position that women took to the streets because of very real physical and economic threats to their homes and families (e.g., 1985b:96, 144).

Blocker challenges the analyses of the Woman's Crusade and the Woman's Christian Temperance Union Bordin (1981) and Epstein (1981) put forward, charging that these two authors "have applied an ahistorical definition of feminism to women who never used that term" (1985a:461). Instead of imputing feminist motives where he feels few were present, Blocker urges that we understand the Crusade on the participants' own terms. The primary justification Crusaders gave for their movement was an attempt to dispose of a threat to themselves and their families from the actual or potential drinking of their husbands, sons, and fathers. They were absolutely opposed to the drinking and selling of liquor regardless of who engaged in these activities. In support of their actions, they emphasized alcohol's threat to women as family members through shame, pain, and economic loss. Crusaders argued they were victimized: The money and time men spent on liquor and in the saloons should have been spent at home. Crusading women and other protemperance groups believed alcohol was an addictive, debilitating substance that impoverished families by destroying men's ability to work. Women also argued that drunken men were violent and likely to beat their wives, children, or other family members; in essence they claimed that John Barleycorn turned normally gentle fathers and husbands into aggressive brutes (Epstein 1981). Crusaders made these claims despite the fact that few of them were directly victimized by men's drinking. Crusaders sketched a picture of women dutifully tending the home while men failed to fulfill their obligation to protect women from the outside world. Occasionally, Crusaders also complained of the threat of harassment or violence from drunks on public thoroughfares. Contra Epstein and Bordin, then, Blocker's position is that "the Crusade did not have to be a women's-rights movement [in the sense of late-twentieth century feminism] to be a movement in defense of women's interests as women" (1985b:145). Women took action on the liquor issue in Truk in the 1970s for essentially the same reasons that American women launched the Crusade in the 1870s: "The threat from male drinking explains why women acted, and the heightening of that threat through the increased availability of liquor . . . explains why they acted when they did" (Ibid.:123).

Yet another reason for women's organized action in both times and places was men's failure to enforce the liquor laws that men had instituted (Ibid.:133). When the events of 1979 chronicled in Chapter Five began to unfold, the women's temperance movement in Truk underwent an important change. Its tactics shifted from lobbying behind the scenes for a prohibition law via petition and referendum to direct public demonstrations in support of continued prohibition. The Woman's Crusaders addressing men in their communities

> Requested that . . . they cease to support the liquor business through their patronage and their non-enforcement of law. At the same time they threatened to continue their embarrassing demonstration of men's unconcern for their women and families until the men withdrew support for the liquor trade. Such a plea could only be effective if the Crusaders [like the women of Truk] acted in such a manner as to emphasize community interests rather than to reinforce community divisions (Ibid.:47).

Trukese women acted in exactly this manner, emphasizing their concern for community interests. The consistent position of Truk's Christian women in combatting alcohol-related problems was that they were "protecting the people," and caring for their families and their communities by seeking to replace *fitikooko,* "trouble, confusion" with *kinamwmwe,* "peace."[5]

Still other parallels exist between the Woman's Crusade of the 1870s and the Trukese women's temperance movement of the 1970s and 1980s. Just as the Truk State Legislature relied on taxes on alcoholic beverages for much of its operating revenue, so the United States federal government also leaned heavily on the liquor trade in an earlier era: "In 1873, liquor taxes amounted to 61 million dollars, more than half of internal revenue receipts and nearly one-fifth of total federal revenues" (Ibid.:57). A nineteenth-century equivalent of Trukese women riding the fire engine and waving signs while the siren wailed during their demonstration at the legislature occurred during the Crusade in Lebanon, Ohio: "The bells of all the churches, public halls and the Court-house were rung at different times in concert. A two-horse wagon, with placards announcing temperance meetings and a large bell continually tolling, was drawn through the streets" (Josiah Morrow quoted in Ibid.:47). And like those Trukese legislators miffed by the women's demonstration outside their chambers, in nineteenth-century America many "men . . . saw the Crusade as a presumptuous interference by women in the sphere of public policy" (Ibid.:77).

THE WOMAN'S CHRISTIAN TEMPERANCE UNION (WCTU)

Most historians accept that the WCTU was "the institutional expression of the energies unleashed by the Crusade" (Bordin 1978:403) and that the Crusade marked the advent of a new phase in the development, organization, and expansion of the temperance movement. From Epstein's (1981) perspective, the WCTU transformed the tradition of female evangelism most latterly expressed in the Woman's Crusade into a basis for social and political action. The WCTU was formally organized in November 1874 in Cleveland, Ohio (Bordin 1980; Morton 1982). Under the leadership of Annie Wittenmyer, it initially operated as a single-issue, women's temperance organization based on conservative social Christianity. But within five years the WCTU leadership shifted to Frances Willard, who dominated the organization and the temperance movement for the remainder of the nineteenth century. More than any other person, Willard converted the WCTU into a general-purpose reform organization that pursued a host of issues of special concern to women. She propounded a feminine vision of social order that gained wide support among the women of the WCTU "because it was limited to the values of social harmony, altruism, and service to society that framed [nineteenth-century American, white, middle-class] women's culture" (Epstein 1981:116). She enunciated a "Home Protection" policy intended to defend the purity of home and family against immorality, drugs, and liquor.

As the WCTU matured, it adopted woman's suffrage as one of its goals, although the organization maintained emphases on "social purity" and the importance of the home as the bastion of Victorian morality. Among the important consequences of the WCTU's support for the women's movement was an identification of the organization with progress and the future. It was hoped that future relations between men and women would be less oppressive, and with this goal in mind the WCTU made dress reform and physical exercise into symbolic acts of rebellion and liberation (Ibid.). Perhaps with a comparable goal in mind, during the 1980s some younger Trukese women began to wear blue jeans, cut their hair short, and play on softball teams (see Chapter Four).

Willard masterminded the international expansion of the WCTU, a development that influenced the attitudes of ABCFM missionaries in Truk during the late nineteenth century. She developed her vision of the World's WCTU in 1883 during a visit to San Francisco's Chinatown, and this international arm of the parent organization was founded officially in 1884, with the goal of a worldwide prohibition on liquor and opium. Frances Willard's concept of the World's WCTU was that the sisterhood of women would be organized "to translate shared consciousness into global power" (Bunkle 1980:57). Even before its charter meeting, Mary Clement Leavitt sailed to Hawaii to begin the work of the World's WCTU in 1883. Following her success there, "temperance friends" in the islands provided funds for her to voyage to New Zealand and Australia beginning in January 1884 (Willard 1889:430–431).[6] At about this time, the ABCFM mission became firmly established in Truk Lagoon, and the WBMPI extended its programs to Micronesia.

By 1890, the WCTU was the largest women's organization in the United States, and probably in the world (Bordin 1985). It was allied with the nation's largest reform party (the Prohibition Party), with the Knights of Labor, and with Edward Bellamy's Nationalists. Although women were still without the vote, under Frances Willard's skillful, pragmatic leadership WCTU women exercised notable political influence. This feat was accomplished via expert use of the petition, the hiring of professional lobbyists, lobbying in their own right, and by authoring and successfully supporting an impressive body of legislation they personally shepherded through the legislative process (Ibid.). Although WCTU women failed to achieve either the vote or national Prohibition during the last quarter of the nineteenth century, these failures do not diminish the significance of the many social reforms they helped bring about. WCTU efforts in the late nineteenth century were crucial to the subsequent success of movements in support of the franchise for women and the Prohibition Amendment during the early twentieth century.

None of the women's clubs in Truk during the 1970s and 1980s rivaled the WCTU for mass appeal, organizational complexity, political influence, and international support. Whether such growth may eventually result from the crusade against alcohol in Truk, as it did from the Woman's Crusade in the midwestern United States, remains to be seen. Should it occur, Truk's temperance movement might be transformed into a more generalized movement for women's equality in the economic, social, and political life of the islands.

SUMMARY

The structural parallels between the Woman's Crusade and what happened in Truk are extraordinary. Both groups of women were excluded from political power and public life. Both groups felt that male drinking was a threat to their well-being and that of their families and communities. In both places there were histories of temperance and prohibition and strong protemperance sentiments, especially among women. In both places women used the ideology and the resources of Protestant churches to organize and sustain themselves and to challenge those who favored drink. In both places alcohol use became the focus of struggle between women and men, and a symbolic arena in which women fought for and gained greater participation in the political process.

Whether comparable structural parallels arise between the WCTU and what may happen in Truk in the future remains to be seen. Certainly, a cadre of bright, well-educated, concerned, increasingly restive women exists in Truk who have gained experience and hope from the temperance movement. Whether someone like Frances Willard will emerge to develop a general-purpose reform organization out of Fin Anisi and Mwichen Maria will determine, to a large degree, the influence women will have in shaping community life on Moen in the years ahead.

In the United States, the Woman's Crusade of 1873–1874 was followed almost immediately by organization of the WCTU. Under the WCTU banner, "by the 1880s temperance had become the issue that drew tens of thousands of women to rally behind general women's and reformist causes and demand a more equal share in the political process" (Bordin 1981:3). Trukese women have had the vote for more than 40 years—from the time the U.S. Naval administration introduced American-style democratic political institutions. Even so, for them to mount a noisy, public political protest against elected male leaders (legislators and councilmen alike) was to step completely outside their traditionally accepted role. A similar set of events in the United States a century ago gave impetus to women's push for suffrage and equal rights. Trukese women have the franchise, but they definitely don't have equal rights. It is too early to tell if a comparable movement for equal rights will take root among the educated elite women of Truk.

There are some signs that key Trukese women have become politicized through their involvement in the prohibition fight. Like the Woman's Crusade, Truk's movement "was a liberating force for a group of church-oriented women who could not have associated themselves directly with the equal rights or suffrage movements ["women's liberation"] (Bordin

1981:33). Also as in the Woman's Crusade, prohibition in Truk "forged a spiritual . . . link between women throughout the country who had been fighting isolated skirmishes against the drink trade in defense of their families" (Dannenbaum 1984:219). Like the Woman's Crusade, then, women's antiliquor activism in Truk posed two major issues: the right of women to participate in public affairs and the sort of public control that should be exercised over use of beverage alcohol (Ibid.). Some of the ways this second issue has been addressed elsewhere in the Pacific islands are explored in the chapter to come.

CHAPTER EIGHT

Alcohol Control Policies in Oceania

> . . . the issue of drunken and violent husbands and the associated squandering of money stands out as the most heartfelt and desperate problem of women in the region (Asian and Pacific Centre for Women and Development 1977:30).

COLONIAL PROHIBITION IN THE PACIFIC

The inhabitants of the Pacific islands were introduced to alcoholic beverages by the European beachcombers, explorers, traders, and whalers who came among them in the late eighteenth and early nineteenth centuries. The first prohibitions against alcohol in the Pacific derived as much from assertions of authority by traditional chiefs as from the preachments of European missionaries. On the island of Abemama, in what is now Kiribati, for example, the chief, Tem Binoka, strictly controlled all trade in liquor and tobacco. Periodically, he lifted these prohibitions and permitted his subjects a spree, but most of the time they were not to manufacture fermented coconut toddy or possess foreign liquor and were only allowed to receive tobacco from Binoka's hand. Given the heavy demand for alcohol and tobacco, such a monopoly gave chiefs like Tem Binoka considerable power over their followers. The chiefs also recognized that a drunken citizenry led to violence and unsettled conditions that might threaten their control. As a consequence, they often made rules to control drinking and decreed severe punishments for those who violated them. Perhaps the most dramatic instance of this was the prohibition Baiteke of Abemama established:

> The drinking of sour toddy was regarded as a threat to the political structure on the same footing as sedition, and the same punishment was provided for both: staking the offender spreadeagled on the lagoon beach for a maximum of forty-eight hours, scorched by the equatorial sun during the day and eaten alive by mosquitos at night. It was said that few survived the sentence and that those who did invariably went mad (Maude 1970:211).

Sometimes, chiefly concerns over political control meshed with the missionaries' efforts to institute prohibition. Writing of Tahiti, Gunson observed that "the chiefs realized that intemperance undermined their authority and disrupted their government. Thus the missionaries were able to influence them to break stills and otherwise control drinking" (1966:52).

As support for first temperance and then prohibition grew in Great Britain, Germany, and the United States during the nineteenth century, these sentiments were reflected in the attitudes of Christian missionaries and colonial administrators in the Pacific.[1] Initially, through the 1820s, the London Missionary Society (LMS) missionaries to Tahiti produced and consumed alcohol quite freely, and several became alcoholics or developed alcohol-related problems that led to censure (Gunson 1966). The official stand of the LMS at that time was one of moderation in the use of alcohol—temperance in its original sense. Eventually, though, abstinence became the rule among LMS missionaries, as it was for Methodists and for the Congregationalist ABCFM missionaries who went to Hawaii in 1820 and Micronesia in 1852.

Some Christian churches sponsoring missionaries to the Pacific islands opposed all four of the major drug substances used in Oceania—alcohol, betel, kava, and tobacco—although most tolerated betel and tobacco. Indeed, Forman claimed that "the faith and the tobacco trade went together" (1982:113). Although kava was incorporated into Christian ceremonies in Samoa (Ibid.:114), its use was sternly opposed by Presbyterians in the New Hebrides [Vanuatu], Methodists in Fiji, the ABCFM on Kosrae and Pohnpei, and by the colonial government (at the instigation of missionaries) in Papua (Forman 1982:114; Marshall 1980:5; Marshall and Marshall 1976:158–160). Beverage alcohol was something quite different, however:

> . . . it was on alcohol, a European importation, that the churches concentrated their major effort. Year in and year out they treated alcohol as the greatest social evil that they had to fight. Protestant churches often made abstinence from liquor a rule of church membership (Forman 1982:114).

Avoidance of alcohol as a symbol of Christian conversion certainly was true for the ABCFM mission in Truk and other parts of Eastern Micronesia (Marshall and Marshall 1976). In fact, the ABCFM required abstinence from kava and tobacco for church membership as well, which doubtless made their conversion of Micronesian men more difficult than it otherwise might have been.[2]

When the WCTU spread to New Zealand in 1885 (Bunkle 1980), it pushed strongly for prohibition and women's suffrage (Grigg 1983; Grimshaw 1975). New Zealand assumed colonial control over the Cook Islands in 1901 at a time when prohibition was a major political issue at home, which probably accounted for the rise of a women's antialcohol organization in the Cooks having certain similarities with the Woman's Crusade in the United States:

> A much more aggressive line of attack on drinking was pursued by a church-sponsored women's organization, the Au Vaine, which dated from the turn of the century. They not only searched out [men's] bush beer sessions but also knocked over the barrels and sang hymns to the drinkers. In 1926 the Au Vaine was reorganized with broader socioeconomic purposes of encouraging cleanliness, planting and conservation of crops. On occasion they marched four abreast wearing garlands of crimson hibiscus and scented leis of frangipani, beating drums and stopping to propagandize wherever groups of men congregated. They patrolled plantations to prevent theft and to scout out beer groups. At times they gave information to the police and testified against beer makers. A Resident Agent on Mauke during one period paid them 3 shillings for each case in which they acted as witnesses (Lemert 1976:579).

By the last quarter of the nineteenth century, as the forces for abstinence and prohibition gained the upper hand in the United States and became extremely influential in Australia, New Zealand, and many parts of Europe, their attitudes began to affect colonial policy. For example, Britain prohibited the sale of alcoholic beverages to Fijians within six months of establishing a Protectorate there in October 1874. Immediately following declaration of the British Protectorate in Papua in October 1884, the sale of liquor was banned in the Territory, and the first ordinance enacted following formal annexation in 1888 prevented Papuans from obtaining firearms, liquor, and opium (Marshall 1980:4). Soon after Germany took possession of German New Guinea, a comparable prohibition against trade in alcohol with the islanders was proclaimed by decree of the imperial chancellor in October 1884 (Ibid.:5). Laws against sale of beverage alcohol to islanders came quite late in some instances. Following years of vigorous campaigning by the Catholic missionary anthropologist, Maurice Leenhardt, who felt the Kanaks of New Caledonia "were committing suicide with alcohol," France passed legislation forbidding the sale of alcohol to indigenes in New Caledonia and the Loyalty Islands in 1917 (Forman 1982:115–116). These various colonial laws were passed to protect Europeans from the depredations of "drunken savages," and to protect the islanders themselves from the ravages of liquor in a situation of rapid culture contact and change. In all of these colonial prohibition declarations, whites could legally possess and consume alcoholic drink. Although today this distinction appears blatantly racist, then it was viewed as enlightened colonial policy.

Following World War I, when Prohibition was the law of the land in the United States and prohibition sentiment was strong in many other parts of the world, some churches in the Pacific tried to stop liquor sales to white people as well as the indigenes.

> The Methodists of Fiji were the most active in this, as they were in the campaign against kava at the same time. The provision for total prohibi-

> tion in [Western] Somoa (for Europeans and Samoans) when New Zealand took over that area from Germany encouraged them. In 1919 and 1920 they made appeals to London for action. A dozen years later, in 1932, they were approaching the Colonial Office again and this time were joined by leading Hindu, Sikh, and Muslim organizations of the Fiji Indian community, those religions having strong teaching against alcohol. But even these combined efforts failed to move London, and white people in Fiji continued to enjoy the privilege of alcoholic drinks (Forman 1982:115).

Since the end of World War II, along with decolonization and the rise of many new Pacific island nations, prohibition legislation has been systematically revoked as an anachronism of the colonial era.

In much of the Pacific, these colonially imposed prohibition laws were in place for 75 to 100 years. The first significant step toward change was not taken until 1947 when the U.S. Navy authorized the general sale of beer on Saipan, Marianas Islands, with the justification that the Saipanese were more acculturated than other Micronesians. New Zealand repealed legal restrictions on the sale and supply of liquor to the indigenous Maori population in 1948, after which "a system of formal control known as Maori Wardens emerged in response to unacceptable levels of Maori drunkenness and disorderly conduct" (Fleras n.d.:2).[3] The New Zealand government also established a Commission of Inquiry in 1952 to look into liquor control questions in Western Samoa, but no fundamental alteration in prohibition laws occurred anywhere in the South Pacific outside of New Zealand until 1955. Beginning then, the French permitted the Kanaks of New Caledonia to drink any brand of beer they chose, and in Papua and New Guinea a Select Committee of the Legislative Council was appointed to consider a proposal to issue alcohol permits to selected Papuans and New Guineans (Blackburn 1969). Few indigenes in Papua and New Guinea pressed publicly for the right to drink at that time; yet relevant to this study, witnesses against the drinking permit proposal reportedly included "a delegation of 'Native' women" (Anonymous 1956). On conclusion of their deliberations, the members of the Select Committee decided against issuing liquor permits.

The Select Committee's decision catalyzed agitation for the right to drink in Papua and New Guinea as early as 1956, and by 1958 traditional leaders and local government councillors alike frequently raised the question. By April 1959, Papuans and New Guineans and Nauruans were the only South Pacific islanders still subject to a total ban on consumption of all alcoholic beverages. By the 1960s the right to drink became a major issue symbolizing inequality, racial discrimination, and political paternalism in Papua and New Guinea (Marshall 1980). Events moved rapidly after 1960, and finally, on November 2, 1962, interim drinking laws the 1962 Liquor Commission proposed and the Legislative Council approved took effect. A permanent ordinance became law on September 26, 1963, allowing for the consumption of all kinds of beverage alcohol.

The year 1963 was significant in the decolonization of liquor legislation in Oceania. In Fiji, Netherlands New Guinea (now Irian Jaya), New Caledonia, Cook Islands, and the Solomon Islands some loosening of the liquor laws had occurred during the mid-1950s, and in 1959 beer consumption became legal for Micronesians throughout the U.S. Trust Territory of the Pacific Islands, including Truk. In 1963, "open-go" drinking of all beverage alcohol became legal for all races in Fiji and New Caledonia. The first important changes in colonial prohibition statutes occurred in 1963 for inhabitants of the New Hebrides Condominium (now Vanuatu) (Casswell 1985:4). American Samoans acquired the right to buy distilled spirits on a ration basis for the first time in 1963, having earlier had the right to drink beer. Passage of right-to-drink laws, or liberalization of such laws already on the books, took effect in the Gilbert and Ellice Islands Colony[4] and in the Cook Islands in 1964; the last liquor restrictions were removed for Solomon Islanders in 1965; and Nauruans could drink intoxicating beverages legally beginning in 1967 (Marshall 1980).

LOCAL PROHIBITION

Truk is not the only place in Oceania where prohibition has been reimposed, or where efforts to reinstate it have been made following the postcolonial experience with alcohol. Casswell (1985:2) mentioned a 1984 call for prohibition in Vanuatu had support from the Vanuatu Christian Council, the Council of Chiefs, and the National Council of Women. Moreover, she noted that "on several of the islands the local chiefs and the local government council have imposed severe constraints on the sale of alcohol in an attempt to contain alcohol related problems" (Ibid.). A bill was introduced in the legislature of American Samoa during 1985 "calling for the prohibition on importation, sale and consumption of any form of tobacco or liquor" (Anonymous 1985:8), and a similar measure recently was introduced in the CNMI Senate (*Marianas Variety News & Views,* December 16, 1988, p. 1). In Kiribati, some islands continue to have local prohibition. A recent magazine report noted, "Peace and order at Buota village Marakei Island . . . is well maintained with the prohibitance [*sic*] of any kind of liquor. Severe punishment such as caning is applicable to the law breakers" (Anonymous 1986b:8). Other news items reported three men in North Tarawa were "punished for breaking a village rule against consuming liquor," and two men from Tobomatang village, Nikunau Island "received forty lashes on their back" for violating the village prohibition law (Anonymous 1985:8).

All the former districts of the U.S. Trust Territory of the Pacific Islands adopted local municipal option laws when drinking was legalized in 1959. Since then, most rural and outer island communities have elected to remain dry whereas the district centers have been wet. In the mid-1970s, the 10 separate municipalities of the Yap Islands proper all permitted the sale and consumption of alcoholic beverages, whereas only Ulithi Atoll, among the outer islands, was legally wet (Mahoney 1974:8).[5] In the Marshall Islands, a similar pattern was found: only three municipalities were wet—the district center of "D.U.D." (Darrit-Uliga-Dalap), Laura (linked to D.U.D. by a paved road), and Kwajalein-Ebeye (the site of a U.S. military missile testing base) (Ibid.). On Pohnpei, in the mid-1970s, sales of liquor and beer were legal only in the district center town of Kolonia (Ibid.). When Kosrae separated from Pohnpei in January 1977, and became a state in its own right, it remained officially dry. Only very recently has the Kosrae State Legislature experimented with this long-standing prohibition statute, passing a revised alcoholic beverage consumption law effective January 1, 1986, permitting on-premises drinking in bars and restaurants, but nowhere else (Ashby 1985b:14).

Following a lump-sum pay increase for government employees in early summer 1971, Ponape experienced an 82 percent increase in alcohol-related arrests over the next two months (Mahoney 1974:38). An alcohol-related homicide in Kolonia led Ponape's district administrator and district legislature to rule, effective July 16, that the bars, which used to close at midnight, should close at 6:30 P.M. (*Micronitor,* July 30, 1971, pp. 1–2). Beginning August 9, Kolonia's 21 bars were shut down completely by Emergency Order 4-71 that the district administrator issued in the wake of a shooting incident three days before in which a policeman was killed and another seriously wounded as they tried to break up a drunken brawl outside one of the bars (*Micronitor,* August 14, 1971, p. 8). These emergency orders did not proscribe all alcoholic beverages; rather, they prevented the sale of liquor by the drink on licensed premises.[6]

By December 1971, pressure mounted from the business community to reopen the bars. In response, more than 150 Kosraen and Kapinga women residing on Ponape marched in the streets on December 2 to keep the bars closed.[7] They carried signs saying, "We do not like the importing of liquor any more for it takes away the lives of our people," as they circled the district courthouse where bar owners were meeting with Ponape's Alcoholic Beverage Control Board to set up new drinking regulations. The women also met with the district administrator for over two hours to make their views known. A leader of the group told a reporter they planned to hold another protest demonstration in February 1972 when the Ponape District Legislature reconvened (*Micronitor,* December 14, 1971, pp. 1 and 8). In mid-February, a Ponapean newspaper columnist wrote "from the rain garden of Micronesia" that "Ponape is still dry. This does not mean that the precipitation goes down. But it means that bars are still closed" (*Micronitor,* February 15, 1972, p. 7).

The legislature did not meet again until April 3, 1972, at which time they began considering Resolution 11 asking the district administrator to rescind his emergency order closing all the bars. The legislators conducted public hearings on this resolution on April 17 before about 60 people. The approximately 30 women who attended were unanimous in wanting to keep the bars permanently closed, on grounds that closure had returned peace and tranquility to Kolonia (cf. Chapters Five and Six); those in favor of reopening the bars were mostly young men (*Micronitor,* May 16, 1972, p. 7).

Two days after the public hearing about 50 Kolonia women marched to the legislature building, saying they did not want any alcoholic beverages to enter Ponape. "The legislators talked with the ladies briefly, and the women walked back to Kolonia peacefully" (Ibid.). A couple of months later "the public and the legislature deliberated over the resolution and wisely decided that it was not in the best interest of the public to have the bars opened" (*Micronitor,* June 13, 1972, p. 4), but the emergency order was lifted soon thereafter and bars resumed operation on July 1, 1972 (*Micronitor,* June 27, 1972, p. 8). According to an observer, only five bars reopened by October, four in Kolonia and one in adjacent Net (*Micronitor,* October 10, 1972, p. 9).

With the reopening, the only major change was that drinkers now were required to have a drinking identification card costing $5 "in order to touch, carry, drink and buy alcoholic beverages" (Ibid.). Economic considerations prevailed in the decision to reopen Ponape's bars. The chair of the legislative committee reviewing the matter told those present at the public hearing on April 17 "that most of the legislature's tax money comes from alcoholic beverages and cigarettes. So the legislature would lose a lot of money if it did not open up the bars" (*Micronitor,* May 16, 1972, p. 7). Similar political controversies over beverage alcohol occurred in other parts of the Trust Territory during the 1970s.

In February 1979, the Yap District Legislature considered Bill No. 6-1 calling for a districtwide prohibition of all imported alcoholic beverages, but allowing the continued legal manufacture of fermented coconut toddy (*tuba*) on a local municipal option basis. The proposed penalty for violation was a fine of no more than $500 or imprisonment of not more than six months, or both. A public hearing on this bill on January 24, 1979, attracted considerable interest. In testimony, the district attorney noted most High Court criminal cases were related to alcohol abuse, cited the failure of prohibition in the United States, and suggested the committee study Truk's experience with prohibition before passing the bill (Yap District Legislature 1979:2). The district treasurer testified the legislature would lose $96,000 per year in alcohol taxes if the bill were passed, and the president of the Chamber of Commerce and the special assistant to the governor echoed this refrain (Ibid.:3). One legislator countered that over $1 million spent on alcohol in Yap each year might better be used to develop the district economically, and another legislator stressed the social benefits of the bill versus the tax revenue issue (Ibid.:4).

Two women testified before the committee. The first, a member of the Alcoholic Beverage Control Board, "pointed out the social, economic and family problems created by alcohol abuse, citing fights, lack of food and divorce, but suggested there may be a better solution than stopping alcohol use completely" (Ibid.:2). The second woman, a Catholic nun, argued that alcohol use was a symptom of the problem rather than the problem itself, that "drunk adults are poor role models for children, and that alcohol use resulted in loss of work and efficiency" (Ibid.:3).

After considering all testimony, the Committee on Government, Health and Welfare recommended to the Speaker that the bill be filed "until such time [as] alternatives to the bill may be explored and a new tax structure can be considered and enacted to avoid the loss of revenues, and the pursuant loss of important district projects and programs" (Ibid.:4). This same fate befell the two alcohol control measures introduced in the Truk District Legislature in 1976 (see Chapter Three). Elsewhere in Oceania, prohibition has fared somewhat better.

In recent years prohibition has been declared in one or more provinces of Papua New Guinea. Largely in response to questions of law and order, but also in an effort to redirect people's expenditures away from alcohol, the provincial government of Simbu Province declared a three-month liquor ban commencing November 10, 1980 (Piau-Lynch 1982). This ban closed 307 licensed liquor outlets, resulted in considerable economic loss for liquor license holders, and was very controversial.[8] In the end it proved only partially effective because it was easy to smuggle illegal alcohol in from adjacent provinces, "but alcohol's accessibility and visibility were greatly reduced" (Ibid.:128).

Problems of law and order and public safety were ostensibly why the Enga Provincial Government imposed a three-month liquor ban beginning February 8, 1981 (Talyaga 1982); however, Wormsley (1987:213) concludes that political threats and competition rather than civic concerns motivated the ban. Unlike Simbu's prohibition, which the provincial government itself initiated, the Enga ban came in response to a strongly worded petition signed by representatives of various churches (Catholic, Lutheran, Pentecostal, and Seventh Day Adventist), and persons representing such groups as teachers, women, community leaders, and public servants (Talyaga 1982:137–138; Wormsley 1987:212–213). Following the three-month ban in early 1981 that totally prohibited sales and consumption of alcohol, prohibition was extended indefinitely with slight modifications giving provincial government leaders legal access to beer (Wormsley 1987:213). Enga's prohibition lasted officially until mid-1984 when it expired through administrative oversight at a time when the national parliament had suspended the Enga Provincial Government (Ibid.:214). In Enga, as in Simbu, the ban only partially stopped drinking, particularly as a black market gradually developed in the province.

More recently, people attempted to bring about a total liquor ban in the five Highlands provinces of Papua New Guinea (Enga, Simbu, Southern

Highlands, Western Highlands, and Eastern Highlands), which have a population of approximately 1 million people (*The Times of Papua New Guinea,* September 5–12, 1986, p. 1). This attempt floundered on the constitutionality of depriving hotels of their liquor licenses, and on an eventual division of opinion among the Highlands premiers: At the last minute the premier of Simbu Province decided not to support the prohibition after all. However, on September 9, 1986, the Eastern Highlands Provincial Assembly passed a liquor licensing act making it illegal to import alcoholic beverages into or transport alcohol through the province (*The Times of Papua New Guinea,* September 19–26, 1986, p. 5). This act effectively blocked all alcohol that might have been trucked up the Highlands highway from the coastal city of Lae from reaching Simbu, Enga, Western Highlands, or Southern Highlands provinces. There was considerable confusion over the legality of this action, and the premier of Simbu Province planned to take his Eastern Highlands counterpart to court. The legitimacy of the ban was still being debated in early November (*The Times of Papua New Guinea,* October 31–November 6, 1986, p. 21), and finally, on December 11, 1986, the prohibition officially ended (*The Times of Papua New Guinea,* December 12–18, 1986, p. 4). Although other provinces allowed the sale of alcohol once again, the premier of Enga declared the ban effective until after the national election in mid-1987 (Ibid.). Recent brief reports in regional magazines indicate a three-month liquor ban was extended in Western Highlands and Southern Highlands provinces (as well as Enga) in early 1987 (Anonymous 1987:8), and reimposed in December 1987 in Southern Highlands Province, following an attack by villagers on the Tari district police station (Anonymous 1988a).

OTHER PATTERNS OF ALCOHOL CONTROL

When it became legal in 1959 for Micronesians other than Saipanese to drink intoxicating beverages, each district passed laws regulating liquor. These laws were similar in setting hours of sale, establishing a minimum age for drinkers, requiring a liquor license to import and sell alcohol, and in levying a special tax on beverage alcohol. In the ensuing 20 to 25 years during which port towns grew in population, U.S. financial support climbed steeply, and alcohol consumption increased markedly. By the early 1970s in most of Micronesia, alcohol-related issues began to draw greater attention. Law enforcement officials unanimously linked alcohol abuse to criminal acts, particularly to acts of violence. Health workers pointed out the heavy toll alcohol abuse took in trauma from drunken fights and drunk driving crashes. Community and church leaders bemoaned the frequent community disruption and family trouble related to alcohol use. Many people felt something had to be done.

During the early 1970s most districts in the Trust Territory inaugurated a drinking permit system in the hope that it might stem growing alcohol problems.[9] The trend began in Ponape District in 1972 as a precondition for reopening the bars in Kolonia after they had been closed following two alcohol-related murders (Mahoney 1974:66). Drinkers had to be at least 21 and possess a valid permit to consume alcohol legally. In December 1986, three Pohnpeians filed suit against the Kolonia municipal ordinance requiring a $10 drinking permit, arguing that because it was unduly vague, it violated the FSM Constitution's due process clause (*The National Union,* February 28, 1987, p. 6). The final disposition of this case has not yet been publicized in the media.

In April 1971, the Marshall Islands District Legislature enacted a comprehensive alcohol control bill making it illegal to drink in any municipality not having an explicit law allowing for the consumption of alcoholic beverages (*Micronitor,* April 24, 1971, p. 1). The legislation raised the drinking age to 21 as well as providing for the establishment of Alcoholic Beverage Control Boards in municipalities where drinking was acceptable and the issuance of districtwide drinking permits.[10] The law also stipulated that any worker serving beverage alcohol must be at least 21. A 1-year permit for residents cost $5, a 30-day visitor's permit cost $2 and "the purpose of the law [was] to keep youngsters out of the bars" (*Micronitor,* July 30, 1973, p. 9). Finally, in August 1973, the Marshall Islands began issuing permits, and enforcement of the new law started at the end of that month (*Micronitor,* August 20, 1973, p. 11; September 3, 1973, p. 15).

The Yap District Legislature also passed a bill the district administrator signed into law in August 1973, requiring both residents and visitors to possess an Alcoholic Beverage Control Permit. The fee was $2 for visitors and $6 for residents beginning September 1, 1973 (*Micronitor,* September 3, 1973, p. 7). Less than four years later, however, Yap's new district administrator came under fire for not enforcing various district statutes, among them the drinking permit law (*Micronesian Independent,* April 29, 1977, p. 9). Despite the law only 54 persons held current legal permits, and "among the scores of known drinkers in Yap . . . who have never purchased a permit are the District Administrator, the District Attorney, and other high ranking administration officials. (Also, the members of the legislature do not have permits and only two members of the Council of Magistrates have been issued permits)" (Ibid.).

Saipan, in what is now the CNMI, has had serious problems with alcohol abuse for years. In an exit interview with the local newspaper, following a two-year stint on the island, the American assistant attorney general stated, "Alcohol is a major social problem that has been a factor in almost every crime [I have] prosecuted" (*Marianas Variety News & Views,* March 27, 1981, p. 1). The same edition reported the sentencing of a man for his fourth drunk driving offense (Ibid.:2), and another article quoted a district court judge who said, "Drinking alcoholic beverages should not be an excuse for criminal acts" (Ibid.:3). In December 1982, the *Marianas Variety* reported that police were to begin cracking down on merchants who did not require proof of age for alcohol sales. This step was a matter of great concern, according to the attorney general, because an estimated 90 percent of juvenile court cases involved some contact with alcohol (*Marianas Variety News & Views,* December 10, 1982, p. 2). The article also mentioned that Saipan police had been using breathalyzers to test drivers' blood alcohol levels since at least November 1982. A new vehicle code signed into law in June 1983 stiffened drunk driving penalties: a blood alcohol level of .10 while driving brought a sentence of not less than 72 hours of imprisonment and a fine of at least $100; those convicted of driving under the influence of alcohol automatically had their driver's licenses suspended for not less than 30 days; and the new law punished vehicular homicide with a fine of no less than $1,000 and a prison term of at least 90 days (*Marianas Variety News & Views,* June 24, 1983, pp. 1–2).[11]

By 1983, various Saipanese attempted to reduce alcohol's toll on society. Catholic Social Services implemented an alcohol information school in mid-July of that year to "provide information on the effect of alcohol on performance and behavior" (*Marianas Variety News & Views,* July 8, 1983, p. 2). This program was designed specifically for persons convicted of drunk driving, and "marks the first attempt here in the Marianas to deal with what is becoming a problem of major proportions" (Ibid.).[12] In 1984 the attorney general's office, the police, and the Alcoholic Beverage Control Board joined together to reduce illegal drinking and related crime through stricter enforcement of the liquor statutes (*Marianas Variety News & Views,* February 17, 1984, p. 2). Recently, the Commonwealth Health Center Volunteers Association and the *Marianas Variety* newspaper launched a campaign to educate the public about the risks of drunk driving. Five hundred antidrunk driving posters proclaiming "The party's over" were printed and posted around Saipan (*Marianas Variety News & Views,* July 10, 1987, p. 3), and the newspaper editorialized in favor of designated driver programs or free rides home for individuals who realized they were too drunk to drive (*Marianas Variety News & Views,* July 17, 1987, p. 2).

Intense concern with alcohol-related problems continues on Saipan. By October 1987 Alcoholics Anonymous and Al-Anon groups were founded (*Marianas Variety News & Views,* October 16, 1987, p. 7), and an Executive Task Force on Combatting Alcohol Abuse began meeting in August 1988 (*Marianas Variety News & Views,* October 7, 1988, pp. 1, 13, 32). Other outgrowths of this heightened concern have been an "Alcohol Awareness Week" at Northern Marianas College (*Marianas Variety News & Views,* October 21, 1988, pp. 4, 16), a proposal from the Executive Task Force to raise alcohol taxes 300 percent (*Marianas Variety News & Views,* November 4, 1988, pp. 1, 5, 30), an alcohol consumption survey to be conducted by the Rotary Club and the Chamber of Commerce (*Marianas Variety News & Views,* December 16, 1988, p. 25), and three different antialcohol bills introduced in the CNMI Legislature at the end of 1988 (*Marianas Variety News & Views,* December 9, 1988, pp. 1, 5; December 16, 1988, p. 1).

The FSM has begun to develop substance abuse programs in recent years. A national workshop for educators at CCM, led by U.S. Army substance abuse education specialists from Hawaii, was held on Pohnpei in 1985 (*The National Union,* April 30, 1987, p. 3). The same U.S. Army team continued this program in Kosrae and Truk during late April and early May 1986, and in June 1986 a visiting alcohol and drug problems specialist from California took it over (Ibid.). FSM Health Services has developed a substance abuse education program for integration into school curricula at all grade levels, and the FSM Education Office has established a resource center where materials on alcohol and drug abuse are made available to the states on request (Ibid.). In March 1984, the Community College of Micronesia on Pohnpei held an Alcohol Awareness Day program to combat alcohol abuse problems among the students (*The National Union,* March 30, 1984, p. 6). The school counselor said, "The main problem is the social problem of fighting, harm to other people and property and interference with others attempting to study" (Ibid.). In summer 1988 a Council Against Substance Abuse was formally chartered on Pohnpei (Ashby 1988:41).

Sale of alcoholic beverages to minors is a problem all over Micronesia. For example, in 1980 the Belau Legislature increased the liquor license fee by 150 percent, and set a mandatory 24-hour jail sentence for anyone who sells or gives alcoholic beverages to a minor (*Marianas Variety News & Views,* May 8, 1980, p. 11). The legislature also established penalties for businesses where minors were found drinking and prohibited drinking in all but a few explicitly designated public places. Belau still has many other alcohol-related problems, however. Quoting from an editorial in Belau's newspaper, *Pacific Islands Monthly* noted that 90 percent of all crimes and 80 percent of road accidents were alcohol related, not to mention a 40 percent drop in work productivity "especially on days after weekends or holidays" (1985:57). Belauan authorities in 1988 requested the World Health Organization to help them draw up measures to reduce alcohol consumption in their islands (Anonymous 1988b:43).

SUMMARY

Historically, alcohol use in Oceania has followed a rather similar pattern. When alcoholic beverages first were introduced in the late eighteenth and early nineteenth centuries, islanders often became quite intoxicated and mimicked the rowdy drinking behaviors of whalers and traders. On some islands, chiefs imposed prohibition on their followers, sometimes enforced by rather severe sanctions. As Christian missions became widely established, and with the advent of colonial rule throughout the Pacific, laws prohibiting islanders from the manufacture, possession, or consumption of alcoholic beverages became the norm. These laws generally proved quite effective although they did not completely eradicate drinking (e.g.,

Lemert 1976). In the era of decolonization during the late 1950s and 1960s, elimination of discriminatory laws preventing islanders from drinking served as a hallmark of political independence. From the beginning of deprohibition, however, disagreement existed among different segments of the populations affected over whether open access to alcohol was a social benefit or a social ill. Women, in particular, proved consistently outspoken against the continued sale of alcohol (e.g., Anonymous 1975; Sumanop 1981).

In most Pacific countries, alcohol-related problems have grown over the years, sometimes (as in Truk) reaching a point where the citizenry demanded some sort of action. Various means of alcohol control have been tried over the years, ranging from restrictions on legal drinking age and on hours of sale to the reimposition of prohibition. As has been the experience of countries and communities elsewhere in the world, none of these alcohol control strategies has proved an unqualified success, and today systems of alcohol control in the region resemble a patchwork quilt of bits and pieces of legislation enacted over the years.

CHAPTER NINE

Conclusions

> The issue of the day is how to address the fieldwork enterprise in a poststructural period, how to understand the fieldwork time as a moment in a sequence, how to understand the place of the small-scale event in the large-scale historical process, how to look at part-structures being built and torn down (Moore 1987:730).
>
> Rare are the issues which can attract any public response at all, rarer still an issue which triggers an instant, vociferous, united reply; rarest of all, an issue which evokes a cry from a group traditionally silent in public (Anonymous 1975:147).

As a strategy for eliminating—or, perhaps more accurately, curtailing—the production, importation, sale, and consumption of alcoholic beverages within a particular political jurisdiction, prohibition has been tried in many times and places. The Aztecs, the ancient Chinese, and feudal Japan tried it; more recently national prohibition was legislated in Iceland, India, Finland, Norway, Saudi Arabia, and the United States (Lemert 1967; Sariola 1954; Unnithan 1985). Many other countries, including Australia, Canada, New Zealand, Norway, South Africa, and the United States, have permitted prohibition under a local option system, whereby members of a community, county, state, or province could vote to enact prohibition within the bounds of their jurisdiction. In the same way that prohibition was imposed on subject peoples in other parts of the world (e.g., North American Indians; May 1977), most colonial governments proclaimed it in Oceania (see Chapter Eight).

Despite the varied social settings in which prohibition has been tried—ranging from large, polyethnic nation states with populations in the millions to small, ethnically uniform societies with communities numbering in the hundreds—America's experiment with national prohibition from 1920–1933 has inordinately shaped contemporary attitudes toward this control strategy. It is widely believed that Prohibition in the United States failed because it attempted to legislate morality (Moore and Gerstein 1981). This conventional wisdom has obscured the positive effects of this strategy and discouraged attempts to use alcoholic beverage control laws as preventive instruments. In our judgment it is time to reassess the potential value of prohibition as a method of alcohol control in certain types of societies and under certain sets of circumstances.

In particular, we believe that prohibition—viewed as a method for containing and controlling alcohol-related problems rather than as a means for wholly eliminating drinking—holds promise for many developing countries.[1] Along with the Western bias against prohibition, noted above, we suggest that the paucity of published data discussing psychosocial research on alcohol problems from developing countries may account for the failure to reexamine prohibition as an alcohol control strategy. In a recent assessment of psychosocial research on alcohol from an international perspective, Rootman (1985) proposed four areas of research that might yield appropriate community responses to perceived alcohol-related problems: (1) to gather information on the extent and nature of alcohol problems nationally, and in particular demographic subgroups; (2) to ascertain how the country, or its constituent communities, actually responds to alcohol-related problems; (3) to acquire data on the organization of and trends in production, distribution, marketing, and control of alcoholic beverages in the country; and (4) to collect information concerning the effects of programs and policies instituted to respond to alcohol-related problems (Ibid.).

In the study presented in the preceding chapters we addressed these four topics for a small developing country in Oceania, giving special attention to the second, third, and fourth priorities Rootman outlined. In the remaining pages we shall analyze the Trukese case in light of other instances of prohibition and draw some conclusions about the relative usefulness of this strategy for alcohol control.

PROHIBITION AS ALCOHOL CONTROL: ANOTHER LOOK

Apparently, prohibition has never been completely successful in eliminating alcohol and drinking. No matter how repressive, governments seem unable to prevent the emergence of illegal sources of supply via smuggling, bootlegging, black markets, home production, and the like. But focusing on this failure draws attention from other effects of prohibition that *are* successful, at least in the short run.

With reasonably vigorous enforcement of prohibition laws, the price of alcohol usually rises, and it becomes more difficult to obtain. Either or both of these effects lower consumption, at least temporarily (e.g., Kendall, Roumanie, and Ritson 1983), and in turn reduce arrests for public drunkenness, hospital admissions for alcoholic psychosis or other alcohol-related maladies, deaths from acute alcohol overdose, and mortality rates due to liver cirrhosis (Moore and Gerstein 1981). Some or all of these effects have been noted as initial consequences of prohibition not only in the United States (Ibid.), but also for the states of Bihar and Tamil Nadu in India (Priyadarsini and Hartjen 1982; Thakur, Sharma, and Akhtar 1982), for Norway (Johansen 1987), for the Pine Ridge Reservation (May 1975), for communities in Alaska (Lonner 1985), and for Canadian Inuit villages (O'Neil 1985). In most of these cases, once prohibition was in place for a year or two, alternative sources of supply appeared, enforcement lapsed, and many of the temporary positive effects of the ban disappeared.

Obviously, the degree of public support for prohibition plays a major role in determining how well people will abide by it. When external authority imposes a law, as in colonial situations and in the prohibition that existed for Native Americans in the United States before 1953, there is a strong likelihood that it will be subverted as a form of protest. And when a majority of voters adopt prohibition, it matters how large the majority was. For example, the partial prohibition (against distilled beverages and fortified wines) approved in Norway in 1919 received a 62 percent favorable vote (Hauge 1978), and prohibition was favored in Iceland in 1908 by 56 percent of the voters (Pinson 1985). In these cases we might expect the substantial minority opposed to prohibition to ignore it and continue drinking illegally. Clearly, this happened in the Norwegian case (Johansen 1987). Alternatively, despite a heavy majority vote for prohibition initially, prohibition-related crime may erode that support, which case seems to account for much of the loss of public support for the Eighteenth Amendment in the United States during the 1920s. A final scenario is one where the citizenry vote strongly in favor of prohibition and maintain that support for a considerable number of years. Such cases include Tamil Nadu in India (dry from 1947 to 1971 and again from 1974 to 1981; Unnithan 1985), well over 60 unincorporated communities in Alaska (dry from 1981 to at least 1985; Albrecht 1985; Richards 1985), 8 Canadian Inuit villages (dry from 1978 to at least 1985; O'Neil 1985), and Moen Municipality in Truk (dry from 1978 to at least January 1989).

Even when prohibition is honored in the breach, and its intitial positive effects on alcohol-related problems have ended, it may still enjoy substantial community support. Such support for an "ineffective" law may seem irrational to an outside observer, but closer inspection usually reveals good reasons for it. For example, the law's existence forces changes in the patterns and places of drinking—what Lonner (1985) calls the "privatization" of alcohol use and behaviors (cf. O'Neil 1985; Thakur, Sharma, and Akhtar 1982). *Public* drunkenness and violence is reduced in such circumstances even if drunkenness and alcohol-linked aggression continue in private. A second reason for continued public support of an evidently "ineffective" prohibition law is largely symbolic: "a gesture made by a community to itself and about itself" (Lonner and Duff 1983:XII–25). This position is the one Millay (1987b:190–191) takes to explain continued support of the Moen ordinance by Trukese women and older men as an affirmation of Christian temperance values. A third factor explaining support for prohibition in the face of its continued violation is that, at least in small communities, such laws seem to support and mobilize internal community controls; hence, "what is achieved by the local option law may not be control over alcohol but control over community" (Lonner and Duff 1983:XII–26). Finally, "ineffective" prohibition laws may continue to receive widespread community support as people recall their original objectives in voting for an alcohol ban.[2]

Contrary to conventional wisdom based on the American prohibition experience, people may vote for prohibition not with the intent of literally eliminating alcohol and drinking from their community, but rather to alter the pattern of alcohol use. In Truk, for example, the major goals were to reduce alcohol-related violence in public places and the amount of general social disruption brought on by public drunkenness.[3] Moen's prohibition law has quite successfully accomplished these ends even though a black market flourishes and enforcement is lax. Prohibition in Truk was more pragmatic than moralistic in tone and primary intent. Most women and their male antialcohol supporters were not out to correct the behavior of immoral people—to save drinkers from sin and damnation; rather, they sought a solution to what they viewed as a series of interlocked social problems all linked to alcohol abuse, with drunken homicide chief among them.[4] Prohibition seemed the most logical and efficient way to accomplish this end. Similar practical concerns were involved in the growing support for prohibition in the mid-nineteenth-century United States:

> When the temperance reformers launched their campaign for prohibition, they . . . correctly sensed a surge in public receptivity to the idea of prohibition. However, this receptivity did not represent a deep-seated commitment to eliminate drinking. Rather, it sprang primarily from growing anxiety over social disorder, and from the hope that prohibition would alleviate social ills (Dannenbaum 1984:107).

Comparable practical concerns also seem to have led to passage of local option prohibition laws in many Alaskan and Canadian Inuit villages. For example, Lonner writes that "the [Alaskan] villagers' concern with alcohol is less a preoccupation with the personal health or moral implications of ingesting alcohol than with the death of village members, *particularly death among young men*" (1985:335, emphasis added). Likewise, O'Neil comments that "several alcohol-related violent deaths involving young people sparked the movement which culminated in prohibition" (1985:341) in the Canadian North. Prohibition via local option laws offers relatively contained and isolated communities suffering from a high incidence of alcohol-related social problems the chance for a breather, an opportunity to take stock and take control when things get out of hand. Quite apparently, alcohol-linked deaths, particularly among young adults, create a community perception that something drastic must be done to stop the carnage.

With several questions in our alcohol survey, we sought people's opinions about alcoholic beverages and the Moen prohibition law. The responses we received, from drinkers and nondrinkers alike, show a

TABLE 9.1 *Responses by gender to the question, "Do you think alcoholic beverages are good? Bad? Other?"*[a]

RESPONSE	FEMALE NUMBER	FEMALE %	MALE NUMBER	MALE %	TOTAL NUMBER	TOTAL %
Good	3	0.6	53	10.4	56	5.7
Bad	459	95.8	388	76.2	847	85.7
Other	17	3.6	68	13.4	85	8.6
TOTAL	479	100	509	100	988	100

[a]*Chi-square and Pearson's* R *significant at the 0.00001 level.*

TABLE 9.2 *Responses by gender to the question, "Do you favor the law banning drinking of alcoholic beverages on Moen?"*[a]

RESPONSE	FEMALE NUMBER	FEMALE %	MALE NUMBER	MALE %	TOTAL NUMBER	TOTAL %
Favor law	471	98.3	403	82.1	874	90.1
Against law	8	1.7	88	17.9	96	9.9
TOTAL	479	100	491	100	970	100

[a]*Chi-square and Pearson's* R *significant at the 0.00001 level.*

general negative attitude toward alcohol and a strong positive attitude toward the Moen ordinance (see Tables 9.1, 9.2, 9.3, and 9.4).[5] These attitudes were more true of women than of men, and of former drinkers than of drinkers. Even so, more than three-quarters of male respondents thought alcoholic beverages were bad; more than two-thirds of the drinkers thought the Moen ordinance was a good law; and over 80 percent of the men said they favored the prohibition law. When one recalls that 93 percent of the voters in the 1977 referendum approved the Moen ordinance, these data make it clear that the law has retained a remarkable degree of support. At one level of discourse, prohibition *does* seem to be an important statement Moen has made about itself.

WHY DO TRUKESE SAY THEY SUPPORT PROHIBITION?

As earlier noted, most Americans believe Prohibition failed because it tried to legislate individual morality. In a land that exalts the individual and individual rights above nearly all else, any perceived attempt to limit or

TABLE 9.3 *Responses by gender to the question, "Is this a good law or a bad law?"*[a]

	FEMALE		MALE		TOTAL	
RESPONSE	NUMBER	%	NUMBER	%	NUMBER	%
Good law	462	97.3	404	83.6	866	90.3
Bad law	13	2.7	79	16.4	92	9.7
TOTAL	475	100	483	100	958	100

[a]*Chi-square and Pearson's* R *significant at the 0.00001 level.*

TABLE 9.4 *Responses by drinking status to the question, "Is this a good law or a bad law?"*[a]

	NONDRINKER		DRINKER		FORMER DRINKER		Total	
RESPONSE	NUMBER	%	NUMBER	%	NUMBER	%	NUMBER	%
Good law	518	97.6	143	68.1	205	94.5	866	90.4
Bad law	13	2.4	67	31.9	12	5.5	92	9.6
TOTAL	531	100	210	100	217	100	958	100

[a]*Chi-square and Pearson's* R *significant at the 0.00001 level.*

control individual freedoms (including the freedom to drink or not to drink) is inevitably opposed. Americans place enormous emphasis on self-reliance—on rugged individualism—and assume that socialization keeps individuals in line, helps them develop a set of internal social controls to keep their behavior within acceptable bounds.[6] A primary cultural focus in America is on self-reliance, or on what Riesman, Glazer, and Denney (1953) refer to as "inner directedness." Indeed, many Americans see alcoholics as people who have "lost control" over their drinking, and Alcoholics Anonymous seems to work successfully for many problem drinkers in part because it helps them "gain control" of their lives again. In Stein's words. "Alcoholism is the most conspicuous 'symptom of choice' for the negation and violation of the values of personal responsibility, self-control, and self-reliance in American society" (1982:358). We contend that this American emphasis on the individual as an autonomous, responsible agent of social action has led to a kind of myopia about prohibition. Specifically, in a subtle, ethnocentric fashion, Americans assume that people everywhere are just like Americans are supposed to be—fully equipped with strong internal controls on individual action—and, thus, that prohibition is everywhere doomed as an alcohol control strategy for the same reasons that it failed in the United States.

Anthropology teaches us that human solutions to the business of getting along in the world—individually and collectively—are numerous and diverse. When we investigate the ethnographic record, we discover that the American cultural glorification of the individual is an aberration when compared with most human societies. Much more commonly the individual is deemphasized, and individual wishes and actions are satisfied or condoned only after the group has received priority. This view certainly holds in Oceania as a region.

Taking a broad overview of the published literature on Polynesia and Micronesia, Alan Howard (1979) identified as a basic cultural pattern a major emphasis on cooperation and interpersonal harmony. The social control of aggressiveness and the individual management of anger and related emotions are key issues for these island communities. In Polynesian and Micronesian social environments "even mildly aggressive behaviour threatens social harmony . . . and much of the cultural apparatus is oriented toward avoiding confrontations and minimizing the probability of affronts, embarrassment, or other anger-arousing circumstances" (Ibid.:124). In Howard's view, these matters lead to a series of questions about the relationship between internal personal and external social systems of control in Pacific societies. Unlike the U.S. pattern, Howard noted that ethnographers of Micronesia and Polynesia repeatedly and consistently emphasize "the importance of external social controls for maintaining behavioural conformity" (Ibid.: 126). Trukese child-rearing practices fit this regional pattern well, making "use of external, rather than internalized controls, for discipline and punishment" (Mahoney 1974:41–42).

These ethnographic findings suggest that social controls of alcohol, including prohibition laws, may succeed. They suggest as well that Pacific islanders may be more amenable to or willing to support and abide by laws that constrain their individual behavior than, say, Americans would be. In this regard, Shore writes that for Samoans "laws and other external impositions of control and authority . . . prevent destructive and selfish acts . . ." and "social control is understood by Samoans as public constraint over private impulses" (1982:158, 186). Mahoney avers that few Micronesian men "believe that it is possible for an individual to control himself once he starts, however tentatively, to drink alcohol" (1974:30), and more specifically, that "Trukese seem most convinced that once a person begins to drink he cannot hope to control himself, and as a consequence cannot be held rigidly accountable for his acts" (Ibid.:42). Similar attitudes may exist in other parts of the world where the rights and autonomy of the individual are not placed ahead of those of the group. For example, Inuit youth in their late teens and twenties admitted to O'Neil "that they were happy to live in a dry town because they considered it the best way to control their drinking" (1985:343).

How can we reconcile these assertions with the reality that many Trukese men continue to drink in the face of the prohibition law?

Although the purchase and consumption of black market alcohol technically violates prohibition, it strikes us as much more important that Trukese drinkers have altered the style and setting of their drinking since the Moen ordinance took effect. Recall that alcohol use had become problematic in Truk—drunken carousing and related violence had intruded into *the public domain.* Drinkers inflicted themselves on others in stores, on public streets, and in the villages both day and night. Potentially dangerous encounters with drunken young men had become an integral part of daily life on Moen and were viewed as increasingly problematic for community (group, public) well-being. An external social control, prohibition, altered this pattern of wanton public drunkenness by chasing drinking underground and restoring the balance of control between individuals and the collectivity.

We suggest further that Trukese reliance on external social controls may explain the apparent anomaly that more than two-thirds of *the drinkers* surveyed on Moen in the summer of 1985 said the prohibition law was a good law (see Table 9.4). They could continue to drink, despite the Moen ordinance, but the presence of the law helped them control where they drank and how they behaved after imbibing. Thus, the prohibition law *did* exercise an important external control over drinking even though it did not eliminate alcohol use.

WOMEN AND MEN AGAIN

Not only have Western attitudes toward prohibition been shaped by its purported failure in the United States, and by an overemphasis on individual rather than communal rights, but most studies of attempts to establish prohibition in different parts of the world have also ignored women's perspectives. The one notable exception to this situation has come only very recently with a reexamination of women's roles in the nineteenth-century temperance movement in the United States (see Chapter Seven). When the general topic of alcohol control and the specific subject of prohibition in Pacific island communities are examined from a woman's point of view, we see alcohol and its impact in a new way. In particular we see that men's unbridled drinking and drunkenness contribute to social problems that perpetuate the subordination of women.

It has been documented elsewhere (Marshall 1987b:73–76) that most Pacific island women do not consume alcoholic beverages, and that those who do so drink much less frequently and in smaller quantities than men. We noted in Chapter One that the overwhelming majority of Trukese women do not drink and that Trukese women and men have different attitudes toward alcoholic beverages. We explored some of the consequences of these differences in subsequent chapters. Our tale of women's opposition to, and eventual mobilization against, men's drinking in Truk, casts quite a different light on alcohol use than do most other accounts of drinking in Oceania. As with feminist critiques in other areas of anthropological inquiry, looking at alcohol use from a female perspective affords a new and different view of the subject.[7]

In most of Oceania women traditionally were denied the full and open access to the arena of public debate that men enjoy. However, women bore the costs of men's drinking more heavily than men, directly via intimidation and physical abuse, and indirectly by, for example, income loss, real and potential, because of men's expenditures on liquor. Throughout most of the Pacific region, women seem to have strong antialcohol sentiments that may embolden them to take joint political action as Trukese women did. In fact, from time to time, women have done just that.

Increasingly, the widespread animosity between Pacific island men and women over alcohol has acquired political overtones, with women speaking out ever more boldly against alcohol's continued availability. The Au Vaine movement of the Cook Islands at the turn of the century, mentioned in Chapter Eight, is the earliest instance we have found of women in a Pacific society formally organizing to oppose men's drinking. Later, in the colonial era, delegations of women periodically appeared before visiting committees or commissions of inquiry to speak vociferously against the sale of alcohol in their communities. Their testimony was duly recorded, but the impression remains that it was not usually regarded seriously, and that the opinions of island males (who generally favored alcohol) counted more. As early as 1950, "a group of Palauan women presented a lucid petition entitled 'The Evil of Drink' " to a U.N. Visiting Mission in Koror (Richard 1957:488–489), and women were prominent witnesses against the first proposal to legalize drinking in Papua and New Guinea in 1955, arguing "that such a measure would result in poverty and degradation" (Anonymous 1956:209).

In the years since legalization of drinking in the 1950s and 1960s, Pacific women have continued to rise up against the social disruption and violence associated with men's drinking.[8] We have already noted that when women threatened physical action in the Teop area of North Solomons Province, Papua New Guinea, they successfully prevented the opening of licensed premises in their area (Chapter Seven, footnote 7). Maskelyne (1975:41) recorded that in 1963 "hundreds" of Tolai women, in what is now East New Britain Province of Papua New Guinea, "marched on Rabaul's council house to protest about the effects of men's drinking on home life." The women complained of drunken fighting and disruption of village life by drunken men, as well as family financial problems because of men's heavy expenditure on drink. By 1965, members of women's clubs on the Gazelle Peninusla of East New Britain "decided [that] they had had enough" (Ibid.:42). Four hundred of them congregated at Rabaul to request that members of a U.N. Visiting Mission withdraw the right to drink the administering authority had approved in 1962. Also in late 1963, church and community women's clubs held joint meetings in Lae to oppose issuance of further liquor licenses in that area (Ibid.:41).

Women organized protests against alcohol in various parts of Oceania throughout the 1970s. Women marched in the streets of Kolonia, Pohnpei, in an effort to keep the bars closed there in 1971 (discussed in some detail in Chapter Eight). In the same year women testified before the Second Commission of Inquiry into Alcoholic Drink in Papua New Guinea (Sumanop 1981). Their complaints centered on men's profligate spending on alcohol to the neglect of their families, wife beating by drunken husbands, and "the increasing rate of community disorders and minor street offences attributed to drunkenness by men in both the urban and rural areas" (Ibid.:20). Women also noted that when men drank, they spent less time in religious activities. About 500 people (mostly women) from different parts of the Asaro Valley attended a meeting in Goroka, Eastern Highlands Province, Papua New Guinea, in September 1975 to demand "that alcohol be sent back to the country from which it had come" (Anonymous 1975:147). Organized by the Goroka branch of the National Federation of Women, the group voted "overwhelmingly in favour of prohibiting alcohol in this area," especially outside of the town proper (Ibid.:149). "The women think that drinking (and the problems associated with it) will stop if alcohol is prohibited, or at least decrease if alcohol is made difficult to obtain" (Ibid.:150).

Women have continued to protest men's drunken escapades into the 1980s. Female students at the University of Papua New Guinea, for instance, called for a temporary liquor ban on their campus in 1981 following allegations of sexual harassment and assault by male students who had been drinking (*Papua New Guinea Post-Courier,* June 3, 1981, p. 12; *The University This Week,* April 30, 1981, p. 3). At a Pacific-wide meeting of women representing most of the countries of the region, the delegates called for "the banning of alcohol and tobacco advertising, with more severe penalties for alcohol-related offenses" (Slatter 1981:23). These examples illustrate that Pacific island women have opposed alcohol in their communities for a long time, primarily because of the social disruption and family dissension associated with male drunkenness. Women have supported prohibition and other means of alcohol control generally because they see men's uncontrolled drunkenness as a threat to themselves, their families, and their communities.[9]

In discussion at a conference on "The Social History of Alcohol," held in Berkeley in 1984, Epstein pointed out "the need for further investigation of the social and cultural bases and meaning of the temperance and prohibition movements," with an area of special interest being "the way in which issues of gender were fought out on the terrain of temperance and prohibition" (Barrows, Room, and Verhey 1987:171). Clearly, Epstein intended her comments to pertain primarily to temperance and prohibition movements in English-speaking countries, especially the United States, but her statements are equally relevant to the Trukese case. In an immediate sense, prohibition in Truk had to do with alcohol control; but at a deeper and more significant level prohibition provided a testing ground for women's emergence as a powerful political force in contemporary Trukese life. As argued in Chapters Four, Five, and Seven, women's greater political awareness and involvement is one consequence of changes in gender roles resulting, especially, from women's increased access to education and wage employment. Whether the prohibition movement in Truk, like the Woman's Crusade, was "the call to arms, if not the opening shot, of a women's revolution" (Blocker 1985b:74) remains to be seen. Whether the struggle over prohibition will allow Trukese women to consolidate their gains and achieve more equal participation in the public political life of their new nation, or whether the prohibition movement was a mere skirmish in a slower but inexorable movement toward increased political power set in motion by opening education, employment, and religious organizations to women remains unclear at present.

Importantly, women's stand against alcohol abuse in Truk does not represent a "war between the sexes," any more than did a similar stand by women in New Zealand around the turn of the century (Grigg 1983). Rather, women's decision to take collective action in favor of prohibition was very much within the bounds of their traditional role as caregivers to family and community. In Rosaldo's words, "At the same time that women often happily and successfully pursue their ends, and manage quite significantly to constrain men in the process, it seems . . . quite clear that women's goals themselves are shaped by social systems which deny them ready access to the social privilege, authority, and esteem enjoyed by a majority of men" (1980:395). Even though women did not consciously use prohibition as a means for pushing "women's liberation" in Truk, there—as in the United States a century before—"the drink issue itself proved subversive to the maintenance of a hard division between the sexual spheres" (Bordin 1978:398).

Hezel (1987b:69) argues that "today in many parts of the Pacific we are witnessing the onset of the war between the sexes." He attributes this development to a breakdown of the formerly clear division between male and female gender roles in which there was a strong note of reciprocity in everything from economic tasks to respect behaviors. Hezel feels that modernization has produced a greater upheaval in men's traditional roles than in women's, and that the complementariness between men and women in traditional society has given way to competition:

> Men see women scrambling for these same positions [salaried jobs, political offices, volunteer organizations, churches, and athletic associations] and intruding in a domain that they regard as rightfully theirs. Women work in government agencies, they drive cars, they play basketball and volleyball and they even run for elected political office. In doing so, they are seen as flouting the traditional cultural distinctions between the genders (Ibid.:71).

But this change is precisely the point! Women in Truk *have* reached beyond the bounds of their traditional roles, in the same way that men have. Gender roles have not remained static in the face of the fundamental, wrenching changes that have swept over Micronesia in the past 40 years any more than other aspects of social life. And there is no reason to contend that men have been more profoundly affected by these changes than women. Indeed, if a comparison is to be made, we think the data (e.g., Chapter Four) show that women have undergone at least as many changes as men.

To give Hezel his due, toward the end of his insightful commentary on the impact of modernization on Pacific societies, he recognizes that it will be difficult to deny women forever the job opportunities to which their talents and education entitle them: "Somehow the society will have to accommodate the presence of both men and women in government and private sector employment" (Ibid.:73). He expects this accommodation will come via a half-measure in which certain job categories are defined as men's work and others as women's work. But this description already obtains: Women held the overwhelming majority of clerical, secretarial, and sales positions in Truk in 1985; men held an equally strong majority of skilled trades, mechanical, and managerial jobs (Truk State Government 1985). Elective political positions at the local, state, and national levels are almost exclusively "men's work." As more men and women obtain formal education beyond high school, and as the outside world continues to impinge on Truk via advisers, new businesses, video and motion pictures, and international development projects. Trukese gender roles will continue to change. If experiences elsewhere in the world are any guide, those changes will be in the direction of greater equality of opportunity and involvement by women in economic and political decision making.

Trukese women leaders of the prohibition movement did not seek to alienate men; indeed, they had significant male support for their cause, without which it would not have succeeded. Male church leaders, the mayor of Moen, the police chief from 1977–1979, the district administrator, some legislators, and a clear majority of the Moen Municipal Council all supported women in their effort to control the chaotic situation that surrounded drinking. Just as the Woman's Crusade in the United States was an implicit rebuke to men for their intemperance and their failure to control the liquor business, so too the women's prohibition movement in Truk. Trukese men's relation to prohibition was every bit as ambiguous as Blocker holds men's relation to the Crusade to have been: "They commanded resources important to the Crusade's success [e.g., money, meeting places, and moral and official support]. Women structured the organizing process so as to elicit maximum male support (while retaining control of the movement themselves), and tried to avoid making too explicit the causative role of men's sins" (1985b:137). It bears repeating here that in addition to trying to avoid alienating men, women—at a deeper level—were doing that which would be most acceptable to men: They were behaving in exactly the way good Trukese women should by caring for the community more than for themselves. In this sense, then, the antialcohol movement was not a "revolutionary" gesture by women but rather a new behavior brought into accord with the conservative canons of Trukese culture.

TAKING STOCK: PROHIBITION AS TEMPERANCE IN TRUK

The Trukese case shows the limits of prohibition while at the same time providing evidence of the positive changes in alcohol-related behaviors it can help achieve. Truk illustrates the kind of social setting and circumstances necessary for prohibition to have a net positive effect on a community.

First, there was strong support in 1977 for the liquor ban, even on the part of many drinkers, because of a widely shared sense that alcohol use was out of control. In Lemert's (1967) terms, the costs of drunkenness were conspicuously high.[10] People believed something drastic had to be done, and the local option procedure provided them with the means to take that drastic action in the form of the Moen ordinance.

Second, Truk is a self-contained, *seemingly* isolated island setting in which behavior deviations have high visibility (Ibid.). But Truk is not really isolated. As noted in Chapter Two, daily commercial airline flights and numerous ships arriving from Pacific Rim countries and elsewhere in Oceania link Moen to the outside world. Moreover, Moen certainly is not isolated within Truk State because it serves as the port town center and state capital. Truk's island setting might have allowed for effective policing of smuggling from outside Truk State had the Moen ordinance not had the transshipment loophole. That necessary legal clause, more than anything else, permitted the black market to develop and prosper. Nevertheless, a relative degree of geographical isolation limits easy access to alternative alcohol supplies and facilitates prohibition (as it has apparently done for Alaskan villages and Canadian Inuit communities). However, attempts to police prohibition in a political jurisdiction bounded by wet communities, as with many North American Indian reservations (Back 1981; May 1975) and with the Papua New Guinea Highlands provinces mentioned in Chapter Eight, seem doomed to failure.

Third, prohibition in Truk retained strong community support at a symbolic level as a statement to the community about itself; that is, the community *did* control its own affairs. (And perhaps hypocritically, many of the power elite who personally profited from black market outlets supported the law.)

Fourth, prohibition created a more temperate drinking climate in Truk, in part because Trukese society is based on the efficacy of external social controls on individual desires. Under these conditions the law seemed less onerous than it might have in a society that relied much more on internal personal controls to achieve behavioral conformity.

Fifth, prohibition seems most likely to succeed in relatively small-scale, culturally homogeneous political units like Truk. A diversity of drinking customs among various immigrant groups in the late nineteenth-century United States was a major barrier to the success of prohibition there.

Sixth, and finally, prohibition as temperance may work best in circumstances of rapid social change. Under such conditions alcohol often is blamed for a multitude of social ills that in fact result from a much more complex constellation of factors. Action against alcohol provides a rallying point for people seeking to preserve institutions and social relationships they value in the face of social transformation.

These six facts about prohibition in Truk demonstrate that the word *prohibition* is a misnomer, for prohibition legislation never actually eliminates alcoholic beverages from a society and never stops people who wish to drink from doing so for more than a short period of time. What prohibition *does* often accomplish is more temperate behavior, either in the sense of lowered consumption levels or in the sense of reduced social disruption and violence associated with drinking, or both. If policymakers recognize this possibility, then prohibition can be viewed as one potentially helpful means for exercising some control over alcohol use in certain social settings.

The Trukese case also teaches us the value of examining alcohol issues from a woman's as well as a man's point of view, particularly in those societies such as most of Oceania where marked gender differences in alcohol use exist. In the process we may come to view alcohol and its social impact in a new light, and we may also gain insight into the changing meanings of gender in the societies we study.

Finally, the Trukese case shows that anthropologists can contribute to our understanding of the processual nature of changes in patterns of use and attitudes toward alcoholic beverages via the well-established tradition of community restudies. Such analyses of what Moore (1987) calls "ethnography as current history" seek to capture change-in-the-making while preserving the webs of meaning and the richness of context that are a hallmark of good anthropological fieldwork. By focusing on appropriate diagnostic events surrounding significant social changes vis-à-vis alcohol use—such as the establishment of legal prohibition—we can move beyond the static structural–functional models of yesteryear toward a truly processual ethnography.

Appendix One

BILL NO. 26-1-29, INTRODUCED IN THE TRUK DISTRICT LEGISLATURE, TWENTY-SIXTH REGULAR SESSION, FIRST SPECIAL SESSION, 1976.

A bill for an act repealing Chapter 1, Title 3, of the Truk District Code, establishing alcoholic beverage control, prohibiting the manufacture, importation, sale, possession and consumption of alcoholic beverage in Truk district; and for other purposes.

Be it enacted by the Truk District Legislature that:

Section 1. Repeal. Chapter 1, Title 3 of the Truk District Code, establishing Alcoholic Beverage Control, is repealed in its entirety.

Section 2. Amendment. Title 3 of the Truk District Code is amended by the addition of a Chapter as follows:

Chapter 1.
Prohibition of Alcoholic Beverages

Section 1. Prohibition. It shall be unlawful for any person to manufacture, import, sell, possess or consume alcoholic beverages within Truk District. For purposes of this Section alcoholic beverages include distilled and fermented liquor, beer, malt liquor, wine or any other liquid which contains one-half of one percent or more of alcohol by volume and which is for beverage purposes, either alone or when combined with other substances. Alcoholic beverages shall not include wine used by religious organizations in the religious rites of such organization.

Section 2. Penalties. Any person who possesses or consumes alcoholic beverages shall be guilty of unlawful possession of alcoholic beverages, and upon conviction thereof shall be imprisoned for a period or not more than six months, or shall be fined not more than one hundred dollars or both. Any person who manufactures, imports or sells alcoholic beverages shall be guilty of unlawful manufacture, importation or sale of alcoholic beverages and upon conviction thereof shall be imprisoned for a period of not more than two years, or shall be fined not more than one thousand dollars, or both.

Section 3. Effective Date. This Act shall take effect on January 1, 1977, upon its approval by the District Administrator or upon its becoming law without such approval.

Introduced by: A. Alex, C. Harper, J. Muritok, I. Simiron.

Appendix Two

MOEN MUNICIPAL ORDINANCE NO. 5-77.

An ordinance to prohibit the sale and consumption of alcoholic beverages.

Section 1. It shall be unlawful for any person to sell or consume alcoholic beverages in Moen Municipality.

Section 2. Definitions. For the purpose of this ordinance, alcoholic beverages mean beer, distilled spirits and wine, and every liquid which contains one-half of one percent or more of alcohol by volume and which is fit for beverage purposes, either alone or when combined with other substances.

Section 3. Exceptions.

A. Notwithstanding the provisions of this ordinance, a religious organization may use wine as part of its religious rites or services;

B. It shall not constitute a violation of this ordinance for a duly licensed merchant to store alcoholic beverages in Moen Municipality for transshipment and sale outside of Moen Municipality.

Section 4. Penalties. Any person who sells or consumes alcoholic beverages in violation of this ordinance shall be fined not more than one hundred dollars or imprisoned for not more than ninety days or both.

Section 5. Effective Date. This ordinance shall take effect upon January 15, 1978, after its approval by the Truk District Administrator.

Certified: Sictus Berdon, Clerk, Moen Municipality

Signed: Fichita Bossy, Mayor, Moen Municipality

Approved this 28th day of October 1977: Erhart Aten, District Administrator Truk, Trust Territory of the Pacific Islands

Appendix Three

PETITION CIRCULATED THROUGHOUT TRUK DISTRICT IN 1979 BY CHURCH WOMEN.

Petition

To: The Honorable Tadashi Wainit, Speaker, and the Honorable Members of the Truk District Legislature

We, the undersigned residents of the Truk District, Trust Territory of the Pacific Islands, respectfully urge our elected representatives to recognize the many social problems, such as violence, alcoholism and disruption of family life, created by the availability of liquor on our islands and the advantages of raising needed government revenues through a sales tax on luxury items and exercising the right guaranteed by Article I, Section 1 of the Truk District Charter respectfully petition our legislators to:

1. Promptly enact a law making illegal in the Truk District the possession, importation, sale and consumption of any and all alcoholic beverages and other substances which can cause intoxication; or

2. Include in any other legislation concerning alcoholic beverages a provision that the law not take effect until it is referred to a vote of the people for their approval or rejection at an election called for that purpose;

And each of the undersigned says that he has personally signed this petition knowing and understanding the contents thereof.

NAME	ADDRESS	DATE

Appendix Four

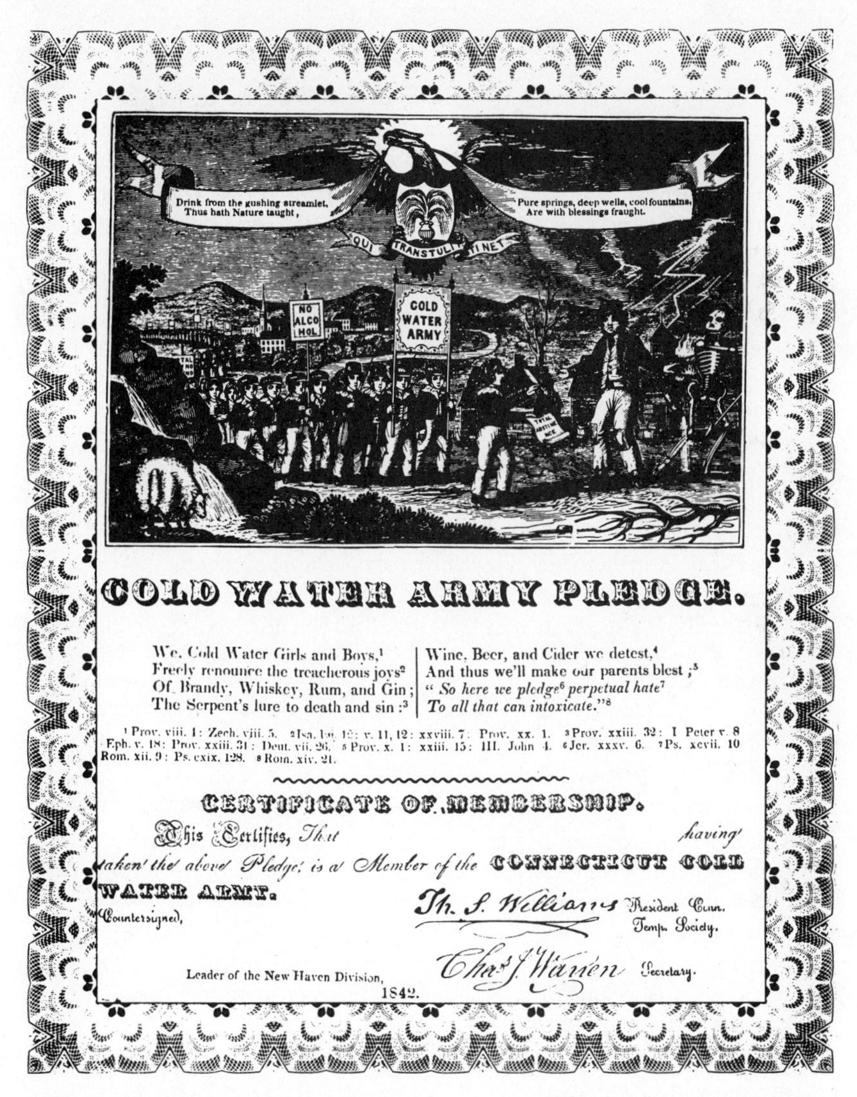

COLD WATER ARMY PLEDGE.

We, Cold Water Girls and Boys,[1]
Freely renounce the treacherous joys[2]
Of Brandy, Whiskey, Rum, and Gin;
The Serpent's lure to death and sin:[3]

Wine, Beer, and Cider we detest,[4]
And thus we'll make our parents blest;[5]
"So here we pledge[6] perpetual hate[7]
To all that can intoxicate."[8]

[1] Prov. viii. 1: Zech. viii. 5. [2] Isa. lvi. 12: v. 11, 12: xxviii. 7: Prov. xx. 1. [3] Prov. xxiii. 32: I Peter v. 8 Eph. v. 18: Prov. xxiii. 31: Deut. vii. 26. [5] Prov. x. 1: xxiii. 15: III. John 4. [6] Jer. xxxv. 6. [7] Ps. xcvii. 10 Rom. xii. 9: Ps. cxix. 128. [8] Rom. xiv. 21.

CERTIFICATE OF MEMBERSHIP.

This Certifies, That ________ having taken the above Pledge, is a Member of the CONNECTICUT COLD WATER ARMY.

Th. S. Williams, President Conn. Temp. Society.

Countersigned,

Leader of the New Haven Division, 1842.

Chas. J. Warren, Secretary.

Copy of the Cold Water Army pledge and membership certificate distributed to participants in the Honolulu conference, "Christians Concerned About Alcohol," November 1976.

Notes

CHAPTER ONE

1. One of the four societies they found to limit alcohol use exclusively to men was Ifaluk Atoll in Yap State, Federated States of Micronesia. Ifaluk is closely related to Truk socially, culturally, and linguistically.
2. A similar gender discrepancy exists in other parts of the Third World. For example, according to Armyr, Elmér, and Herz (1982:161), an official estimate made for India in 1977 "states that 42 percent of the men and 98 percent of the women have never tasted alcohol."
3. In a recent account of changing patterns of alcohol consumption among the Gwembe Tonga of Zambia, Colson and Scudder (1988) also give great attention to historical changes affecting drinking, in their case between 1950 and 1982. The difference is that unlike Trukese, Gwembe Tonga made beverage alcohol traditionally, and they have not experienced legal prohibition.

CHAPTER TWO

1. The 1986 population projection for Truk State was 47,724, or just over half of the projected FSM population for that year of 94,534 (Ashby 1986). The 1988 total population estimate for the FSM was 101,155 (*The National Union,* March 1988, p. 3).
2. In the 1970s nearly all outboard motors in Truk were Johnsons or Evinrudes (usually 25 hp) from the United States; in 1985, well over 90 percent of the engines were Yamaha, Suzuki, or (more rarely) Tomatsu from Japan, and most were 35 hp or higher.
3. During 1983 Air Nauru flights, through Pohnpei to Kiribati and the Solomon Islands, serviced Truk. These flights were discontinued for economic reasons.
4. Although not everyone in the wage economy is so well paid, mid-level to senior public servants earn salaries of $10,000–$15,000. Upper-level bureaucrats and elected state government officials have incomes between $15,000 and $30,000.
5. Only eight of the privately owned vehicles on Moen in 1985 were U.S. built (four sedans and four pickups, three with camper tops); the overwhelming majority were made in Japan.
6. A few elite families owned kerosene refrigerators or freezers before electricity became widely available.
7. At 13 percent in 1969–1970, Truk District had the lowest percentage of actual wage earners to total potential work force of any of the Trust Territory's six districts. Comparable figures for the other districts were Ponape 17 percent, Yap 18 percent, Marshall Islands 19 percent, Palau 23 percent, and Marianas Islands 38 percent (U.S. Department of State 1970:95). Although an exact percentage is not available for the mid-1980s, this figure has risen significantly since 1970.

8. The Truk radio station began broadcasting in late 1961, and it has become indispensable to the state's social and political life. As of the end of summer 1986, Truk had a second radio station—WSZP—owned and operated by the Liebenzell Mission (Anonymous 1986a).
9. Video has taken Truk by storm and has largely replaced movie theatres in the town. Wealthy residents own VCRs that run nearly every evening and often during the day in front of crowds of kin and friends. Videotapes are sometimes purchased in Hawaii or on Guam, sometimes rented from one of the outlets on Moen (one of which supplied pornographic videos), and sometimes pirated off television on Guam or in the United States and sent back to Truk by relatives living there. Both video cameras and VCRs are now found in Trukese communities outside the port town. One outer island community with which we are familiar boasted four VCRs in 1985. Local events and happenings were filmed and then shared with kin residing in the town to help maintain a sense of connectedness, mutual commitment, and involvement.
10. Work was in progress during summer 1985 to continue the blacktop out to the remotest villages.
11. Tuition in 1985 ranged from $8 per month at St. Cecelia's School to $20 per month at the SDA School, and $35–$40 per month at Berea Christian School depending on the grade.
12. Fischer reports that pupils for the three-year elementary school on Dublon were chosen on a quota basis, and "apparently only boys were selected at first, although girls were soon added" (1963:516).
13. As with many other gender issues in the tale to follow, striking parallels exist between the post–World War II situation in Truk and that of the United States in the nineteenth century. For example, compare Epstein writing about America in the early 1800s: "The education of girls was still regarded as less important than that of boys and girls were likely to be withdrawn from school earlier than their brothers" (1981:72).
14. The Truk extension program increased its enrollment dramatically between 1980 and 1985. In summer 1980, 69 students were signed up; this number grew to 119 in winter 1982, 140 a year later, 245 in winter 1984, and 256 during winter quarter 1985.
15. The UCC faction is composed of the Logan Memorial Church in Mwáán, Newúwé (old church), Peniyesene, Sópwúúk (one church), and Tunnuuk. The Nómwoneyas group consists of the remaining eight Moen churches: Epinupw, Mechchitiw, Nantaku, Newúwé (new church), Peniya, Sópwúúk (two churches), and Wiichap.

CHAPTER THREE

1. However, the inhabitants of some Polynesian outliers (e.g., Tikopia) chew betel.
2. But other Pacific islanders were later still: Due to the effectiveness of colonially imposed prohibition laws, many inhabitants of Papua New Guinea were insulated from first contact with alcoholic beverages until the 1960s (Marshall 1980). Even today, peoples exist in the interior of Papua New Guinea among whom alcohol has yet to appear (Poole 1982).

3. Produced in homemade stills hidden in the bush, a bottle of *chooriyú* cost $10 during the first year or two of prohibition. *Chooriyú* was available on the black market in 1985 but commanded only about $5 per liter by then.

4. Presumably, the cases of blindness referred to here resulted from ingestion of nonbeverage alcohols (e.g., methanol and isopropanol) from duplicating fluid, industrial cleaners, and hospital supplies (see Marshall 1988 for a discussion of the public health consequences of such consumption elsewhere in the Pacific).

5. The committee consisted of Dr. Michi (a Medical Officer trained at the Fiji School of Medicine and stationed at Truk Hospital) who was chair, Napoleon DeFang (Assistant Educational Administrator and a member of the Moen Municipal Council), Tosiwo Nakayama (later to become the first President of the Federated States of Micronesia), Chief Enis Nedelec (from Feefen Island), and Sheriff Keigo Ezra. Raymond Gosda, George Gavora, L. K. Anderson, and Associate Justice Philip R. Toomin advised the committee (*Truk Review,* January, February, March 1959, p. 10).

6. The beer tax yielded $18,724 as against $17,568 from the import tax (*Truk Review,* November 1959, p. 3).

7. We have not been able to locate information on the disposition of the second bill.

CHAPTER FOUR

1. We are well aware of the problems that inhere in a simplistic gender analysis in which women are seen to operate primarily in the domestic realm and men in the public sphere (e.g., Collier and Yanagisako 1987; Rosaldo 1980:396ff.). We use the domestic-public dichotomy here purely in a descriptive and not in an analytic or explanatory sense. Indeed, our focus is on how Trukese women have moved *beyond* the domestic realm.

2. Thick, long, jet-black hair is considered beautiful in Truk, and wearing it loose and unbound is viewed as immodest (Akapito 1982:3). A small but increasing number of younger, educated women in the islands have gotten short haircuts, partially to symbolize their advocacy of a new role for women in Truk.

3. Note was taken, beginning in the early 1950s, that departure from customary practices had begun to occur in the district centers "where foreign influence has to some extent lessened the rigidity of sanctions pertaining to occupations of the sexes" (U.S. Department of State 1954:70).

4. Only 7 of 51 students who graduated from Truk Intermediate School in 1958 were girls (*Truk Review,* October, November, December 1958, p. 12).

5. Between 1970 and 1973, graduating classes ranged in size from 127 to 188; in 1974, 242 students graduated, and the next year more than 300 (Ilon 1978).

6. In Truk, these parental attitudes have altered over the last decade. Many parents now realize that at investment in their daughters' education "pays off" better, in most cases, than a similar investment in a son's schooling. This is because women find it somewhat easier to obtain wage employment these days, and because a man must give a significant portion of his salary to his wife's family. A daughter's pregnancy while away at school is no longer humiliating, so long as she marries the father, brings the baby home to Truk, and then returns abroad to complete her schooling.

7. The Marshall Islands, Palau, Ponape, and Yap Districts all had active women's interests programs by the mid-1960s (U.S. Department of State 1966).
8. This woman's career is illustrative of the lives of younger, outward-looking, educated Trukese women. She was married for a time to an American Peace Corps lawyer, and subsequently has returned to Honolulu on several occasions to further her education. During 1986, she attended graduate school at the University of Hawaii, nearly completing the requirements for a Master's of Public Health degree.
9. The Girl Scouts involved a number of women leaders as well as the girls they organized. Girl Scouts began in Truk in 1965, and in 1985 there were five troops in Truk State, all in Truk Lagoon, two of which were on Moen. The coordinator of the scouting program in 1985 was the governor's wife, and during June 1985 Truk hosted an international workshop for scouting leaders from Micronesia, Sri Lanka, and South Pacific countries. The scouting program in Truk concentrates on fostering good citizenship and socially acceptable behavior.
10. Interestingly, all three Trukese women legislators were of the new educated elite; two were nurses and one was trained as a teacher.
11. At least one of these women candidates, from Pohnpei, exemplified many of the characteristics of newly emergent Pacific women leaders. Mother to seven children, she was married to a Samoan doctor and had lived abroad for a number of years. In 1972, she was the self-employed operator of a sawmill on Pohnpei, with plans to build Kolonia's first laundromat (*Micronitor,* November 7, 1972, pp. 1 & 4).
12. Although it is true that some elective offices, particularly in municipal government (e.g., councillor), do not require English language skills, some elective positions in state government (e.g., legislator, governor, lieutenant governor) have an unstated but basic requirement for facility in English. This is because state government officials must meet and deal with persons from elsewhere in the Federated States or from the United States who do not speak or understand Trukese. Even by 1970, responses to a political attitudes questionnaire administered to citizens of Namoluk Atoll revealed the importance of English language ability for offices such as legislator (Marshall and Borthwick 1974).
13. Several male informants emphasized that men wishing to run for political office in Truk find it advantageous to have assumed a lay leadership position in their church. Consequently, they noted, a number of church offices now are occupied by men of dubious religious sincerity.

CHAPTER FIVE

1. This phrase is the motto of the Woman's Board of Missions for the Pacific Islands.
2. Examples of these pamphlets include ACAP's "Booze and You" by Ann Landers; NIAAA's "Alcohol—Some Questions and Answers" and "Someone Close Drinks Too Much"; the AMA's "How Teens Set the Stage for Alcoholism"; DISCUS's "If You Choose to Drink, Drink Responsibly"; ADAB's "What Everyone Should Know About Alcohol"; and AA's "Alcoholism: A Merry-Go-Round Named Denial" and "What Do You Do About the Alcoholic's Drinking?"

3. Like these Trukese women, most leaders of the Woman's Crusade in the United States a century before shared two organizational forms in their backgrounds: Woman's Christian Associations (cf. Fin Anisi) and foreign missionary societies (cf. the Woman's Board; Blocker 1985b:136).
4. In this regard compare Blocker (1985b:214) who writes: "Only recently have historians examining women's temperance activity raised the possibility that men and women responded differently to the same stimuli. Such divergent responses seem particularly likely when men's and women's drinking behaviors differ radically. At such times, gender roles will affect responses to the liquor issue indirectly, acting through drinking behavior and attitudes toward drinking. One might expect to find among both men and women a link between personal abstinence and attitude toward the liquor business. But when personal abstinence is common among one group and rare in the other, the aggregate or collective responses of the groups to questions of liquor control will be different. This difference will of course be exacerbated when the more abstinent group depends upon the less abstinent for material support and physical protection, both of which are threatened by drinking."
5. Truk State has 39 municipalities. Moen Municipality encompasses the entire island of Moen, including the port town serving Truk State. Registered voters in Moen Municipality comprise a subset of Moen's overall population that includes many immigrants who remain registered to vote in their home municipalities.
6. On Moen, the municipal magistrate also is called the mayor. In many municipalities the incumbent in this office is referred to as *saamon,* "chief." The root *saam-* is also a kinship term, meaning "father," which is more than a passing coincidence. Just like a father, a chief or magistrate has a primary duty to take care of his people and his community. Women told us that this is one reason the mayor of Moen was a staunch supporter of the prohibition law: He saw it in the best interests of those for whom he was responsible.
7. The staff of the Trust Territory's most widely read newspaper of the day seemed ignorant of where the power lay to regulate liquor by editorializing that the Truk District Legislature would be asked to approve legislation forbidding sale and consumption of alcohol on Moen. Staff of the *Micronesian Independent* advocated keeping Truk wet in their editorial; yet, in the same issue, they reported passage of Moen's dry law (August 5, 1977, pp. 4, 6).
8. The mayor was appointed on October 21, 1971, to complete the unexpired term of the much-revered Petrus Mailo, who had died in early September. Subsequently elected in his own right in 1972, he has served as Moen's magistrate ever since (*Micronitor,* September 30, 1971, p. 8; May 16, 1972, p. 6).
9. This response mirrors a similar event in March 1875 in which the Ohio legislature "undercut the McConnelsville Ordinance, withdrawing from municipal corporations the power to prohibit ale, beer, and porter shops" (Blocker 1985b:220). McConnelsville had adopted an ordinance in September 1869 that added a prohibition against the above kinds of shops to an already existing state law against sale of distilled liquor by the drink (Ibid.:126).
10. By the first week of April 1979, the women had gathered nearly 10,000 signatures (*Truk Chronicle,* April 6, 1979, p. 3).

11. The committee consisted of seven persons appointed by the Speaker of the legislature. The chief of police was to serve as committee chair, but for unrecorded reasons he was superseded by the chair of the legislature's Resources and Development Committee. Others on the committee were the Truk tourism officer, a Catholic priest, a local businessman (who finished high school as a foreign exchange student in Illinois, and graduated from the University of Hawaii), and the senior land commissioner (who also was a former district administrator and a Protestant lay minister) (*Truk Chronicle,* April 20, 1979, p. 7).
12. Protest posters also were nailed up outside major stores, the hospital, and various government offices on Nantaku.
13. The Hotel Maramar no longer existed in 1985, having been converted into a dormitory for Maeda Construction Company workers. It originally opened in 1968 on a location just toward the downtown area from the Communication Station (see Figure 2.7).
14. Some friction earlier existed between the chief of police and the legislature, perhaps over his determination to apply the prohibition law equally to everyone, whether elected official or no. This friction was reflected in Resolution No. 1-1-19 that the legislature passed in their first regular session of 1978, directing the Speaker to appoint a special investigating committee of five legislators to look into district police activities. This resolution was passed, among other reasons, because "there appears to be no check on the unbridled action of the Chief of District Police" (FSM 1979c).
15. Although they did not participate in the protest march itself, some older male church leaders sat outside with the women during the sit-in phase of the demonstration in the days that followed. Still, the overwhelming majority of participants were women.
16. At least one other protest demonstration—having to do with the legislature's failure to act on a cost of living adjustment for government workers' salaries—was held at the legislature in recent years. When the legislature was in session in 1985, barriers were erected on the road adjacent to their building to prevent through traffic. Despite this symbolic gesture, no one has been prosecuted under this law.
17. Not only Third World women are kept outside the chambers of power on issues that directly affect their lives. Scutt writes of Australian women in the 1980s who became involved in the drafting and eventual passage of a new law against rape in New South Wales. After noting that women demonstrated outside Parliament House, she mentions that "women had to sit mute at the sides of the chamber, gazing 'admiringly' upon male legislators debating a measure which had been brought into the Parliament as a result of unflagging work of women's groups, continuing over more than eight years" (1985:20).
18. Millay's analysis (1987b) of the facts surrounding tourism in Truk revealed no significant decline as a result of Moen's prohibition law. If anything negatively affected the number of tourists visiting Truk after prohibition began, it was the cholera epidemic of 1982–1983 that received extensive international coverage.
19. This scene is reminiscent of America's nineteenth-century Woman's Crusaders: "The slow march of women in single file or column of twos down a main

street, the women silent or singing a hymn, invariably attracted a crowd of onlookers . . ." (Blocker 1985b:43).

20. A story in the *Truk News Chronicle* for April 1983 claimed a legal opinion rendered by Truk's state attorney general, reaffirming the rights of municipalities to regulate liquor within their jurisdictions, may have been a decisive factor influencing the council's vote.
21. Much information in this section was obtained in letters from persons in Truk in response to our specific inquiries.
22. Reportedly, this liquor was returned to the owner in January 1987 after a court hearing determined a technical defect existed in the police department's warrant.
23. Truk District first required all drinkers to have a valid identification card (drinking permit) beginning November 1, 1974 (Marshall 1979a:139). At that time the cards cost $6 per year. The police department suspended sale of identification cards in January 1978 because of the Moen ordinance and the unavailability of the cards themselves (*Truk Chronicle,* March 8–21, 1980, p. 3). In March 1980, the Alcoholic Beverages Control Board again approved issuance of drinking permits by the state police department; at that time the cards still cost $6 per year ($3 for a temporary permit) (Ibid.).

CHAPTER SIX

1. This presents an interesting instance in which the ethnographer's gender apparently limited access to sensitive data. MM inquired of women about alcohol-linked domestic violence in 1976, but he was told that it did not occur; when LBM interviewed women in 1985, she was regaled with stories—some volunteered, rather than prompted by questions—of domestic violence by drunken men.
2. The senior author made some of these points earlier in a rejoinder to publicity surrounding Dale's study (*Marianas Variety News & Views,* April 13, 1979, p. 9).
3. Alcohol continues to be implicated in most serious crimes in the FSM. For example, decisions in two cases of Assault With a Dangerous Weapon the FSM Supreme Court on Pohnpei recently adjudicated specified the defendants must refrain from drinking alcoholic beverages during the probationary periods of 18 months. (*The National Union,* April 15, 1987, p. 6). The clear implication was that the defendants had been drunk at the time of their crimes.
4. It was necessary to hold a state importer's license for a businessman to legally import goods of any sort, including alcoholic beverages for transshipment. In 1983, 48 establishments held importer's licenses; in June 1985, this number had grown to 65. Only a minority of those owning importer's licenses chose to import alcohol.
5. By 1985, commercially produced distilled beverages were being marketed in 750-mL bottles rather than in fifths (one-fifth of 1 U.S. gallon = 757 mL). Bootleg liquor in Truk was cheap in comparison to prices customers paid in dry villages in Alaska. In the town of Bethel, which allows importation of alcohol but not its sale, a bottle of whiskey that sells for $7 in Anchorage can be sold for $40, and the same bottle bootlegged into villages where both importa-

tion and sale are banned may command as much as $120 (*Anchorage Daily News,* January 15, 1988, p. A-1).

6. By comparison, in Iowa City, Iowa, in October 1987, a case of twenty-four 12-ounce cans of Old Style beer sold for $5.99, a liter of Seagram's bourbon was $8.99, and a 1.75-liter bottle of Skol vodka was marked at $8.99.
7. The owner of one black market on Moen in 1985 had 204 cartons of Bacardi rum in stock at 12 bottles per carton. At the then-operative market price of $10 per bottle, this cache represented over $20,000 in potential revenue, and the owner stood to realize a net profit of about $6,000 on his investment when it was all sold.
8. Ethanol is the active ingredient in all beverage alcohol (beer, wine, and distilled spirits). Nicotine is the major active substance in tobacco, whereas caffeine plays the same role in coffee and most soft drinks. THC (tetrahydrocannabol) is the primary pharmacologically active substance in marijuana. The police, major political figures, and persons in social-work-type jobs generally believed no hard drugs (such as cocaine or heroin) were available on Moen in summer 1985. Trukese knew of these substances, however, from movies and videos and by reading newspapers and magazines from Guam and the United States. Hard drugs *have* become a problem elsewhere in Micronesia on Guam, Saipan, and Belau.
9. When the Moen Council drafted the prohibition law in 1977, the official Trust Territory monthly newspaper rather confusingly reported that "the [Truk District] legislature recently collected an average of $108,000 from taxes on alcoholic beverages alone . . . [in an unspecified time period]" (*Highlights,* August 1, 1977, p. 2). This report was hardly clarified three months later when the same newspaper stated that "the [Truk District] legislature collects over $300,000 from the tax on alcoholic beverages [again in an unspecified period]" (*Highlights,* November 1, 1977, p. 5).
10. By comparison, the state and local tax per 12 ounces of beer in Pohnpei State only reached 20 cents in mid-1985 (Ashby 1985a:26).
11. The Congress of Micronesia levied a comparable duty beginning in 1965.
12. Although he is not responsible for the calculations presented here, we are grateful to Robin Room for urging us to undertake this rough estimate of prohibition's effect on overall consumption.

CHAPTER SEVEN

1. Frances Willard used this phrase in referring to the Woman's Crusade (1889:470).
2. Trukese men frequently comment on how foolish and incapable Trukese women supposedly are and use this prejudice to keep women from participating openly in the political arena.
3. With the islands of Hawaii designated as a prime target for evangelization, the ABCFM was formed in 1812 at the Congregationalist General Association meeting in Boston (Crawford and Crawford 1967). (Giving no source for her information, Aberley [1975:8] says the ABCFM was organized in 1810.)

4. Epstein (1981:93–94) claims that "sporadic, spontaneously organized women's attacks on saloons" took place "from at least the 1830s on" in New England "and especially the 'New England belt' of settlement through the Midwest," whereas Dannenbaum (1984) dates these activities to the 1850s and 1860s. Because Dannenbaum documents his case more thoroughly on this point, we have accepted his dates as more accurate. Carrie Nation's much more widely publicized exploits as a one-woman, ax-wielding crusader against saloons were not begun until 1900 (Knight 1976:202). In one Pacific island location (the Teop area of Bougainville Island, North Solomons Province, Papua New Guinea), women reportedly threatened similar direct action: "Women . . . opposed the renewal of storekeeper liquor licenses which happened to have been the only type of liquor license in the Teop area. The women protested strongly at the annual sittings of the Liquor Licensing Commission and said that if the licenses were renewed they would attack the stores. The Commission revoked all three licenses. Some time later the women had a victory celebration and now claim they can move freely about without being bothered by drunks" (Maskelyne 1975:47).
5. Those Trukese who have adopted a more Western lifestyle, principally younger adults who have lived and studied abroad, seem to feel that it is possible to drink *appropriately* (in a controlled manner) and still be one who cares for the community.
6. In 1885, the WCTU became New Zealand's first national women's organization. It spread quickly in New Zealand, and Leavitt's "visit stimulated the formation of associations throughout the country" (Bunkle 1980:57; Grimshaw 1975:5). Her sojourn in Melbourne in the same year "produced a handful of local unions . . . and a dozen or so more in rural centres . . ." (Hyslop 1976:29; cf. Tyrrell 1983). By 1888, Leavitt had helped organize WCTUs in Japan and China, in addition to those in Hawaii, Australia, and New Zealand (Paulson 1973). She had also visited India, Ceylon, Madagascar, and Africa in her quest, while other American WCTU representatives visited and organized in Switzerland, Norway, and France during the late 1880s (Willard 1889:431–432). All told, by the mid-1920s, organizers, lecturers, and missionaries for the World's WCTU had helped launch affiliate organizations in 42 countries (Tyrrell 1987).

CHAPTER EIGHT

1. Those areas of the Pacific the French missionized and colonized generally did not experience temperance and prohibition sentiments to nearly the same degree. Forman (1982:115) noted that during the nineteenth century the French forbade alcohol for the Leeward and Tuamotu islanders and put some restrictions on it in the Marquesas and on Wallis, but elsewhere in French Oceania set no limitations.
2. Forman (1982:123) states that today few churches insist on abstinence from alcohol as a necessary condition for membership. However, the Mormons, the New Caledonian Evangelicals, the Samoan Methodists, the Seventh Day Adventists, and the South Sea Evangelical Church continue the requirement.
3. Maori Wardens are men and women organized into a national voluntary association appointed under provisions of the Maori Community Development

Act. Their duties are to monitor hotels to prevent disorderly conduct and drunkenness by Maori patrons and to prohibit the illegal sale or consumption of alcoholic beverages in the vicinity of a *marae,* "Maori ceremonial center." Essentially, the Wardens serve as an informal or secondary police force helping maintain order in this ethnic population (see Fleras n.d. for more details).

4. This former British colony has divided into the two independent nations of Kiribati and Tuvalu.
5. Of course, this does not mean that drinking never took place in dry municipalities.
6. As a result a major drop in monthly liquor sales occurred, drinkers began to partake at home with friends and relatives, and commercial bars selling Pohnpei's traditional kava opened (Mahoney 1974).
7. The island of Kosrae (Kusaie) lies to the southeast of Pohnpei (Ponape), and the atoll of Kapingamarangi is situated more or less due south of Pohnpei almost on the equator. Kosraens are Micronesians whereas the Kapinga are of Polynesian derivation. People from these and other islands in the vicinity of Pohnpei have established ethnic communities on Pohnpei.
8. Rather than prohibition, several provinces of Papua New Guinea instituted "village drinking clubs" (e.g., Sumanop 1982). Such clubs certainly did not discourage drinking; they were, rather, an effort to control several widely perceived problems linked to alcohol use: road accidents, bar fights in towns among men from different villages or ethnic groups, and the general social disruption surrounding drinking. This effort to achieve controlled drinking seemed quite successful in some places and much less so in others.
9. As noted in Chapter Three, Truk District required drinkers to have a valid permit obtained from the police department beginning in 1974.
10. The implementation of drinking permits in the Marshall Islands did not happen right away. Therefore, with the start of the school year in September 1972, Marshall Islands High School announced a policy whereby they would issue their own ID cards to all students over age 21. The school's hope was that liquor outlets would request ID before serving students, and the school let it be known it would prosecute any bar where underage students were found drinking (*Micronitor,* September 26, 1972, p. 9).
11. In 1983, 90 percent of all crimes committed on Saipan and over 90 percent of traffic fatalities were alcohol related (*Marianas Variety News & Views,* July 8, 1983, p. 2). Sixty-three percent of all arrests the Department of Public Safety made in 1986 were for drunk driving (*Marianas Variety News & Views,* June 5, 1987, p. 11). Deaths from drunk driving crashes have been particularly vexing: 14 of 15 traffic fatalities in the 1980–1982 period involved drunk drivers. In 1986, drunk drivers caused 5 of 8 traffic deaths, and in the first six months of 1987 this was true for all 7 vehicular deaths (*Marianas Variety News & Views,* July 10, 1987, p. 3). Two more fatal drunk driving wrecks occurred on Saipan in mid-July 1987 (*Marianas Variety News & Views,* July 19, 1987, pp. 1, 7).
12. This program was still functioning in June 1987 (*Marianas Variety News & Views,* June 5, 1987, p. 11).

CHAPTER NINE

1. This view accords with Kolstad's (1986) observation that the temperance movement is rapidly expanding in many Third World countries, notably in Africa and Asia. Kolstad attributes this expansion to the fact that the International Order of Good Templars has more than doubled its membership in four years (Ibid.). Self-imposed prohibition as prevention may also prove helpful for certain populations in developed nations, for example, Australian Aborigines (Sargent 1983:93, 100) and Native Americans in Canada and the United States (May 1977; May and Smith 1988; Smart 1979).
2. Unnithan (1985:592) mentions five reasons why prohibition has been thought a worthwhile alcohol policy: (1) for moral reasons; (2) to end the negative effects of excessive use on physical and mental health and on the number of deaths from alcoholism; (3) to eliminate a source of family discord and a drain on individual and family income; (4) to redirect money being spent on liquor to the purchase of more useful things; and (5) to reduce delinquency, crime, and alcohol-related deviance. Of course, proponents of prohibition may have several of these goals in mind when seeking to ban alcoholic beverages (see, e.g., Chapters Six and Seven).
3. Lonner (1985) and O'Neil (1985) provide other examples where local prohibition has retained significant community support, despite the inevitable rise of illegal drinking, primarily because alcohol-related violence diminished.
4. A few of the major antialcohol leaders *did* see prohibition as a moral crusade to save drinkers from sin, although they also mentioned pragmatic reasons as well and even realized these statements were essential if they wished to achieve their goal.
5. In examining the socioeconomic impact of removal of prohibition in the state of Karnataka in India (formerly Mysore), Thimmaiah (1979:45–46) found that "the majority of the respondents" were still in favor of total prohibition, even those from "drinking households."
6. Stein has some interesting observations on self-control in American culture: "Self-control is not only valued on its own merit, but instrumentally implements the values of autonomy and self-reliance. To admit that one is not fully in charge of one's 'faculties' and behavior, that one is irresponsible, is to forfeit one's right to be free, and an open invitation for another to take control of one's life. From the Revoluntionary War slogan 'Don't tread on me' to the Midwestern motto 'Don't fence me in,' Americans pride themselves on their fierce personal independence" (1985:211). Riches' (1976:73) comment on the "perennial Canadian sermons to the effect that Eskimo drinkers should exercise a great deal more self-control . . ." suggests that these assumptions about the individual are widespread elsewhere in Western society, not merely in the United States.
7. According to Feinberg (1986), knowledge of how to ferment coconut toddy only diffused to the remote Polynesian outlier atoll of Nukumanu (in Papua New Guinea's North Solomons Province) in the early 1950s. Toddy drinking has been thoroughly incorporated into the masculine world view in the years since, and men "consume it in large quantities despite a host of seemingly dysfunctional consequences" (Ibid.: 278). Women rarely drink. Feinberg states that "I never heard any male seriously suggest that toddy drinking should be

banned" (Ibid.), whereas women express a different view: "Sexual imposition and domestic quarrels following men's drinking parties have become commonplace, and many women have grown openly and vehemently opposed to toddy drinking" (Ibid.:279).

8. Women in parts of Asia also have demonstrated against alcohol. In 1984, for example, activists surrounded liquor shops in Chaukhutia, western Almora (Uttar Pradesh), and "women led a large demonstration outside the district office at Almora. . . . The activists' aim is to declare the entire hill area dry" (Pathak 1988:9).
9. That this is the case elsewhere in the developing world is shown in Gakuo's recent article concerning Kenya. She discusses the problems women have with drunken husbands and then, in a list of "strategies for improvement," advocates that "the government should stop sale of alcoholic drinks so that men mainly in the urban areas can spend more time at home with their families rather than spending the after-office hours and money in the bars" (1985:378).
10. We are tempted to suggest, although we cannot prove, that certain societies with a particular pattern of drinking may profit from prohibition and find it more acceptable. This pattern involves high rates of public drunkenness, a great deal of alcohol-related violence and death, and binge drinking at irregular intervals when great quantities of alcohol are consumed. Such a pattern describes drinking in Alaskan villages (Lonner 1985; Lonner and Duff 1983), Finland (Sariola 1954), Canadian Inuit communities (O'Neil 1985), and Truk (Mahoney 1974; Marshall 1979a). All these societies have had reasonable success with prohibition as temperance.

Bibliography

AAMES, JACQUELINE SNYDER

1976 The role of education in affecting change in attitudes and values toward strategies of elite selection: Micronesia under an American administration. Ph.D. dissertation, University of California, Santa Barbara.

AARON, PAUL AND DAVID MUSTO

1981 Temperance and prohibition in America: A historical overview. In *Alcohol and Public Policy: Beyond the Shadow of Prohibition,* eds. Mark H. Moore and Dean R. Gerstein. Washington, DC: National Academy Press. pp. 127–181.

ABERLEY, JENNIFER

1975 Robert W. Logan, the "soldier-saint" of Micronesia. B.A. (Honours) thesis, Australian National University.

AKAPITO, VITA J.

1982 Reverse cultural shock experienced by Trukese female students. Unpublished paper for Public Health 792, University of Hawaii, on file in the Pacific Collection, Hamilton Library, University of Hawaii, Honolulu, Hawaii.

ALBRECHT, C. EARL

1985 Alcohol: Availability and abuse. In *Circumpolar Health 84. Proceedings of the Sixth International Symposium on Circumpolar Health,* ed. Robert Fortuine. Seattle: University of Washington Press. pp. 327–331.

ALKIRE, WILLIAM H.

1968 Porpoises and taro. *Ethnology* 7: 280–289.

———

1989 Land, sea, gender, and ghosts on Woleai-Lamotrek. In *Culture, Kin, and Cognition in Oceania: Essays in Honor of Ward H. Goodenough,* eds. Mac Marshall and John L. Caughey. American Anthropological Association Special Publications, No. 25. Washington, DC: American Anthropological Association. pp. 79–94.

AMBROS, INC.

1984 Trust Territory price list effective January 9, 1984. Typescript. [current as of August 7, 1985; copy in authors' files]

ANONYMOUS

1956 Supply of liquor to New Guinea natives. *South Pacific* [Australian School of Pacific Administration] 8(10): 209–211.

———

1975 Women vote for prohibition. *Point* [Melanesian Institute for Pastoral and Socio-Economic Service, Goroka] No. 2, pp. 147–152.

———

1985 News-Gram. *Pacific Magazine* 10(3): 8.

———

1986a FSM, Marshalls, Palau. *Pacific Magazine* 11(5): 29.

———

1986b News-Gram. *Pacific Magazine* 11(2): 8.

———

1987 News-Gram. *Pacific Magazine* 12(1): 8.

———

1988a High spirits quelled. *Pacific Islands Monthly* 59(1): 25.

———

1988b Palau fights alcohol abuse. *Pacific Islands Monthly* 59(8): 43.

ARMYR, GUNNO, ÅKE ELMÉR, AND ULRICH HERZ

1982 *Alcohol in the World of the 80s: Habits, Attitudes, Preventive Policies and Voluntary Efforts.* Stockholm: Sober Forlags AB.

ASHBY, GENE

1985a Pohnpei tax bite on beer/smokes. *Pacific Magazine* 10(3): 26.

———

1985b Kosrae swings to wet under new legislation. *Pacific Magazine* 10(6): 14.

———

1986 Population is 94,534 says FSM statistics. *Pacific Magazine* 11(5): 12.

———

1988 Substance abuse council organized on Pohnpei. *Pacific Magazine* 13(6): 41.

ASIAN AND PACIFIC CENTRE FOR WOMEN AND DEVELOPMENT

1977 Report of the Expert Group Meeting on the Identification of the Basic Needs of Women of Asia and the Pacific and on the Formulation of a Programme of Work, 4–10 December, Tehran, Iran.

ATWOOD, MARGARET

1986 *The Handmaid's Tale.* Boston: Houghton Mifflin Co.

BACK, WILLIAM DOUGLAS

1981 The ineffectiveness of alcohol prohibition on the Navajo Indian Reservation. *Arizona State Law Journal* 1981(4): 925–943.

BARBACH, LONNIE, ED.

1984 *Pleasures.* New York: Harper & Row.

BARROWS, SUSANNA, ROBIN ROOM, AND JEFFREY VERHEY, EDS.

1987 *The Social History of Alcohol: Drinking and Culture in Modern Society. Proceedings of a Conference held in Berkeley, California, January 1984.* Berkeley: Alcohol Research Group, Medical Research Institute of San Francisco.

BLACKBURN, N.

1969 The debate on changing the liquor laws, 1955 and 1962. In *Select Topics in the History of Papua and New Guinea,* eds. H. N. Nelson, N. Lutton, and S. Robertson. Waigani: University of Papua New Guinea. pp. 43–48.

BLOCKER, JACK S., JR.

1985a Separate paths: Suffragists and the Women's Temperance Crusade. *Signs: Journal of Women in Culture and Society* 10(3): 460–476.

———

1985b *"Give to the Winds Thy Fears:" The Women's Temperance Crusade, 1873–1874.* Contributions in Women's Studies No. 55. Westport, CT: Greenwood Press.

BORDIN, RUTH

1978 "A baptism of power and liberty": The Women's Crusade of 1873–1874. *Ohio History* 87(4): 393–404.

———

1980 Marching for temperance: The Woman's Crusade in Adrian. *Chronicle* [Historical Society of Michigan] 15(4): 16–23.

———

1981 *Woman and Temperance: The Quest for Power and Liberty, 1873–1900.* Philadelphia: Temple University Press.

———

1985 Frances Willard and the practice of political influence. *Hayes Historical Journal: A Journal of the Gilded Age* 5(1): 18–28.

BRUNTON, RON

1988 The disappearing narcotic: Kava and cultural instability in Melanesia. Ph.D. dissertation, La Trobe University.

BRUUN, KETTIL, ET AL.

1975 *Alcohol Control Policies in Public Health Perspective.* Finnish Foundation for Alcohol Studies, Volume 25. Helsinki.

BRYSON, LOIS AND BETSY WEARING

1985 Australian community studies—a feminist critique. *Australian and New Zealand Journal of Sociology* 21(3): 349–366.

BUNKLE, PHILLIDA

1980 The origins of the women's movement in New Zealand: The Women's Christian Temperance Union 1885–1895. In *Women in New Zealand Society,* eds. Phillida Bunkle and Beryl Hughes. Sydney: George Allen & Unwin. pp. 52–76.

BUTHING, MARTINA, ET AL.

1984 New religions in Truk State. Senior Town Project, Xavier High School, Moen, Truk.

CASSWELL, SALLY

1985 Prevention of Alcohol-Related Problems, Fiji and Vanuatu. Report of an Assignment, February 1984–April 1985. World Health Organization Western Pacific Regional Office.

CHILD, I. L., H. BARRY III, AND M. K. BACON

1965 A cross-cultural study of drinking: III. Sex differences. *Quarterly Journal of Studies on Alcohol,* Supplement No. 3. pp. 49–61.

COLLIER, JANE F. AND SYLVIA J. YANAGISAKO, EDS.

1987 *Gender and Kinship: Essays Toward a Unified Analysis.* Stanford, CA: Stanford University Press.

COLSON, ELIZABETH AND THAYER SCUDDER

1988 *For Prayer and Profit: The Ritual, Economic, and Social Importance of Beer in Gwembe District, Zambia, 1950–1982.* Stanford, CA: Stanford University Press.

CRAWFORD, DAVID AND LEONA CRAWFORD

1967 *Missionary Adventures in the South Pacific.* Rutland, VT: Charles E. Tuttle Co.

DALE, PAUL W.

1979 Restriction of alcoholic beverage sales in Truk: Effect on hospital emergency room visits. Typescript. [copy in authors' files]

DANNENBAUM, JED

1981 The origins of temperance activism and militancy among American women. *Journal of Social History* 15(2): 235–252.

——

1984 *Drink and Disorder: Temperance Reform in Cincinnati from the Washingtonian Revival to the WCTU.* Urbana and Chicago: University of Illinois Press.

DOLAN, SUSAN A. BALLARD

1974 Truk: The Lagoon area in the Japan years 1914–1945. M.A. thesis, University of Hawaii.

DUPERTUIS, LUCY

1988 Religious abstinence styles and cultural identity in Micronesia. Paper read at the Annual Meeting of the Kettil Bruun Society for Social and Epidemiological Research on Alcohol, 5–11 June, Berkeley, California.

EDWARDS, GRIFFITH

1978 *Alcohol Problems in Developing Countries.* Report prepared for Division of Mental Health, World Health Organization, Geneva.

——

1979 Drinking problems: Putting the Third World on the map. *The Lancet* Volume II for 1979, No. 8139 (25 August): 402–404.

EPSTEIN, BARBARA LESLIE

1981 *The Politics of Domesticity: Women, Evangelism, and Temperance in Nineteenth-Century America.* Middletown, CT: Wesleyan University Press.

FAGER, CHUCK

1984 The new prohibition. *The Drinking & Drug Practices Surveyor* 19: 70–73.

FALCAM, LEO A., JR., ET AL.

1978 Moen—"Dry Season 1978": Report on Prohibition of Alcohol. Senior Town Project, Xavier High School, Moen, Truk.

FEDERATED STATES OF MICRONESIA (FSM)

1979a Truk State Law No. 1-1-4. In *Laws and Resolutions, Truk State Legislature, First Regular Session, First and Second Special Sessions, 26 September–6*

December 1978 and 20 February–17 March and 19 April 1979. Truk, Eastern Caroline Islands: Public Affairs Office. p. 39.

——

1979b Truk State Law No. 1-1-13. In *Laws and Resolutions, Truk State Legislature, First Regular Session, First and Second Special Sessions, 26 September–6 December 1978 and 20 February–17 March and 19 April 1979.* Truk, Eastern Caroline Islands: Public Affairs Office. pp. 70–71.

——

1979c Truk District Resolution No. 1-1-19. In *Laws and Resolutions, Truk State Legislature, First Regular Session, First and Second Special Sessions, 26 September–6 December 1978 and 20 February–17 March and 19 April 1979.* Truk, Eastern Caroline Islands: Public Affairs Office. p. 122.

——

1980 Truk State Law No. 2-1-2. In *Laws and Resolutions, Truk State Legislature, Second Regular Session, First and Second Special Sessions, 7 May–2 July 1979, 4–22 September 1979, and 14–31 January 1980.* Truk, Eastern Caroline Islands: Public Affairs Office. pp. 36–38.

——

1982 *Code of the Federated States of Micronesia,* Vol. I, 1982 edition, Constitution, Titles 1-31. Seattle: Book Publishing Co.

——

1984 Truk State Law No. 5-103. In *Laws and Resolutions, Truk State Legislature, Third Regular Session, May 1984.* Truk, Eastern Caroline Islands: Public Affairs Office. pp. 1–6.

——

1985 Federated States of Micronesia Tax Information. Kolonia: Division of Revenue, Department of Finance.

FEINBERG, RICHARD

1986 Market economy and changing sex-roles on a Polynesian atoll. *Ethnology* 25(4):271–282.

FIGIRLIYONG, JOSEDE

1976 The contemporary political system of Ulithi Atoll. Master's thesis, California State University, Fullerton.

FISCHER, JOHN L.

1963 The Japanese schools for the natives of Truk, Caroline Islands. In *Education and Culture,* ed. George Spindler. New York: Holt, Rinehart & Winston. pp. 512–529.

FLERAS, AUGIE

n.d. Maori Wardens as formal social control: Transforming the politics of policing among the Maori of New Zealand. Unpublished manuscript. [copy in authors' files]

FORMAN, CHARLES W.

1982 *The Island Churches of the South Pacific: Emergence in the Twentieth Century.* American Society of Missiology Series, No. 5. Maryknoll, NY: Orbis Books.

GAKUO, MUMBI

1985 The Kenyan women and situation and strategies for improvement. *Women's Studies International Forum* 8(4): 373–379.

GOODENOUGH, WARD H. AND HIROSHI SUGITA

1980 *Trukese-English Dictionary.* Philadelphia: American Philosophical Society.

GRIGG, A. R.

1983 Prohibition and women: The preservation of an ideal and a myth. *New Zealand Journal of History* 17(2): 144–165.

GRIMSHAW, PATRICIA

1975 *Women's Suffrage in New Zealand.* Hamilton: Waikato Art Museum.

———

1985 New England missionary wives, Hawaiian women, and "the cult of true womanhood." *The Hawaiian Journal of History* 19: 71–100.

GUNSON, NIEL

1966 On the incidence of alcoholism and intemperance in early Pacific missions. *Journal of Pacific History* 1: 43–62.

GUSFIELD, JOSEPH R.

1963 *Symbolic Crusade: Status Politics and the American Temperance Movement.* Urbana and Chicago: University of Illinois Press.

———

1976 The prevention of drinking problems. In *Alcohol and Alcohol Problems: New Thinking and New Directions,* eds. W. J. Filstead, J. J. Rossi, and M. Keller. Cambridge, MA: Ballinger. pp. 267–291.

———

1982 Prevention: Rise, decline and renaissance. In *Alcohol, Science and Society Revisited,* eds. E. L. Gomberg, H. R. White, and J. A. Carpenter. Ann Arbor: University of Michigan Press. pp. 402–425.

HADDON, A. C.

1947 Smoking and tobacco pipes in New Guinea. *Philosophical Transactions of the Royal Society of London,* Series B, Volume 232. London: Cambridge University Press for the Royal Society.

HAUGE, RAGNAR

1978 *Alcohol Research in Norway.* Oslo: National Institute for Alcohol Research.

HEZEL, FRANCIS X.

1970 Catholic missions in the Caroline and Marshall Islands: A survey of historical materials. *Journal of Pacific History* 5: 213–227.

———

1973 The beginnings of foreign contact with Truk. *Journal of Pacific History* 8: 51–73.

———

1979 The education explosion in Truk. *Pacific Studies* 2(2): 167–185.

———, ED.

1981 *Youth Drinking in Micronesia: A Report on the Working Seminar on Alcohol Use and Abuse Among Micronesian Youth.* Kolonia, Pohnpei: Micronesian Seminar.

———

1984 Cultural patterns in Trukese suicide. *Ethnology* 23(3): 193–206.

———

1985 A report on child abuse and neglect in Truk. Completed for TOCA Headstart, Truk State by Micronesian Seminar and Youth Link, September 1, 1985. Typescript. [copy in authors' files]

———

1987a Truk suicide epidemic and social change. *Human Organization* 46(4): 283–291.

———

1987b The dilemmas of development: The effects of modernization on three areas of island life. In *The Ethics of Development: The Pacific in the 21st Century,* eds. Susan Stratigos and Philip J. Hughes. Port Moresby: University of Papua New Guinea Press. pp. 60–74.

———

n.d.a In the aftermath of the education explosion. Unpublished manuscript. [copy in authors' files]

———

n.d.b The Catholic Church in Truk. Unpublished manuscript. [copy in authors' files]

HOLDER, HAROLD D. AND MICHAEL T. STOIL

1988 Beyond Prohibition: The public health approach to prevention. *Alcohol Health and Research World* 12(4): 292–297.

HOOPER, PAUL F.

1976 Feminism in the Pacific: The Pan-Pacific and Southeast Asia Women's Association. *The Pacific Historian* 20(4): 367–377.

HOWARD, ALAN

1979 Polynesia and Micronesia in psychiatric perspective. *Transcultural Psychiatric Research Review* 16: 123–145.

HYSLOP, ANTHEA

1976 Temperance, Christianity and feminism: The Woman's Christian Temperance Union of Victoria, 1887–97. *Historical Studies* 17(66): 27–49.

ILON, LYNN

1978 Trukese high school graduates: A statistical report (preliminary findings). Unpublished manuscript. [copy on file in Pacific Collection, Hamilton Library, University of Hawaii, Honolulu]

INSTITUTE OF MEDICINE.

1987 *Causes and Consequences of Alcohol Problems, An Agenda for Research.* Report of a Study by a Committee of the Institute of Medicine, Division of Health Sciences Policy. Washington, DC: National Academy Press.

ISETTS, CHARLES A.

1979 A social profile of the Women's Temperance Crusade: Hillsboro, Ohio. In *Alcohol, Reform and Society: The Liquor Issue in Social Context,* ed. Jack S. Blocker, Jr. Contributions in American History No. 83. Westport, CT: Greenwood Press. pp. 101–110.

JAPAN, NANYŌ-CHŌ (SOUTH SEAS BUREAU)

1931 *Nanyō Gunto Tōsei Chōsa-sho, Showa 5 nen [A Summary of Conditions in the Japanese Mandated Territories, 1930].* 4 volumes. Palau: Nanyō-chō.

———

1937 *Nanyō Gunto Tōsei Chōsa-sho, Showa 10 nen [A Summary of Conditions in the Japanese Mandated Territories, 1935].* 2 volumes. Tokyo: Nanyō-chō.

JOHANSEN, PER OLE

1987 Alcohol prohibition in Norway: 1917–1927. Paper read at the 33rd International Council for Alcohol and the Addictions, International Institute on the Prevention and Treatment of Alcoholism, 4 June, Lausanne, Switzerland.

KAY, A.

1974 Population growth in Micronesia. *Micronesian Reporter* 22(2): 13–22.

KENDALL, R. E., M. DE ROUMANIE, AND E. B. RITSON

1983 Influence of an increase in excise duty on alcohol consumption and its adverse effects. *British Medical Journal* 287: 809–811.

KERR, K. AUSTIN

1985 *Organized for Prohibition: A New History of the Anti-Saloon League.* New Haven: Yale University Press.

KIENER, ROBERT

1977 They don't make stores like this anymore. *Glimpses of Micronesia and the Western Pacific* 17(4): 36–39.

KIM, MARIANA

1981 Impact of college education on Trukese women. Unpublished paper prepared for Women's Studies 420. [copy on file in the Pacific Collection, Hamilton Library, University of Hawaii, Honolulu, Hawaii]

KNIGHT, VIRGINIA C.

1976 Women and the temperance movement. *Current History* 70(416): 201–203.

KOHL, MANFRED WALDEMAR

1971 *Lagoon in the Pacific. The Story of Truk.* Schooley's Mountain, NJ: Publications Committee, Liebenzell Mission.

KOLSTAD, HELGE J.

1986 Public enlightenment and alcohol policy: The impact of voluntary organizations on public opinion. Paper read at the 32nd International Council on Alcohol and the Addictions, International Institute on the Prevention and Treatment of Alcoholism, 5 June, Budapest, Hungary.

LARSON, R. BRUCE

1987 A note on marijuana in Truk. In *Drugs in Western Pacific Societies,* ed. Lamont Lindstrom. ASAO Monograph No. 11. Lanham, MD: University Press of America. pp. 219–230.

LEMERT, EDWIN M.

1967 Alcohol, values and social control. In *Human Deviance, Social Problems, and Social Control,* by E. M. Lemert. Englewood Cliffs, NJ: Prentice-Hall. pp. 72–87.

———

1976 *Koni, kona, kava:* Orange-beer culture of the Cook Islands. *Journal of Studies on Alcohol* 37(5): 565–585.

LEVINE, HARRY GENE

1978 The discovery of addiction: Changing conceptions of habitual drunkenness in America. *Journal of Studies on Alcohol* 39(1): 143–174.

———

1980 Temperance and women in 19th-century United States. In *Alcohol and Drug Problems in Women,* ed. Oriana Josseau Kalant. Research Advances in Alcohol and Drug Problems, Volume 5. New York: Plenum. pp. 25–67.

———

1985 The birth of American alcohol control: Prohibition, the power elite, and the problem of lawlessness. *Contemporary Drug Problems* 12(1): 63–115.

LEWTHWAITE, GORDON R., CHRISTIANE MAINZER, AND PATRICK J. HOLLAND

1973 From Polynesia to California: Samoan migration and its sequel. *Journal of Pacific History* 8: 133–157.

LINDSTROM, LAMONT, ED.

1987 *Drugs in Western Pacific Societies.* ASAO Monograph No. 11. Lanham, MD: University Press of America.

LOEB, EDWIN M.

1943 Primitive intoxicants. *Quarterly Journal of Studies on Alcohol* 4: 387–398.

LONNER, THOMAS D.

1985 Village alcohol control: Traditional methods and the "Local Option Law." In *Circumpolar Health 84. Proceedings of the Sixth International Symposium on Circumpolar Health,* ed. Robert Fortuine. Seattle: University of Washington Press. pp. 335–339.

LONNER, THOMAS D. AND J. KENNETH DUFF

1983 *Village Alcohol Control and the Local Option Law. A Report to the Alaska State Legislature.* Anchorage: Center for Alcohol and Addiction Studies, School for Health Sciences, University of Alaska.

LOOMIS, ALBERTINE

1970 *To All People: A History of the Hawaii Conference of the United Church of Christ.* Honolulu: Hawaii Conference of the United Church of Christ.

MACANDREW, CRAIG AND ROBERT B. EDGERTON

1969 *Drunken Comportment: A Social Explanation.* Chicago: Aldine Publishing Co.

MAHONEY, FRANCIS B.

1974 *Social and Cultural Factors Relating to the Cause and Control of Alcohol Abuse Among Micronesian Youth.* Prepared for the Government of the Trust Territory of the Pacific Islands under Contract TT 174-8 with James R. Leonard Associates, Inc.

MÄKELÄ, KLAUS

1985 Lessons from the postwar period. In *Alcohol Policies,* ed. Marcus Grant. WHO Regional Publications, European Series No. 18. Copenhagen: World Health Organization Regional Office for Europe. pp. 9–22.

MÄKELÄ, KLAUS, ET AL.

1981 *Alcohol, Society, and the State 1. A Comparative Study of Alcohol Control.* Toronto: Addiction Research Foundation.

MANCHESTER, CURTIS A., JR.

1951 The Caroline Islands. In *Geography of the Pacific,* ed. Otis W. Freeman. New York: John Wiley & Sons. pp. 236–269.

MARGOLD, JANE AND DONNA BELLORADO

1985 Matrilineal heritage: A look at the power of contemporary Micronesian women. In *Women in Asia and the Pacific: Towards an East-West Dialogue,* ed. Madeleine J. Goodman. Honolulu: University of Hawaii Press. pp. 129–151.

MARSHALL, LESLIE B. AND MAC MARSHALL

1982 Education of women and family size in two Micronesian communities. *Micronesica* 18(1): 1–21.

MARSHALL, MAC

1975a The politics of prohibition on Namoluk Atoll. *Journal of Studies on Alcohol* 36(5): 597–610.

———

1975b Changing patterns of marriage and migration on Namoluk Atoll. In *Pacific Atoll Populations,* ed. Vern Carroll. ASAO Monograph No. 3. Honolulu: University of Hawaii Press. pp. 160–211.

———

1976 A review and appraisal of alcohol and *kava* studies in Oceania. In *Cross-Cultural Approaches to the Study of Alcohol: An Interdisciplinary Perspective,* eds. Michael W. Everett, Jack O. Waddell, and Dwight B. Heath. World Anthropology Series. The Hague: Mouton. pp. 103–118.

———

1979a *Weekend Warriors: Alcohol in a Micronesian Culture.* Palo Alto, CA: Mayfield Publishing Co.

———, ED.

1979b *Beliefs, Behaviors, and Alcoholic Beverages: A Cross-Cultural Survey.* Ann Arbor: University of Michigan Press.

———

1980 A history of prohibition and liquor legislation in Papua New Guinea, 1884–1963. IASER Discussion Paper No. 33. Boroko: Institute of Applied Social and Economic Research.

———

1981a Tobacco use in Micronesia: A preliminary discussion. *Journal of Studies on Alcohol* 42: 885–893.

———

1981b Sibling sets as building blocks in Greater Trukese Society. In *Siblingship in Oceania: Studies in the Meaning of Kin Relations,* ed. Mac Marshall. ASAO Monograph No. 8. Ann Arbor: University of Michigan Press. pp. 201–224.

———

1982b Introduction: Twenty years after deprohibition. In *Through a Glass Darkly: Beer and Modernization in Papua New Guinea,* ed. Mac Marshall. IASER

Monograph No. 18. Boroko: Papua New Guinea Institute of Applied Social and Economic Research. pp. 3–13.

———

1984 Alcohol and drug studies in anthropology: Where do we go from here? *The Drinking & Drug Practices Surveyor* 19: 23–27.

———

1987a An overview of drugs in Oceania. In *Drugs in Western Pacific Societies,* ed. Lamont Lindstrom. ASAO Monograph No. 11. Lanham, MD: University Press of America. pp. 13–49.

———

1987b "Young men's work": Alcohol use in the contemporary Pacific. In *Contemporary Issues in Mental Health Research in the Pacific Islands,* eds. Albert B. Robillard and Anthony Marsella. Social Science Research Institute Monograph Series. Honolulu: SSRI, University of Hawaii Press. pp. 72–93.

———

1988 Alcohol consumption as a public health problem in Papua New Guinea. *The International Journal of the Addictions* 23: 573–589.

———

1989 Rashōmon in reverse: Ethnographic agreement in Truk. In *Culture, Kin, and Cognition in Oceania: Essays in Honor of Ward H. Goodenough,* eds. Mac Marshall and John L. Caughey. American Anthropological Association Special Publications, No. 25. Washington, DC: American Anthropological Association. pp. 95–106.

———

1990 Two tales from the Trukese taproom. In *The Humbled Anthropologist,* ed. Philip DeVita. Belmont, CA: Wadsworth Publishing Co.

MARSHALL, MAC AND MARK BORTHWICK

1974 Consensus, dissensus, and Guttman scales: The Namoluk case. *Journal of Anthropological Research* 30(4): 252–270.

MARSHALL, MAC AND LESLIE B. MARSHALL

1975 Opening Pandora's bottle: Reconstructing Micronesians' early contacts with alcoholic beverages. *Journal of the Polynesian Society* 84(4): 441–465.

———

1976 Holy and unholy spirits: The effects of missionization on alcohol use in Eastern Micronesia. *Journal of Pacific History* 11(3 & 4): 135–166.

MARTIN, PETRUS

1986a Truk Chamber opposes senatorial allowances. *Pacific Magazine* 11(1): 12.

———

1986b Doone's dry reign withers Truk alcohol. *Pacific Magazine* 11(5): 26.

———

1986c Untitled. *Pacific Magazine* 11(5): 60.

MASKELYNE, GEOFF

1975 Alcohol problems and women in Papua New Guinea. *Administration for Development* [Journal of the Administrative College of Papua New Guinea] No. 5, pp. 41–49.

MAUDE, H. E.

1970 Baiteke and Binoka of Abemama, arbiters of change in the Gilbert Islands. In *Pacific Islands Portraits,* eds. J. W. Davidson and Deryck Scarr. Canberra: Australian National University Press.

MAY, PHILIP A.

1975 Arrests, alcohol, and alcohol legalization among an American Indian tribe. *Plains Anthropologist* 20: 129–134.

———

1977 Alcohol beverage control: A survey of tribal alcohol statutes. *American Indian Law Review* 5(1): 217–228.

MAY, PHILIP A. AND MATTHEW B. SMITH

1988 Some Navajo Indian opinions about alcohol abuse and prohibition: A survey and recommendations for policy. *Journal of Studies on Alcohol* 49(4): 324–334.

MC MILLIN, JAMES D.

1973 Drinking patterns in Sweden. Ph.D. dissertation, Southern Illinois University, Carbondale.

MELLER, NORMAN

1969 *The Congress of Micronesia.* Honolulu: University of Hawaii Press.

MICRONESIA INSTITUTE, THE

1987 *Annual Report 1987.* Washington, DC: The Micronesia Institute.

MILLAY, JOHN R.

1987a Prohibition Pacific style: The emergence of a law banning alcohol in Truk. *Legal Studies Forum* 11(2): 165–187.

———

1987b Prohibition Pacific style: The impact of a law banning alcohol in a Micronesian society. In *Contemporary Issues in Mental Health in the Pacific Islands,* eds. Albert B. Robillard and Anthony Marsella. Social Science Research Institute Monograph Series. Honolulu: SSRI, University of Hawaii Press. pp. 177–214.

MISSIONARY HERALD: A PERIODICAL PUBLISHED BY THE AMERICAN BOARD OF COMMISSIONERS FOR FOREIGN MISSIONS. Cambridge, Massachusetts: The Riverside Press.

1881 Rev. E. T. Doane, The Lagoon of Ruk. *MH* 77: 208–210.

1886 Letters from Mr. Logan. *MH* 82: 15–18.

1888 Letter from Mr. Treiber. *MH* 84: 323–326.

MITCHINSON, WENDY

1981 The Woman's Christian Temperance Union: A study in organization. *International Journal of Women's Studies* 4(2): 143–156.

MOORE, MARK H. AND DEAN R. GERSTEIN, EDS.

1981 *Alcohol and Public Policy: Beyond the Shadow of Prohibition.* Washington, DC: National Academy Press.

MOORE, SALLY FALK

1987 Explaining the present: Theoretical dilemmas in processual ethnography. *American Ethnologist* 14(4): 727–736.

MORTON, MARIAN J.

1982 Temperance, benevolence, and the city: The Cleveland Non-Partisan Woman's Christian Temperance Union, 1874–1900. *Ohio History* 91: 58–73.

MOSER, JOY, COMP.

1979 *Prevention of Alcohol-Related Problems: An International Review of Preventive Measures, Policies and Programmes.* Geneva: World Health Organization.

O'NEIL, JOHN D.

1985 Community control over health problems: Alcohol prohibition in a Canadian Inuit village. In *Circumpolar Health 84. Proceedings of the Sixth International Symposium on Circumpolar Health,* ed. Robert Fortuine. Seattle: University of Washington Press. pp. 340–343.

PAN-PACIFIC WOMEN'S ASSOCIATION

1958 *Women of the Pacific.* A Record of the Proceedings of the Eighth Conference of the Pan-Pacific and Southeast Asia Women's Association, 20–31 August 1958, Tokyo, Japan.

PATHAK, SHEKHAR

1988 Fighting alcohol in Uttarakhand. *Himal* 1(1): 9.

PAULSON, ROSS EVANS

1973 *Women's Suffrage and Prohibition: A Comparative Study of Equality and Social Control.* Glenview, IL: Scott, Foresman.

PEASE, DR. E. M. AND MRS. E. M. PEASE, TRANSLS.

1894 The W.C.T.U. Primary Temperance Catechism in Marshallese. *Nan in Katak kin Dren in Karek, kin Tobako, im kin Kejbarok Enbwiner.* Boston: Samuel Usher.

PIAU-LYNCH, ANDONIA

1982 The Simbu liquor ban of 1980–1981. In *Through a Glass Darkly: Beer and Modernization in Papua New Guinea,* ed. Mac Marshall. IASER Monograph No. 18. Boroko: Papua New Guinea Institute of Applied Social and Economic Research. pp. 119–129.

PINSON, ANN

1985 Temperance, prohibition, and politics in nineteenth-century Iceland. *Contemporary Drug Problems* 12: 249–266.

POEHLMAN, JOANNE

1979 Culture change and identity among Chamorro women of Guam. Ph.D. dissertation, University of Minnesota.

POOLE, FITZ JOHN PORTER

1982 Cultural significance of "drunken comportment" in a non-drinking society: The Bimin-Kuskusmin of the West Sepik. In *Through a Glass Darkly: Beer and Modernization in Papua New Guinea,* ed. Mac Marshall. IASER Monograph No. 18. Boroko: Papua New Guinea Institute of Applied Social and Economic Research. pp. 189–210.

POPHAM, ROBERT E., WOLFGANG SCHMIDT, AND JAN DE LINT

1975 The prevention of alcoholism: Epidemiological studies of the effects of government control measures. *British Journal of Addiction* 70: 125–144.

———

1976 The effects of legal restraint on drinking. In *The Biology of Alcoholism, Volume 4, Social Aspects of Alcoholism,* eds. B. Kissin and H. Begleiter. New York: Plenum. pp. 579–625.

PRIYADARSINI, S. AND CLAYTON A. HARTJEN

1982 Legal control and alcohol in the United States and India. *The International Journal of the Addictions* 17(7): 1099–1106.

RAMARUI, DAVID

1976 Education in Micronesia: Its past, present and future. *Micronesian Reporter* 24(1): 9–20.

RICHARD, DOROTHY E.

1957 *United States Naval Administration of the Trust Territory of the Pacific Islands. Volume 3. The Trusteeship Period, 1947–1951.* Washington, DC: Office of the Chief of Naval Operations.

RICHARDS, BILL

1985 Alcohol-related health problems in Alaska—preventive strategies. In *Circumpolar Health 84. Proceedings of the Sixth International Symposium on Circumpolar Health,* ed. Robert Fortuine. Seattle: University of Washington Press. pp. 322–326.

RICHES, DAVID

1976 Alcohol abuse and the problem of social control in a modern Eskimo settlement. In *Knowledge and Behaviour,* ed. Ladislav Holy. The Queen's University Papers in Social Anthropology, Volume 1. Belfast: Department of Social Anthropology, Queen's University. pp. 65–80.

RIESMAN, DAVID, NATHAN GLAZER, AND REUEL DENNEY

1953 *The Lonely Crowd. A Study of the Changing American Character.* Garden City, New York: Doubleday.

RITTERBUSH, S. DEACON

1987 These days, Pacific women mean business. *Centerviews* [East-West Center] June–July, p. 5.

ROOM, ROBIN

1978 Evaluating the effect of drinking laws on drinking. In *Drinking Alcohol in American Society—Issues and Current Research,* eds. J. A. Ewing and B. A. Rouse. Chicago: Nelson-Hall. pp. 267–289; 414–419.

———

1982 Alcohol, science and social control. In *Alcohol, Science and Society Revisited,* eds. E. L. Gomberg, H. R. White, and J. A. Carpenter. Ann Arbor: University of Michigan Press. pp. 371–384.

———

1984 Alcohol and ethnography: A case of problem deflation? *Current Anthropology* 25(2): 169–191.

ROOTMAN, IRVING

1985 Afterword: Psychosocial research on alcohol problems from an international perspective. In *Alcohol Patterns and Problems,* ed. Marc A. Schuckit. Series in Psychosocial Epidemiology, Volume 5. New Brunswick, NJ: Rutgers University Press. pp. 267–271.

ROSALDO, MICHELLE Z.

1980 The use and abuse of anthropology: Reflections on feminism and cross-cultural understanding. *Signs: Journal of Women in Culture and Society* 5(3): 389–417.

RUBINSTEIN, DONALD H.

1980 Social Aspects of Juvenile Delinquency in Micronesia. Conference report for the Micronesian Seminar and Justice Improvement Commission, Micronesian Area Research Center, May 8–13, 1980, University of Guam.

———

1983 Epidemic suicide among Micronesian adolescents. *Social Science and Medicine* 17(1): 657–665.

———

1987 Cultural patterns and contagion: Epidemic suicide among Micronesian youth. In *Contemporary Issues in Mental Health Research in the Pacific Islands,* eds. Albert B. Robillard and Anthony J. Marsella. Social Science Research Institute Monograph Series. Honolulu: SSRI, University of Hawaii Press. pp. 127–148.

SARGENT, MARGARET

1983 *Sociology for Australians.* Melbourne: Longman Cheshire.

SARIOLA, SAKARI

1954 Prohibition in Finland, 1919–1932: Its background and consequences. *Quarterly Journal of Studies on Alcohol* 15: 477–490.

SCUTT, JOCELYNNE A.

1985 United or divided? Women "inside" and women "outside" against male lawmakers in Australia. *Women's Studies International Forum* 8(1): 15–23.

SHORE, BRADD

1982 *Sala'ilua: A Samoan Mystery.* New York: Columbia University Press.

SINGLE, ERIC, PATRICIA MORGAN, AND JAN DE LINT, EDS.

1981 *Alcohol, Society and the State 2. The Social History of Control Policies in Seven Countries.* Toronto: Addiction Research Foundation.

SINGLETON, JOHN

1959 Education for paradise: Improving elementary education in the Truk District, United States Trust Territory of the Pacific Islands 1955 to 1959. Unpublished manuscript. [copy on file in Micronesian Seminar Library, Moen, Truk]

———

1970 Cross-cultural strains in development education: An analysis of American-sponsored schooling on Truk. Paper read at the Interdisciplinary Conference on Processes of Change in Contemporary Asian Societies, 5–7 November, Urbana-Champaign, Illinois. [copy on file in Micronesian Seminar Library, Moen, Truk]

SLATTER, CLAIRE

1981 The Pacific decides on a plan of action for women of the subregion. *Social Development Newsletter* [Economic and Social Commission for Asia and the Pacific] No. 2, pp. 21–23.

SMART, REGINALD G.

1979 A note on the effects of changes in alcohol control policies in the Canadian North. *Journal of Studies on Alcohol* 40(9): 908–913.

STEIN, HOWARD F.

1982 Ethanol and its discontents: Paradoxes of inebriation and sobriety in American culture. *The Journal of Psychoanalytic Anthropology* 5(4): 355–377.

———

1985 Alcoholism as metaphor in American culture: Ritual desecration as social integration. *Ethos* 13(3): 195–235.

SUMANOP, FRANCIS H.

1981 The involvement of women's groups in alcohol issues in Papua New Guinea: 1960–1981. B.A. Honours Thesis, University of Papua New Guinea.

———

1982 Village clubs on the Gazelle Peninsula. In *Through a Glass Darkly: Beer and Modernization in Papua New Guinea,* ed. Mac Marshall. IASER Monograph No. 18. Boroko: Papua New Guinea Institute of Applied Social and Economic Research. pp. 379–387.

TALYAGA, KUNDAPEN K.

1982 Liquor sale and consumption in Enga Province: Some personal observations. In *Through a Glass Darkly: Beer and Modernization in Papua New Guinea,* ed. Mac Marshall. IASER Monograph No. 18. Boroko: Papua New Guinea Institute of Applied Social and Economic Research. pp. 131–138.

THAKUR, CHANDRESHAWAR PRASAD, RAM NARESH SHARMA, AND HAFIZ SHAH MOHAMMAD QURBAN AKHTAR

1982 Prohibition and alcohol intoxication. *British Journal of Addiction* 77: 197–204.

THIMMAIAH, G.

1979 *Socio-Economic Impact of Drinking, State Lottery and Horse-Racing in Karnataka.* Institute for Social and Economic Change, Bangalore. New Delhi: Sterling Publishers Pvt. Ltd.

TIFFANY, SHARON W.

1987 Politics and gender in Pacific Island societies: A feminist critique of the anthropology of power. *Women's Studies* 13: 333–355.

TRUK DISTRICT

1954 *Truk District Third Annual Conference of Island Magistrates, November 29 to December 3, 1954.* 32 pp. Mimeographed. [copy on file in Truk State Legislature Library, Moen, Truk]

———

1956 *Truk District Fourth Annual Conference of Island Magistrates, January 17–24, 1956.* Mimeographed. [copy on file in Truk State Legislature Library, Moen, Truk]

TRUK DISTRICT GOVERNMENT

1970 *Puken Annuken Truk District. Truk District Code.* Seattle: Book Publishing Co.

TRUK DISTRICT LEGISLATURE

1967 *Truk District Public Laws, 1-1 1958–15-20 1967*. Mimeographed. [copy on file in Truk State Legislature Library, Moen, Truk]

——

1976a Report No. 18 to the Speaker of the Truk District Legislature, Twenty-Sixth Regular Session, First Special Session, from the Political Committee on Bill No. 26-1-29. Typescript. [copy on file in the Truk State Legislature Library, Moen, Truk]

——

1976b Minutes of the Truk District Legislature, July 13, 1976, comp. Herter E. Sorim, Assistant Clerk. Typescript. [copy on file in the Truk State Legislature Library, Moen, Truk]

TRUK STATE GOVERNMENT

1985 Local resident workers, first quarter reports from January to March 1985. Truk State Labor and Manpower Development Division, Department of Resources and Development, Moen, Truk.

TRUK STATE LEGISLATURE

1980a Audit Report Fiscal Year Ending September 30, 1979. Saipan: Touche Ross and Co.

——

1980b Accountants' Report, Financial Statements, Fiscal Year Ending September 30, 1980 and Management Letter, March 10, 1981. Agana, Guam: Touche Ross and Co.

——

1981 Audit Report, Financial Statements and Letter of Findings and Recommendations, Fiscal Year Ending September 30, 1981. Agana, Guam: Touche Ross and Co.

——

1983 Annual Financial Report, Year Ended September 30, 1982. Kolonia, Ponape: Touche Ross and Co.

——

1984 Federated States of Micronesia, Annual Financial Statements, Year Ended September 30, 1983. Kolonia, Ponape: Touche Ross and Co.

TRUK STATE OFFICE OF PLANNING AND STATISTICS

1981 *Statistical Yearbook, Truk State, FSM*. Moen: Truk State Office of Planning and Statistics.

TYRRELL, IAN R.

1982 Women and temperance in antebellum America, 1830–1860. *Civil War History* 28(2): 128–152.

——

1983 International aspects of the woman's temperance movement in Australia: The influence of the American WCTU, 1882–1914. *The Journal of Religious History* 12(3): 284–304.

——

1987 Women and temperance in international perspective: The World's W.C.T.U., 1880s–1920s. In *The Social History of Alcohol, Drinking and*

Culture in Modern Society, eds. Susanna Barrows, Robin Room, and Jeffrey Verhey. Berkeley: Alcohol Research Group, Medical Research Institute of San Francisco. pp. 163–164.

UNITED STATES DEPARTMENT OF COMMERCE, BUREAU OF THE CENSUS

1983 *1980 Census of Population,* Volume 1. Characteristics of the Population, Chapter B, General Population Characteristics, Part 57B, Trust Territory of the Pacific Islands, Excluding the Northern Mariana Islands. Washington, DC: U.S. Government Printing Office (PC80-1-B57B).

UNITED STATES DEPARTMENT OF STATE

1954 *Seventh Annual Report of the Administration of the Territory of the Pacific Islands, July 1, 1953, to June 30, 1954.* Washington, DC: U.S. Government Printing Office.

———

1955 *Eighth Annual Report on the Administration of the Trust Territory of the Pacific Islands, July 1, 1954 to June 30, 1955.* Washington, DC: U.S. Government Printing Office.

———

1956 *Ninth Annual Report on the Administration of the Trust Territory of the Pacific Islands, July 1, 1955 to June 30, 1956.* Washington, DC: U.S. Government Printing Office.

———

1959 *Twelfth Annual Report on the Administration of the Trust Territory of the Pacific Islands, July 1, 1958 to June 30, 1959.* Washington, DC: U.S. Government Printing Office.

———

1960 *Thirteenth Annual Report on the Administration of the Trust Territory of the Pacific Islands, July 1, 1959 to June 30, 1960.* Washington, DC: U.S. Government Printing Office.

———

1962 *Fifteenth Annual Report on the Administration of the Trust Territory of the Pacific Islands, July 1, 1961 to June 30, 1962.* Washington, DC: U.S. Government Printing Office.

———

1963 *Sixteenth Annual Report on the Administration of the Trust Territory of the Pacific Islands, July 1, 1962 to June 30, 1963.* Washington, DC: U.S. Government Printing Office.

———

1964 *Seventeenth Annual Report on the Administration of the Trust Territory of the Pacific Islands, July 1, 1963 to June 30, 1964.* Washington, DC: U.S. Government Printing Office.

———

1966 *Nineteenth Annual Report on the Administration of the Trust Territory of the Pacific Islands, July 1, 1965 to June 30, 1966.* Washington, DC: U.S. Government Printing Office.

———

1967 *Twentieth Annual Report on the Administration of the Trust Territory of the Pacific Islands, July 1, 1966 to June 30, 1967.* Washington, DC: U.S. Government Printing Office.

———

1968 *Twenty-first Annual Report on the Administration of the Trust Territory of the Pacific Islands, July 1, 1967 to June 30, 1968.* Washington, DC: U.S. Government Printing Office.

———

1969 *Twenty-second Annual Report on the Administration of the Trust Territory of the Pacific Islands, July 1, 1968 to June 30, 1969.* Washington, DC: U.S. Government Printing Office.

———

1970 *Twenty-third Annual Report on the Administration of the Trust Territory of the Pacific Islands, July 1, 1969 to June 30, 1970.* Washington, DC: U.S. Government Printing Office.

———

1971 *Twenty-fourth Annual Report on the Administration of the Trust Territory of the Pacific Islands, July 1, 1970 to June 30, 1971.* Washington, DC: U.S. Government Printing Office.

———

1972 *Twenty-fifth Annual Report on the Administration of the Trust Territory of the Pacific Islands, July 1, 1971 to June 30, 1972.* Washington, DC: U.S. Government Printing Office.

———

1973 *Twenty-sixth Annual Report on the Administration of the Trust Territory of the Pacific Islands, July 1, 1972 to June 30, 1973.* Washington, DC: U.S. Government Printing Office.

———

1980 *Thirty-third Annual Report on the Administration of the Trust Territory of the Pacific Islands, October 1, 1979 to September 30, 1980.* Washington, DC: U.S. Government Printing Office.

———

1982 *Thirty-fifth Annual Report on the Administration of the Trust Territory of the Pacific Islands, October 1, 1981 to September 30, 1982.* Washington, DC: U.S. Government Printing Office.

———

1985 *Thirty-eighth Annual Report on the Administration of the Trust Territory of the Pacific Islands, October 1, 1984 to September 30, 1985.* Washington, DC: U.S. Government Printing Office.

UNITED STATES DEPARTMENT OF THE NAVY

1948 *Information on the Trust Territory of the Pacific Islands Transmitted by the United States to the Secretary-General of the United Nations Pursuant to Article 88 of the Charter.* Washington, DC: Department of the Navy.

———

1951 *Report on the Trust Territory of the Pacific Islands for the Period July 1, 1949 to June 30, 1950.* Washington, DC: Department of the Navy, Office of the Chief of Naval Operations.

UNITED STATES TRUST TERRITORY OF THE PACIFIC ISLANDS (USTTPI)

1974a Truk District Law No. 24-4. In *Laws and Resolutions, Truk District Legislature 24th Regular Session.* Truk: Public Affairs Office. n.p.

———

1974b Truk District Law No. 24-23. In *Laws and Resolutions, Truk District Legislature, 24th Regular Session.* Truk: Public Affairs Office. n.p.

———

1975a Truk District Law No. 25-30. In *Laws and Resolutions, Truk District Legislature, 25th Regular Session.* Truk: Public Affairs Office. pp. 99–103.

———

1975b *Alcohol and Drug Abuse Plan for the Trust Territory of the Pacific Islands.* Saipan: Division of Mental Health, Department of Health Services.

———

1976 Truk District Law No. 26-11. In *Laws and Resolutions, Truk District Legislature, 26th Regular Session.* Truk: Public Affairs Office. p. 11.

———

1977a Truk District Law No. 27-34. In *Laws and Resolutions, Truk District Legislature, 27th Regular Session.* Truk: Public Affairs Office. p. 42.

———

1977b *Annual Report to the Secretary of the Interior, 1977.* Saipan: U.S. Trust Territory of the Pacific Islands.

———

1977c Truk District Law No. 27-17. In *Laws and Resolutions, Truk District Legislature, 27th Regular Session.* Truk: Public Affairs Office. pp. 18–19.

———

1979 Trial Division of the High Court, Truk State, Criminal Case No. 7-79. TTPI vs. Kanesus, Kaki and Angfaso, Otto. *Order.* November 29, 1979. Chief Justice Harold W. Burnett.

UNNITHAN, N. PRABHA

1985 A cross-national perspective on the evolution of alcohol prohibition. *The International Journal of the Addictions* 20(4): 591–604.

WAGENAAR, ALEXANDER C.

1982 Three natural experiments in changing alcohol availability. Paper read at the 13th Annual Medical-Scientific Conference of the National Alcoholism Forum, 2–5 April, Washington, D.C.

WALTHER, JOSEPH

1982 Statistical data on imported alcoholic beverages. Truk State Tax Office. Typescript. [copy in authors' files]

WILLARD, FRANCES E.

1889 *Glimpses of Fifty Years. The Autobiography of an American Woman.* Chicago: H. J. Smith and Co.

WOLFE, ARTHUR C.

1960 Taxation in Truk. Moen: Truk Education Department. Mimeographed. [copy on file in Truk State Legislature Library]

WOMAN'S BOARD OF MISSIONS FOR THE PACIFIC ISLANDS [WBMPI]

1976 *105th Annual Report of the Woman's Board of Missions for the Pacific Islands.* Honolulu: WBMPI.

———

1984 *113th Annual Report of the Woman's Board of Missions for the Pacific Islands.* Honolulu: WBMPI.

WORMSLEY, WILLIAM

1987 Beer and power in Enga. In *Drugs in Western Pacific Societies,* ed. Lamont Lindstrom. ASAO Monograph No. 11. Lanham, MD: University Press of America. pp. 197–217.

WUORINEN, JOHN H.

1931 *The Prohibition Experiment in Finland.* New York: Columbia University Press.

YAP DISTRICT LEGISLATURE

1979 Standing Committee Report No. 6-8, regarding Bill No. 6-1, "A bill for an act to repeal Part E of the Yap District Code, on Alcoholic Beverage Control, to enact a new Part E prohibiting alcoholic beverages except tuba, and for other purposes." 1st Regular Session, 6th Yap District Legislature. Colonia, Yap, USTTPI.

Index

Pages on which there are figures or illustrations are indicated by **bold** type.